The Falcon Five

By Julie Atlas

Chapter 1: Charles Mitchell

He heard about his destruction just by being at 7-Eleven when the fire trucks and ambulances drove noisily by.

"What's going on?" asked the burly customer in front of him. The brown-skinned cashier answered in his heavy accent.

"Down the street there was some big high school senior partytime. Like always those rich kids all came in here trying to buy beer underage. Cops are always flying by here with sirens blazing trying to catch those sneaky little khabeezes!" He paused and his eyes narrowed. "They think Aman is dumb that he doesn't know! But Aman knows and I don't give them nothing!"

The boy—well, he was almost 18, so almost a man—looked defiant as he said, "Hey Arab," his voice coming out hoarse because he rarely used it. "Are you talking about Ray Balachek's place on Columbia Pike?"

Aman started for a brief moment at being called "arab" but decided to ignore it. Instead he answered with great irritation. "Yes of course, boy," he said spitting out the word "boy" as if it were something nasty. "All those high school beeg shot kids go there on the weekends," Aman leaned over the counter and looked closely at the boy studying him from feet to head. He stared at the boy's dirty tennis shoes that looked like they were a size too big. "No socks—stinky feet!" observed Aman to himself. Aman studied his '70s looking brown cords that just may have been bellbottoms but the boy had sloppily rolled them up. "Must have been his Father's old pants," thought Aman. Next his eyes fell on the boy's enormous untucked, red and yellow plaid flannel shirt. "Perhaps this was another hand-me-down," pondered Aman. When he got to the boy's face, Aman was surprised to see that among the scattered acne and very greasy unkempt hair, the boy's eyes were bright green framed by long eye lashes. Aman spoke again in a teasing manner.

"Boy, why aren't you there? Not a beeg shot like the rest of them, eh? Aman thinks you're what the beeg shot kids call a nork!" Aman elbowed the customer first in line "Nork right? Heh heh."

The beefy customer turned and studied the boy for a second and replied to Aman "I think you mean 'dork,' Aman. The kid's a big dork." Together they chuckled while the boy blushed furiously.

"Hey keed," said Aman. "You see a dermanonlgeest, you get better clotheengs! Get clean, boy! You will not be a nork anymore, yes?" As Aman spoke he nodded to the first customer, who corrected him.

"No, Aman—this one's doomed. No one recovers from wearing bellbottoms at his age!" The customer shrugged his shoulders at the boy. "Sorry kid, but you'd better find out now rather than later, this is it for you."

The boy was silent. His green eyes glared out from under his greasy bangs. He was used to this kind of treatment at school, but to have this experience at a convenience store was beyond humiliating. He clenched his fists tightly thinking to himself, *Arab sinner, redneck cowboy. They don't matter. They will suffer. God helps those who help themselves.* He smiled, his lips lifting only on one side so the smile looked more like a snarl. He paid for his Coke and walked out feeling smug, his backpack full of at least a case of his Aman's beer that he'd lifted when the storekeeper's back was turned (*Help themselves!*). As the boy walked outside, more fire trucks and ambulances rushed by. The boy smiled. *Time to get on over to the beeg shot party*, he thought to himself. *Us dorks know how to shake things up.* He walked over to his dad's 1975 off-white and brown-paneled station wagon—kids at school called it the "Loser-mobile"—and climbed in. *This was shaping up quite nicely*, he thought slyly. *I hadn't expected quite this many ambulances.* The boy pulled out into the street and followed the sound of sirens to Bielksi's place. As he drove away from the 7-Eleven he heard loud crash as a wild wind suddenly ripped a branch from a nearby tree and hurled it through the front window. He smiled at the sound of glass breaking and the screams of agony from within the convenience store's walls.

He headed toward Balachek's place, parking one street over to avoid having anyone spot the Loser-mobile. He snuck through the woods behind Balachek's house and sat in his usual place in the middle of a dense thicket of overgrown honeysuckle bushes. In front of him was the backyard. It was big split-level home, old and dumpy—a rental that Ray's college-aged brother lived in with his friends. Ray's brother would go out of town on weekends, leaving Ray free to throw raucous parties with no parental supervision. It was the place to see and be seen if you were a Severna Park High School senior. The boy had never been invited to a party there, but he did try to go once.

At the back of the house was a decrepit second-story deck. This ancient deck was the main event at each party. This is where Ray and his friends would put the kegs of beer, play their loud music, and try to make out with the drunken party girls. The boy spent many hours watching and listening to the "beeg shots" on the deck. The drinking and debauchery disgusted him: girls being compelled to flash the boys, boys doing keg stands and choking down beer bongs. He'd seen some girls kiss two and three boys in a night! These people had no morals and it outraged him. The boy paused for a second and considered the one time that he should have stepped in. He saw big, burly Todd Hemar take the petite head cheerleader and school beauty queen Jenny Mercer under the old deck and kiss her. It wasn't much to watch at first, until he heard Jenny say, "Todd, no." The boy strained his eyes in the night to see that Todd had gotten bolder and had shrugged off his letterman's jacket and was pawing at Jenny's fuzzy, pink shirt. Aggressively, Todd shoved his thick knee between her tiny legs. Jenny asked quietly for Todd to stop, but he grunted his refusal. "No!" was all the boy could hear. Todd became frenzied, pushing Jenny down. Jenny struggled and scratched and screamed for help, but the music was so loud up on the deck none of the party-goers could hear a thing. The boy had considered rescuing her—being her knight in shining armor and stopping the terrible thing that was happening to her. But he knew that God had a way of punishing those who strayed away from Him, like she had.

Jenny was one of the boy's biggest troubles at Severna Park High School. He'd let her cheat off of him all semester long in their Algebra class. She smiled at him and even brought him chocolate treats to thank him for allowing her to use his smarts. She treated him nicely in class and laughed at his unfunny jokes—and she had the most beautiful laugh. When he saw Jenny in the hallway during a break between classes, he felt it was okay—even friendly—to smile and say hello to her as she passed. He knew this was a no-no at Severna Park, but he thought for sure Jenny was beyond that sort of silliness. After all, the other day after getting a 98% on her pop quiz she'd even touched his arm to say thank you. They were *friends*.

He could not forget the look of confusion and disgust on her pretty face when he squeaked out his "Hi, Jenny."

"Oh Charles," she'd sighed, as if the boy had just spoken inappropriately to the Queen of England. She did not return his greeting, and a split second later the boy was pinned against the locker by testosterone-fueled Severna Park football hero Todd Hemar. Todd held him by the throat for a few seconds, watching him struggle to breathe. When Charles turned red, then purple, Todd let him go. As the boy slid to the floor coughing and choking, Todd snickered and turned to walk away, but stopped.

He quickly turned back, swiftly kicked Charles in the stomach, chuckled "That oughta do it, eh Charlie?" and was gone. Charles Mitchell coughed violently and tears welled up in his eyes. Not only had he been attacked; Todd called him "Charlie." That infuriated him. *My name is Charles!* His head had ached and his throat burned, but his mind was sharp. *This would stop now*, he remembered thinking. *I will carry out God's will and bring the devil to his knees.*

And so it was quite easy for Charles to watch Todd punch Jenny, knock her out and then rape her. God was on his side and Charles was pleased to see Jenny get what she deserved. The boy had been so thrilled that Jenny got hers (*God is good!*) he crossed her off his list. Todd was still at the very top of the list, as were several other boys on the football team. Then there were "the five": Tricia, Holly, Allie, Zoe, and Skylar were all very popular girls who did a terrible thing to Charles, something he would never forget. Each one of these characters would be at Ray's party to play out the torturous and righteous scene in Charles' mind. Charles knew that God would be pleased when he culled the popular kids. This was God's will. Charles would be rewarded handsomely by God himself.

"In fact," thought Charles, "He already had."

He surveyed the damage slowly. Charles was pleased to see the old deck had fallen to the ground, just as he knew it would when he'd willed it to collapse violently just hours earlier. He'd been injecting himself with a mixture he'd created in his father's laboratory, and he'd been thrilled with the results. Frank Mitchell was not the husband of Charles' mother, Constance King. Charles had been the product of a one-night stand back when his mother was an alcoholic, well before her parents threatened to throw her out on the street if she didn't embrace Christ. Charles always found it interesting that his mother was once anything but a woman of God. He preferred not to hear the small town gossip that told the story of the night that Frank met Constance. He'd often heard bits and pieces of it whispered behind his back when he was in school or at the store, (that's the bastard son of Constance and Frank) or heard it from his bullies at school (your mom is a whore). Everyone knew that Constance was the daughter of an Evangelical minister who was so staunchly religious that he started his own church out of his basement. In constant rebellion, Constance was known to be wild and sneaky, and on her 15th birthday she snuck out and managed to hitchhike her way to a biker bar just outside of town. It was there she met a 22-year old Frank Mitchell. Frank had never been to a bar before and had only stopped in to use the bathroom. On his way out of the bar he bumped into her as she was coming in. She'd grabbed his arm and dragged him back in and they spent the next few hours drinking (or she did, anyway) and it was when another older man tried to kiss her that Frank decided to give her a ride home. That night, in the car in front of his grandparent's home/church, Charles was conceived. Frank didn't know that Constance was 15.

Constance tried desperately to hide her pregnancy and she even kept it from Frank. But eventually she could hide it no longer. Charles always enjoyed this part of the story as it was her account of actually entering the Kingdom of God. She'd told her parents on a Sunday morning, just as her father was about to conduct church services, figuring he would not have time to deal with her. She was very, very wrong. Constance's mother cried and cried upon hearing the news and her father said nothing. He just left the room and returned with a small whip. He took Constance by the hand and brought her to the basement where there was a congregation waiting. He asked her to remove her shirt and sit on a stool with her back to the people. Charles' grandfather proceeded to whip his mother across the back. In between smacks of the whip she could hear the murmuring and praying of the congregation. He screamed to her that he had known of her sin and that the only way she could get back into God's good graces would be to suffer as Jesus did. Constance always got very animated when she told this part of the story because this is when she finally understood what her father had been teaching all of these years. "I knew that you were the key to my suffering, Charles," she would always say. "You were whipping me, you were making me bleed. You caused all of my suffering, you left these scars on my back." It was that day that Constance gave her life to God and Jesus and her father's church. It was that day that her father baptized her again and almost drowned her as he held her in the water that was awash with her own blood. Constance never looked back, she often said. And she believed that it was her destiny to teach Charles about suffering and pain. The ultimate sacrifice.

When Charles turned 2, Constance decided to bring him to meet Frank. Charles had a vague memory of a man in a cold room wearing a long white coat. Frank hadn't said much – he just shook his head and scribbled out a check that he handed to Constance in silence. Over the years, Charles had a few interactions with Frank similar to that but nothing that anyone would call loving or even remotely close to a father-son relationship. Sometimes, as a young child, Charles would accompany Frank to work at his lab where Frank was a lab tech who took care of the test animals that the scientists were using in their various experiments. Charles always marveled at the pain and torture that these animals endured. He often found himself jealous of their suffering, but was often instrumental in helping them achieve their pain. When his father would leave the lab for meetings or even to use the bathroom Charles would experiment by adding soap or other chemicals to their food dishes or sometimes he'd poke the sharp needles into their furry little bodies just to hear them scream. The more they whined or cried or screamed the more Charles felt he was helping them achieve a higher state, closer to God. He also found their suffering made him feel powerful. And he thought about power a lot.

Tall, lanky, slightly balding and blind as a bat, Frank Mitchell was as bad a lab technician as he was a father. He did the minimum amount of work and then went home to his television. When he wasn't at work, Frank Mitchell was sure to avoid Charles's mother at all costs by dropping Charles off a few houses down and when Charles turned 16 handing over his car so he wouldn't have to pick him up at all. If Frank did happen to catch orange-haired Constance King outside when he dropped Charles off, he was met with a pale, scrawny woman with wild green eyes going around in her head howling various bible verses and begging him to repent. Frank would speed off as fast as one could in a small suburban neighborhood but Constance would often run after his car, her frizzy, unkempt hair flying around her head as she ran on the tips of her toes reminding him he was going straight to hell for his bastard child.

Without a real father and no other family, Charles was raised in an intensely religious, often violent household. Frank never directly explained science to Charles – he just let the boy figure it out on his own. One of his mother's rules, Charles was strictly forbidden to go the lab but Frank took him anyway and told Charles to tell his Mother that they tossed the football or watched movies. When Charles returned home from his rare visits with his father, Constance would whisk Charles into her home-made shrines of candles, incense and bible verses for forgiveness. While other children were in preschool learning about shapes and colors, Charles was taught each and every word of the Bible. By the age of 5 he could recite the old testament. In first grade Charles would stand up and admonish his peers for participating in such pagan rituals as Halloween and Santa Claus. His strict views made him a constant target of ridicule and torment every single day but when he shared his pain with Constance she only reminded him that to be close to God meant to suffer.

While Charles endured constant physical and mental abuse at home with his mother, school was no different. Charles already stood out as an outcast and a loser to most of the students. Friendless and weird, he was shunned at every level. Charles never forgot a particular day during his 4th grade year when he had to stay late after school in detention. He'd gotten caught squeezing the class hamster again. Charles loved to get the hamster out and hold it tight around its middle. He'd heard a hamster will struggle until it's eyes pop out and he would watch in excited anticipation as it suffocated and squirmed

- waiting for the moment the eyes would come loose. He wondered if they would fly across the room or would they just explode into a bloody pulp – would it make a sound? The first time he gotten caught he'd made up a lame story about worrying that the hamster might fall out of his hand. The squeezing was an accident, he'd told Mrs. Stitz. Only that day Mrs. Stitz spotted him the second he'd gotten his fist around the animal and not only forbade him from feeding the animal anymore she'd also punished him by making him stay late and help decorate the classroom for the holidays.

Charles remembered her writing yet another troublesome note for him to bring home to his mother. He tried to avoid giving these notes to his mother because more often than not they would result in a beating. She often would heat up a wire hanger in the oven and whip it across his back. These were good beatings, she'd always say. Because pain and suffering bring you that much closer to peace. Still, Charles tended to keep the notes himself preferring to torture other things to keep on that path to peace.

As Charles left the school that day he shuffled down the long hallway and stopped in front of the cafeteria where he heard girls' voices singing. He paused in the doorway observing five girls, dressed as angels in white, on stage practicing a song over and over while the music teacher fussed from the floor in front of them. Behind the music teacher stood a girl dressed as a golden angel and a few other boys who were wearing long robes. Charles surmised that there must be some holiday school production rehearsal going on – he stopped to listen and watch a little bit longer – Christmas did have something to do with God, right? After a few minutes, he grew disgusted with the watered-down songs they sang for his Lord and he decided to leave. As he was turning to go he heard a girl's voice yell out "Stop that!" He turned back around and the several boys backing away from the golden angel girl. They were shaking their heads vigorously and pointing at Charles. The golden angel turned her angry eyes on him and she grabbed a bag that was nearby and began to walk toward him at a fast pace – the boys were right behind her. Charles froze in his tracks.

He was not used to being looked at, ever and he waited fearfully. The angel took him angrily by his arm and pulled him out the front door of the school. "Think you're going to grab my bottom, Charles Mitchell?" she'd said.

"I don't…I never…I didn't…" he stammered.

"I'll teach you to never, ever touch me or talk to me ever again," said the angel. With that she swung her bag around and hit Charles squarely in the jaw knocking him backwards and off of his feet. The bag had felt so heavy and hard, Charles couldn't imagine what she'd hit him with. From the ground Charles looked up and found himself surrounded by the boys in robes.

"Charles got beat up by a girl!" one of them taunted.

"And I'm going to do it again!" said the golden angel. She slammed her heavy bag hard down on Charles head and hands. The boys joined in the fight by kicking Charles to keep him down while the girl continued her beating. Charles knew these school beatings well and he was sure to keep his hands around his head and face to protect himself while it lasted. He knew soon they would get bored with him and leave him alone.

As the beating let up the boys wandered off, leaving Charles bleeding, bruised and sobbing on the ground – with the angel. He would never forget her leaning over him, the spit flecks from her mouth warm on his scraped skin and hearing her taunt that soon everyone would know he'd been beaten up by a girl.

"I'm not even going to tell them what was in my purse," she'd said to him. As she stood the angel opened her bag and pulled out a large, black tape recorder. "It's barely even damaged!" she laughed. "The whole school will think it was just a plain old purse that did this." A horn sounded and Charles heard the angel say "Daddy! I'm coming! Oh look you brought Fluffy Dog!" When Charles determined he was alone he got up, wiped himself off as best he could and started walking home.

When Constance heard the story, she did what she always did when he would share his tales of abuse. She'd quote to him from John 16:33 – "These things I have spoken unto you, that in me ye might have PEACE. In the world ye SHALL HAVE

TRIBULATION: but be of good cheer; I HAVE OVERCOME the WORLD." Constance never missed a chance to remind her only son that pain was power. She believed he was responsible for her glorious scars and he reveled in her pain. The more he was abused at school by students and even teachers, Constance would remind him that with God on his side, everyone would pay.

Charles took these words to heart and remembered fondly that it had been a cold and terrible Christmas morning at the golden angel's house. When she awoke that morning and ran down to see the new fallen-snow in the yard, she discovered her beloved Fluffy Dog swaying by the neck on the brightly lit Christmas tree on the front lawn. The dog's eyes were bulging and its tongue was purplish and hanging out of the side of it's mouth. The noose had been fashioned from an electrical cord and it was most curious to the golden angel's parents why the killer would have left the portable tape recorder attached to the other side.

Chapter 2: The Deck

It had been easy for Charles to get access to his father's lab. All he had to do was ask for a visit. Frank responded that Charles could drive himself and that he'd be at work until 10 P.M. that night. Very briefly, Charles thought that his father might actually spend some time with him and show an interest in him. He'd even made up a story about a fake experiment for school credit story in the faint hope that maybe his dad would work with him, for once. But Charles was disappointed as usual as his father dropped him off in the cold, white lab, mumbled something about a meeting he had to attend and left Charles to experiment with all of the vials, tubes and flasks.

Charles was delighted as he wandered through the lab reading the various labels. "Chemical – genetic interaction: Cranial Hypertrophy," read one. Another label read "Complex genetic modification *Dicotyledoneae*," in black, block letters. Delighted to find such interesting and clearly terrible liquids, Charles mixed both in a flask and watched as it turned a bright blue and bubbled. He vaguely recognized the terms on the labels.

"Hypertrophy had something to do with increasing strength," he thought. "And cranial obviously has something to do with the head, maybe the brain." He wasn't sure at all what dicotyledoneae meant but he figured since it said genetic modification that it was an agent to change the make-up of the chemicals. "Perhaps in addition to poisoning my oppressors I can create something to make myself stronger," he wondered to himself. Charles continued his inspection of the lab and walked slowly down the aisle with cold, metal counters on either side of him until he came to the mice. He leaned forward, studying the mice as they ran around and around, completing various tasks like pressing a lever to receive food or running around in a wheel to create the force to pour water into a dish.

He came upon one mouse who was just sitting silently in his bed of straw. This mouse looked overweight and had enormous black eyes. Charles quickly grew bored watching the fat mouse sitting lazily in his nest so he decided to move on. But just before he took his eyes off of the creature something amazing happened. A little tiny piece of corn from the mouse's food dish lifted awkwardly and floated clumsily through thin air and into the tiny paws of the chubby mouse. Shocked at what he was seeing, Charles watched in amazement as the mouse began chewing on the corn hungrily. As Charles watched another tiny piece of corn lifted and rode the air straight into the paws of the pot-bellied rodent. Again, the mouse ate quickly and noisily before curling up into a ball and going to sleep.

Charles was floored - and ecstatic. He studied the label on the mouse cage closely. It read "Psychokenetic Easter Island Compound, see notebook." Charles flipped through the black notebook sitting to the right of the cage. "Treating tumors with a-KG and Easter Island compound rapamycin yields unprecedented telekinetic behaviors in standard gray laboratory mice," was the title of the first page. The article went on to describe how when scientists were trying to discover a way to use a chemical combination of rapamycin – a compound first discovered in the soil of the South Pacific island found to increase the lifespan of mice – and a-KG a compound virus that when modified can treat deadly brain cancer tumors, that unexpected telekinetic behaviors emerged. Charles flipped through the pages excitedly reading the details of the mouse who had been cured of brain tumors and had also now developed the ability to feed itself through thought. He ran through the lab searching for the "a-KG/rapamycin" vials, not noticing that he still held his blue flask tightly. Charles threw open one of the laboratory refrigerators and stared impatiently at each label on the shelf. "No, no, no, no," he thought angrily. "Oh my," he thought suddenly, "God IS good." He reached in with his free hand and pulled an orange-colored vial off of the second shelf. Charles held it up to his face and read the label outloud in his scratchy voice. "a-KG/rapamycin – top secret" he said.

A loud throat-clearing sound at the door startled Charles and he whirled around to discover his father standing in the doorway. In an attempt to hide what he'd discovered from his father, Charles held both the blue flask and the orange vial behind his back. His father spoke stiffly.

"I see you're busy," he said half closing his eyes as he spoke. Charles' father rarely ever looked at Charles directly. It had been so long since they'd made eye contact Charles often wondered if his father even remembered what he looked like. His father lumbered into the room causing Charles to startle, and unbeknownst to him the *orange vial spilled silently and completely into the blue one.*

"Dad," Charles stammered "What are you doing?" Just as his father had startled Charles, Charles' scratchy voice in turn startled him right back.

"I, uh," his father replied once again closing his eyes. "Your, uh, mother called," he finally said. "She wants you home for prayers."

"Yessir," Charles replied dutifully. "Can I just finish up my project?"
"Uh hurry it up, you know how she gets." said his father, "I'll be back in 5 minutes to walk you out, so finish up."

As soon as he could no longer hear the soft click of his father's black loafers, Charles pulled the flask and the vial from behind his back. The orange vial was completely empty and as Charles looked to the floor to see where it had spilled he noticed that his bright blue vial had now changed colors to a deep brown color. Anxiously, Charles looked at the clock. He had 3 minutes to figure out what to do. He rushed to the laboratory supply closet and grabbed a huge syringe marked "epidural" and filled it as high as he could with his brown concoction. Two minutes left. Charles had no time to think about what to do next and decided that if this was his last day on earth that he would welcome seeing God in Heaven (*if that's where you go*). "If I live after injecting this then it is God's will," he thought. He began to pray, whispering the Psalm 23:4 "Yea though I walk through the valley of the shadow of death, I will fear no evil," he said. One minute. Charles took the enormous needle and stabbed directly into a big blue vein in the cradle of his arm. He shoved the plunger down violently, trying to get as much of the brown liquid into his body as he could. The pain was immense and overwhelming. And as soon as Charles was able to get the last drop into his flowing blood stream it was all he could do to toss the needle into the radioactive trash and pass out on the hard lab floor. He sank into darkness.

He woke up with a start and discovered he was laying in his own bed in his own room. There was a small, bright light from the old wooden lamp next to his bed and he heard the monotone voice of his mother speaking in religious tongues at the foot of his bed.

"Mother," he croaked. Constance Mitchell's wild, orange hair flipped back as her head popped up and her vacant blue eyes peered at Charles. She leaped to her feet and waved her hands around manically.

"Believe in the Lord Jesus Christ and you will be saved!" she howled. Charles' eyes hurt from the brightly lit lamp and rolled back into his head. As his mother danced around his bed shouting various bible verses, one after another, they slowly closed. Neither one of them noticed the wooden lamp lifted up for a bit and then put itself back down as Charles entered into a deep slumber.

After a full 24 hours of sleep, Charles had recovered completely and he made the discovery that by accidentally mixing up the different genetic compounds that he found in his father's lab, he'd unlocked the power of the mind. The brown liquid seemed to have altered Charles permanently, and he remembered spending hours upon hours in his room using his new-found telekinesis to move different objects around. Charles remembered thinking that his father might have actually been proud, if he'd ever been around.

Controlling his will was difficult at first. Charles had accidently killed his mother's beloved Foo Foo Kitty, who'd kept meowing while Charles was trying to concentrate. He hadn't meant for the pencil he was using to fly out of his hand and violently pierce the feline's tiny gray head, but he was thrilled when it did. Charles didn't mind cleaning up blood, brains, and fur from his mother's linoleum kitchen floor because he knew this was just the beginning. Oh, how his mother had wailed and screamed when she found her furry baby all covered in gore. Charles feigned feeling terrible about the accident because he loved his mother and God dearly, but secretly he was elated. Even still, to appease his mother he sat and prayed and sang with her all night for their kitty candlelight vigil.

The death of his mother's beloved kitty was just the beginning of his new power, and he didn't bat an eye when there was a rash of kitty deaths-by-pencil in his neighborhood. Constance King thought it meant the beginning of the apocalypse. Frank Mitchell didn't even know about it. Charles thought of it simply as target practice. *First cats, then my classmates.*

There was one weakness to Charles' new power. He could influence only wooden objects. After researching the one vial from his father's lab that he hadn't recognized he discovered that *Dicotyledoneae* was the class from the subdivision of Angiosperms. Charles knew that Angiosperms were trees. But what he discovered was that Dicotyledoneae was made up of all the hardwood trees. He reasoned that the a-KG/rapamycin, mixed with the cranial hypertrophy chemical combined with the dicotyledoneae was the reason that he was able only to move hardwood materials.

His affinity for wooden pencils penetrating kitty skulls was small potatoes once Charles learned how to manipulate trees, furniture, fences, and, of course, decks. The Balachek deck had been easy to manipulate—it was old and wobbly already. All Charles had to do was concentrate quietly on one post. When the entire party moved outside, he squeezed his hands tightly and directed his anger towards that post. To inspire his anger, Charles pictured the time he actually attempted to go to one of the Balachek parties. It had taken him hours to get up the courage to knock on the door. He didn't know why, but all five of those horrible girls answered at the same time. Charles remembered the looks on their faces when they saw him.

"Charles?" Tricia had said. "What are you doing here? You need to leave now!" Charles remembered looking at all ten eyes watching him warily.

"Charles, get the hell out of here," said Zoe quickly. Charles remembered hearing laughter behind the girls. He assumed they were laughing at him.

"Go. Get out of here, Charles," said Skylar. "You're not smart for coming here. Go!" Charles remembered being so confused. These five girls had always been cordial to him at school, sometimes even nice—now they were shunning him? What had he ever done to them? All of a sudden the door opened wider and there was the grinning Todd. In his big hands was an oversized wooden University of Maryland Phi Delta Theta fraternity paddle. Todd pushed hard past the girls as they continued to implore Charles to go - and swung the paddle at Charles.

"Hey, Charlie, you fag—wanna spanking?" he said menacingly. Charles was surprised at Todd's comment, but quickly became disgusted.

"Don't call me Charlie. My name is Charles." Todd grabbed Charles by the shoulder and started dragging him into the street.

"Come on Charlie!" Todd taunted. As Charles struggled weakly against Todd's strong hold, he was so sure he could hear the five girls at the door laughing and carrying on. Screaming to Todd for "More! More!" He would never forget the sounds of laughter in between smacks of the paddle on his back and bottom. Todd held Charles down and pounded him with the wooden paddle. Each smack and slap of the paddle brought Charles closer to unconsciousness. *Please God,* he thought. *I think I'm going to die tonight.* He had sobbed and begged Todd to let up.

"I'll do anything you want!" he cried to Todd. "Please, show me mercy." But there was no mercy for Charles from Todd. Todd was drunk and wild with bully fervor.

"Don't. Come. Here. Again. You hear me, Charlie?" Each word was separated by another stinging smack of the paddle.

Mercy comes only from God, thought Charles deliriously as he lay in the street, curled up in a fetal position. Charles recalled thinking that Todd would have killed him then and there if the police cruiser hadn't suddenly pulled up. *God is good,* thought Charles as he was bathed in the red and blue flashing lights of the cruiser. *I have been saved so that I may help God punish those deserving because God is good.* Charles was beaten to a pulp, black and blue, and he was sure he could still hear the laughter and jeers of the five girls. He twisted his head slightly to the side and looked to the door to see if they were still there. The door was ajar and only Todd and his friends were there talking to one of the cops.

"Officer, he came here and started it," Todd had said. "My whole defensive line was in this living room and they saw him provoke me. There was nothing I could do— that kid is freakin nuts. Have you ever met batshit crazy Constance King?"
The other officer helped Charles to the curb and called an ambulance.

"You look like shit, kid" she said, "But it's gonna be alright, okay? I'll tell you what—God takes care of his own, right? Good thing we showed up!" Charles made a mental note to not ever hurt female police officers in his quest to rid this town of evil doers. She would be spared.
The other officer would not be. Charles overheard him remark to Todd, "Hey, man, I saw you play last Friday and you were fantastic! You know, I used to play ball at Severna Park—they retired my number…"

The rest of the evening was a blur of doctors and nurses, police officers and reports. Charles considered pressing charges but felt confident that he was going to inflict way more permanent damage on Todd and his cronies. He knew there would be another party the following weekend. He would be there.

Charles Mitchell sat crouched in the bushes looking excitedly at the carnage that lay before him. He wanted to remember every second of their pain. Every moan, every scream, every cry was a triumph to him! A triumph to God! The yard was chaos. Boards from the deck were strewn everywhere. There were dozens of red plastic cups tipped on their sides, spilling their contents everywhere and filling the night air with a stench of warm beer. The keg had actually rolled away from the party and had stopped near where Charles was hiding. The music was still playing—Charles recognized Bob Marley's "Three Little Birds." He was excited to hear voices and words, full of confusion, fear, and pain.

"What the hell happened?" he heard one bloodied boy say to no one in particular. "GOD HELP ME," screamed a girl Charles recognized as Zoe Lewis. She sat crying in the middle of the mess surrounded by wood and bodies. No one could even get to her, so she suffered alone. She was one of the five! (*God help her indeed!*) Charles felt keyed up as he appraised the scene that he'd created, and he smiled his snarling smile as he surveyed the damage. Students—*beeg shots*—were scattered all over the lawn. Some were holding their broken arms, some staring in shock at their own broken ankles. He could see several kids' faces covered in blood. Tricia Salmons (*another of the five, thanks be to God!*) was sobbing and begging for help. It looked to Charles as if she were sitting in between two bloody pieces of one broken timber. Charles couldn't be sure, but it looked as if the board had broken between her legs and cut her badly—there was an unbelievable amount of blood on her upper thighs. He scanned the yard looking for the other three girls. One by one he found them. Holly looked unconscious as she lay crooked and still in the grass next to the debris. Allie had removed her shirt (*slut!*) and sat hunched over, moaning and holding it to her face. He spotted Skylar rocking back and forth and muttering, holding her left arm. The planks had cracked and broken and his peers were bleeding, broken, and almost destroyed. Emergency personnel were having difficulties stepping over and around the splintered boards to reach the injured students. The red and blue lights flashed as they called to each other to bring stretchers and to call for more ambulances. To his delight, most of the students were moaning and writhing in pain. To his chagrin, some were not. He could see Todd limping around in the wreckage, calling out to his friends on the ground. Charles crossed his arms and sighed in frustration. How had God allowed this? Was Todd not the sinner to be destroyed? Charles frowned as he realized that some kids, like Todd, would likely go to the hospital and get a simple Band-Aid for their injuries. He had hoped the devastation would be greater and that he wouldn't have to use the compound on them—specifically on Todd— just yet.

Charles fingered the vials in his pocket. Once he'd discovered the way to harness the powers of his own mind he had determined that his days as a chemist had just begun. In the event that some of the students on his list didn't sustain enough injuries to maim them for life or to kill them, Charles created what he called a "death compound." This concoction was made up of a few bottles of liquid he'd found in his father's lab. Each liquid he used had been marked "toxic" or "hazardous." So far he'd tested his death compound only on his own pet hamsters and had only packed a handful of vials for this occasion. Charles spent many demented hours injecting the rodents watching the animals suffering in pain. The first two died awfully fast, he'd noted, so he on a whim he added some aspirin and ibuprofen to his mix to see if it would prolong the effect to at least a few minutes. To his delight, his pets died slowly and miserably. Using a chemical detection blot card from his father's lab, Charles was able to check the hamster's blood level. Just by putting a drop of the hamster's blood on detection cards he could discover if the compound was detected. Once again, to Charles' glee, the compound was undetectable. "If only I'd had more time to test it!" he thought. He'd run out of hamsters and had no money to purchase new ones for testing. Charles knew it was important to make sure that it wouldn't react with other chemicals in the blood, but unfortunately he had no real way of knowing if the compound could do anything other than cause death. These partly injured people would be his first human subjects. *God has prepared me for this night,* he thought. *He wouldn't give me anything that I cannot handle. The compound will kill those deserving and I will be rewarded.*

Charles backed away quickly into the woods to get back to his dad's station wagon. The firefighters had already cleared a lot of the wooden wreckage and he knew that it wouldn't be long before the paramedics could reach the students. Not long after, the ambulances would be rushing to the closest and most unprepared hospital in the area, Anne Arundel County Hospital. Charles needed to get to his dad's station wagon, put on his costume, get the compound needles, and get to the hospital before the injured patients arrived. It was time to administer his punishment to the evil ones, to bring God's punishment to those who wronged him. They would all pay tonight and he would be rewarded. Charles took a pencil out of his pocket and threw it hard so it would land near the deck. This would be his calling card. *God is good.*

Chapter 3: The Hospital

"Get ready for a busy night!" yelled the feathered-haired nurse to the emergency room employees at Anne Arundel County Hospital. "We got a load of drunken teenagers who fell off a deck or somethin'," she hollered, her harsh inner city Baltimore accent carrying easily over the din. "Believe it or not, we also got some fishermen from the Chesapeake who all got water moccasin bites, too," she continued loudly. "The antivenom is on its way. Kids are gonna be here in minutes and I got a mom about to pop with twins in room 2!" She gestured down a short hallway for emphasis. "GET MOVING!" she roared.

The emergency room had turned into pure pandemonium. Overworked and tired nurses were running back and forth grabbing blankets, beds, and clipboards. Doctors names were being shouted: "Doctor Sherman! Please come to room two immediately!" "Doctors Rattan and Wilcox, you are needed in emergency stat!" The sound of sirens was getting closer. Through the door first were the five snake bite victims. One at a time they came rolling in rickety wheelchairs, pushed in succession by the same orderly.

One of the men said drowsily to his wheelchair pusher, "You're young for hospital work…" Another fisherman also addressed the young orderly but his tongue was so swollen he was almost unintelligible.

"What'd you do to that other nurse? Saw him fall down. You see?" His head fell to the right and his red, swollen eyes closed. The three other fisherman looked similar, their eyes swollen and red, their cheeks purplish and puffy, their heads lolling about as their chairs were pushed. The orderly paused briefly at the front desk.

"Where you want em?" he asked in an accent similar to hers . She barely looked up and barked back at him.

"Find a room, put 'em all in there! I gotta tell everybody everything? It's a freakin' emergency." He nodded and pushed his greasy hair out of his bright green eyes.

"Room 3 it is then," a raspy voice responded. Charles Mitchell smiled hideously as he pushed the first fisherman into room 3 and then ducked into a hallway to wait for his victims.

A man dressed in white walked into the chaotic emergency room carrying a big brown box marked with yellow tape and the words "Water Moccasin Antivenin" written on it in large black letters.

"Where does this go?" he asked politely of the receptionist whose nametag read "Donna." "Donna," he said amiably "Where does the antivenin go?"

Donna looked up with stress in her eyes. "What do I look like, a friggin' pharmacist?" she responded sharply.

"AMY!" she screeched, reaching out and grabbing a very young nurse who'd just happened to be rushing by. "Come help Mr. Snake Guy find a place for his drugs, okay, hon?"

Amy paused and considered telling Donna that she had just started working at this hospital just two weeks ago and was still learning the ropes but then thought better of it. *I'll figure it out*, she thought to herself and motioned for Mr. Snake Guy to follow her into the lab. The man picked up his box and followed the nurse into the stark white room filled with vials and test tubes.

"You can just put it here," Amy said motioning to the hard, metal table. The man looked confused.

"Hon," he said "This here antivenin has to be kept in the fridge or it ain't gonna work for nothin'." Right at that moment there was an announcement on the hospital loudspeaker.

"All medical personnel to the ER *stat*. Ambulances bringing the teenagers from the accident are arriving! Repeat—*all* medical personnel needed in the emergency room *stat*!"

Amy looked at the man who was waiting for further instructions from her. She motioned to the small refrigerator nearby and turned to leave.

"You heard that—I gotta go. Can you just put it in the fridge? I gotta go!"

In a flash, Amy was gone and the man in white was left to do the job. He was irritated that she'd asked him to put the meds in the fridge himself. He wasn't supposed to touch the meds and had no idea where they should go in the fridge. *Ah well*, he thought to himself, *I guess it's a real emergency. I guess I can step up and do the job*. The man grabbed his knife from his belt, stabbed it into the seam on top of the box and dragged it down the center. Inside were 5 vials with the tiniest writing on their yellow labels. The man opened the refrigerator and found a whole shelf with vials that also had yellow labels and tiny writing. *Might as well put all the yellows together.* He placed the five vials next to the other yellow vials, lining them up perfectly. The first set of vials was marked "Antivenin" and the slightly lighter yellow set right next to them was marked "Antibiotics."

The students were arriving quickly and Charles had no trouble blending into the madness of the emergency room. Nurses and doctors alike were requesting that he bring blankets, pillows, and bandages to those in need. He fingered the needles in his pocket as he watched the door, patiently waiting for his favorite victims to arrive. He'd only brought 5 in each pocket so he wouldn't be able to kill all of his victims tonight, but to think of what devastation just killing 10 students would bring on the town! The town would thank him someday. He'd be ridding them of many vandals, underage drinkers, and immoral sluts. Once they got over their initial feelings of sadness they would see that Charles was actually a hero. He couldn't wait.

Suddenly, in came the top six sinners on Charles' list. Todd ambled in and sat on a nearby chair while "the five" were all ushered into the same room, number 4. What luck! All five girls in one spot. *(God is good!)*

Charles walked over to Todd and leaned closely in. He spoke in his raspy voice. "Do you need a wheelchair?"

Todd's eyes were closed as he answered. "No, man, I don't even need to be here. I hardly bumped my head."

Charles persisted. "Todd, you simply must have a wheelchair because you're not going to be sitting up much longer!"

Todd's eyes flew open at the mention of his name and he stared in shock as he faced Charles nose to nose. In less than a second Charles had stabbed Todd in the leg with the needle and pushed the plunger in. Todd fell backwards in his chair and lay tensed with his fists clenched as he fought for air. His eyes searched Charles' and he managed to choke out "Charlie?" before a violent spasm jolted his body.

"You must be in shock, young man!" Charles said too loudly and awkwardly. "I'll cover you up with this blanket!" He covered Todd's shaking body up and pushed his head down onto the chair next to him so that it looked as if Todd was just taking a nap. He sat and watched Todd convulse a few more times. Charles made a mental note that Todd had an enormous amount of bloody drool coming from his mouth. He used the corner of the blanket to wipe up the mess and tucked it discreetly under Todd. Not that anyone would notice. The emergency room was still in great disarray and looked as if it would be for quite some time. Charles smiled his snarl and patted Todd on the head. "I told you not to call me Charlie," he told Todd's lifeless body.

There was so much going on. Amy could barely focus as the doctor screamed out orders to her.

"I need five vials of Vancomycin antibiotics *stat,* these patients are at risk for infection! Amy! Are you listening?"

Amy's eyes were wide behind her coke bottle thick glasses and she nodded quickly.

"Yes, Dr. Ratterman. Yes, sir. You said antibiotics? The ones in the fridge?"

Dr. Ratterman seethed when he looked at the inexperienced Amy.

"You hopeless disaster do they teach you nothing in nursing school? Do I need to find them myself?" he shouted, purple veins popping out of his forehead. "I will spell it out for you! A-N-T-I—BIOTICS!" he howled inches from her nose. "Vancomycin, yellow labels, in the medical cooler. We have ZERO time for this Amy—go now!!"

Frazzled, intimidated, and frightened, Amy sprinted from room 4 into the medical supply room, knocking her glasses off in the bedlam. She skidded past the metal table not even noticing the now empty brown box with the yellow tape or even bothering to remember why it was there in the first place. Amy threw open the refrigerator door with a slam and searched for the yellow vials.

"Yellow tubes, yellow tubes," she muttered to herself. Ah ha! She'd spotted them. Dr. Ratterman would stop berating her, for now. Which ones? So many yellow labels and suddenly Amy realized that everything was blurry. She started as she heard Dr. Ratterman bellowing for her from room 4. Amy squinted at the tiny black letters on the labels. She could make out the capital letter "A"—they are all antibiotics! She grabbed the darker yellow vials because they looked newer, remembering that Dr. Ratterman yelled at her yesterday for not looking at expiration dates. With five vials in her hands and five needles for injections, Amy hurried quickly back to Dr. Ratterman, who had already started the patients' IVs. He demanded that she fill the needles with 25 cc's each and hand them over to him. Amy did as she was told.

Dr. Ratterman walked to each individual patient and, whether they were conscious or not, told them, "This is going to help you with infection and make you feel better," before quickly and expertly injecting each IV bag with water moccasin antivenin.

One down, five to go, thought Charles eagerly, wiping his greasy hair from his forehead. He paused for a moment, pleased at his successful evening. The deck had fallen easily. It was old and no match for Charles' mind control. His power had even managed to gravely injure Aman, that nosy, inappropriate clerk at the 7-Eleven. When Charles arrived at the hospital, he'd fit in easily in his lab uniform that he stole from his father's work. He hadn't planned on taking out the orderly standing outside but had made a brilliant snap decision to send a nearby crutch through his neck and take his place. The men in wheelchairs had served as vehicles for his grand entrance. Fortunately for Charles, the men were so out of it no one would believe anything they said anyway. The perfect plan—*God IS good*! Additionally, he thought about how easy it was to fell Todd with one simple injection (*He's not so strong, is he?*) and not a single person in the entire, poorly organized hospital had even noticed him (*not*) napping yet. He gently placed a pencil into Todd's hand and closed Todd's fingers around it.

Charles had nine compound vials left and his orderly outfit would be an easy way in to see the girls and an easy way out after he'd murdered them. Charles watched an irritated-looking doctor and a skittish nurse exit room 4. The doctor was yelling something at the nurse about calling parents or guardians. Charles knew this was his only chance to get in the room and take care of the sinners. He feigned a busy expression and walked briskly past the doctor who was still yelling at the nurse. No one noticed. Not a soul. *Did Todd have a soul?* Charles slipped into the room and gently shut the door behind him. He knew he had only minutes before family members were going to arrive.

What a surprise they would get! His eyes narrowed as he studied the room—he didn't want to miss a thing. The staff had managed to squeeze five beds in here, two on each wall and one in the middle. They were separated by light pink hospital sheet dividers.

Zoe was to his left, her hair was a tangled mess of leaves and dirt and her face was grimy and red. She was sleeping soundly—they all were. Charles knew it was the sedatives they'd been given upon their arrival. Her left leg was mangled and Charles surmised they would soon call for x-rays. Next to her was the fair-skinned Skylar. Her hair had probably been pulled back in a relaxed bun, he thought. When the deck fell, most of it had blown out of place. She was on her side, her broken wrist sticking off the bed. In the middle was big-mouthed Tricia. The sheets where she lay were covered with fresh blood and she looked very pale and fragile. To the right of Tricia up against the wall lay Allie, or at least it looked like it was Allie at one time. Her swollen eyes were blue, black, purple, and yellow. Her nose looked like it had been broken and her lips were caked with blood, as if she'd lost a nasty fight. To the right of Allie lay Holly. She was silent and motionless. Charles wondered if maybe she broke her back or neck because she was just so still. None of these injuries mattered to Charles anyhow because they would all be dead in a matter of minutes. Suddenly, the door opened for a brief moment. Charles could hear a nurse talking just outside.
"Who am I bringing in for x-rays? HELLO? Amy? Donna? Anyone??" The nurse sighed loudly and closed the door. Charles knew he had to act quickly. He ran to Zoe's bed, stabbed her in the leg, and pushed the plunger in. She let out a low moan but didn't stir. Next he rushed to Skylar and violently injected her with the serum. She whimpered and her eyes fluttered, but then she was quiet. The next three were totally anticlimactic: Tricia, Allie, and Holly were all silent and still as he quickly moved from one to the next.

Charles was in a frenzy. He paced back and forth shoving his oily hair from his wild eyes, looking from bed to bed, waiting for the girls to start convulsing and shaking. Where were the seizures like he'd observed watching Todd and the hamsters? No bloody, drooling mess? For a second he thought heard Zoe make a noise, but it was just the air conditioner switching on. All at once, the girls started shaking, but not in the same way Todd had. This was different. This shaking started at their feet, then traveled to their knees, to their stomachs and backs, and finally to their necks and heads. And they weren't really seizing, Charles noticed; they trembled as if there were a battle going on inside of them—like something was fighting the serum he'd injected.

Their eyes were open now and their trembling began to ease. They were looking around wildly at each other and at Charles. No one made a sound as Charles stepped methodically from bed to bed, placing pencils carefully at the foot of each bed. "Then the anger of the Lord will burn against you and He will destroy you," he whispered. He stopped suddenly and faced his victims slowly taking in each girl's terrified and confused expression one at a time —his victims were not only awake now but their eyes were bright. They weren't just alert; they were almost glowing. This was an unexpected side effect. Charles thought that this must be a separate side effect that Todd had not experienced. But why were they all experiencing it? And at the same time? Where was the bloody drool? Why were they still alive? Before Charles could observe any more, he heard the x-ray nurse outside the door again.
"Getting patient Zoe Lewis from room 4 for x-ray machine number 5, okay Donna?" she hollered. The door handle turned and the x-ray nurse walked briskly in and stopped in her tracks as she looked at Charles. "What the hell are you doing with those needles?" she asked angrily. "Who ARE you?" She watched this strange boy's eyes roll around in his head. He opened his palms and reached them up toward the ceiling.
"I...I...I," he stammered. What should he say? Charles decided to let God take care of him. (*God helps those...*) "I AM DOING GOD'S WILL. THEY ARE DYING! TODD IS DEAD! I HAVE CULLED THIS TOWN OF EVIL IN GOD'S NAME!" he howled.

The next few minutes were a blur after the nurse pressed the red security button. In seconds, 911 was called and several orderlies and hospital security rushed in and subdued Charles. They dragged him as he kicked and screamed religious epithets to the emergency breezeway and stuffed him into the back of the waiting police car. Charles didn't see the doctors rush in and check the girls he'd injected. They determined that their patients just had a small reaction to antivenin (Amy got fired that night). He never saw them find Todd's lifeless body on the chairs in the waiting room where they determined he'd been injected with something but they had no idea what. Charles didn't know that each girl had not only survived the deck collapsing and his attempted attack; they all had miraculously healed. He didn't know that the doctors and nurses just chalked it up to a clerical error, that the girls must have just hit their heads during the fall—no broken legs or wrists, no black eyes, no bleeding legs, no fractured necks or spines. They all went home that night. Except Todd. Charles had no idea.

Charles didn't put up a fight when he was arrested. He didn't put up a fight the next day either when he plead guilty to murder and attempted murder. The judge agreed when the defense lawyers and the district attorney deemed Charles mentally unfit to stand trial and he placed him directly into Crownsville Psychiatric Hospital for care. It took only a few weeks overall for Charles to be sentenced there for life.

Charles went along with his sentence agreeably, even earning good patient comments from the hospital staff until the day he happened upon a local Severna Park newspaper that an absentminded psychiatric ward nurse had left in the trash in the psychiatric hospital game room. Charles was calm and collected when he saw the picture of students with navy caps and gowns and gold tassels. He smiled when he read the headline "Severna Park Graduates Class of '91." It wasn't until he read the caption below the picture that he lost his cool. It read "Severna Park graduates Tricia Salmons, Holly Spencer, Allie Kasmir, Zoe Lewis, and Skylar Stewart managed a smile in the face of the tragic loss of would-be fellow graduate Todd Hemar." Charles stood and bellowed unintelligibly. He raised his arms into the air and every wooden chair and table in the room lifted simultaneously. They swirled around him like a tornado, and he controlled them with just a twitch of his eye. One twitch and down went the comatose patient who'd been staring at the television. Another twitch, down went the nurse who was frantically calling for help on the phone. Charles was lost in agony and fury and didn't notice the big, beefy, black orderly sneaking up behind him, armed with a cocktail of medicines forumlated to subdue him for a very long time. Charles whirled around and faced him just after being stuck several times with the heavy tranquilizers. One last twitch broke a table leg off a floating table and stabbed it directly into the big man's chest, killing him. Charles fell to his knees and fought to keep his eyes open. Though he resisted, his eyes finally closed. As he drifted off, the tables and chairs all fell to the floor in a crashing cacophony of broken wood. The last thing Charles remembered seeing was a thin, black-haired nurses' assistant standing a few feet away, looking awe-struck. A very sleepy, subdued Charles Mitchell was then taken to his secure, solitary, padded cell (with no wood in sight). The nurse's assistant stared at the big metal door as it closed. There he would stay, thought the nurse's assistant, for the rest of his life.

Chapter 4: Letting Go

We slowly pulled away from the curb, my husband Jimmy at the wheel of my sand colored Toyota FJ Cruiser and me in the passenger seat. I stared out the window and waved to my two beautiful little blonde-haired, blue-eyed boys, 6-year-old Max and nearly-4-year-old Pierce.

Behind them in the doorway were my parents waving back. I could hear my mother saying loudly, "Enjoy yourself! They will be fine, Zoe! It's just one Halloween!" I couldn't believe I was leaving my babies and missing a Halloween with them. Halloween was the ultimate mommy moment: to dress children up in cute or scary costumes and parade them around door to door. I was just leaving Nashville for three nights to Washington D.C., a place I knew very well; I'd been pulling my hair out as a stay-at-home mom, so I deserved and needed this trip; and I'd be seeing great friends who I hadn't seen in person since high school. Nevertheless, I felt awful, selfish, and guilty for leaving. What mother leaves her family at *Halloween* to do fun things on her own? Wouldn't they need me? What if they got hurt? I had looked at so many different airplane ticket options, but Jimmy couldn't take off work to watch the boys, so I needed a time that that coincided with my globe-trotting parents' being in town. I trust only my parents to watch my babies if their Daddy couldn't, and this was the only weekend they had free. It was now or never, Jimmy had told me. When would I get a chance like this again?

I rolled the window down and blew kisses to the boys, which they returned enthusiastically. Another wave of guilt washed over me and I fought to keep my smile intact so that they wouldn't notice. *I need this trip*, I told myself emphatically. *It is okay for me to take time away, and Oprah Winfrey herself would agree with that.* Sometimes I felt like that—as if I never left the house. I never was much of a typical June Cleaver housewife, though. I generally wore my long blonde hair pulled back in a ponytail. I wore minimal make up—usually just a little blush, mascara and lipstick—and could regularly be seen wearing black yoga pants, a tank top, and tennis shoes. That day for my trip, however, I'd traded the yoga pants for dark stretchy Lucky brand blue jeans, my favorite red Lynrd Skynrd skull t-shirt, and flip flops—probably not that much different from my usual uniform, but I loved being the mom who wore a t-shirt with a skull on it. It felt rebellious, and my sons thought it was cool because they equated the skull with pirates, the ultimate in cool for them.

Though I always thought of myself as a fantastic mother and a decent wife, I'd always felt like a square peg in a round hole when it came to normal stay-at-home mom activities: grocery shopping, cleaning, laundry, endless mommies groups (that covered topics of conversation like grocery shopping, cleaning, laundry), mommy-and-me classes, mommy exercise classes, mommy cooking—and on and on. Though I viewed all of these as unpleasant tasks, I participated as much as I could stand it because some things are necessary evils (laundry) and some were evil necessaries (mommies groups). I think I could have tolerated the mommy clubs a little more if we had more wine drinking and less potty training discussion. However, ask any Southern first-time mom to have a glass of wine around her newborn and you'll find yourself ostracized faster than you can say "poopy." It had gotten harder and harder for me over the years to find places to fit in, but I smiled and tried to be a good sport. However, it got increasingly difficult to tolerate my life as it was, so Jimmy and I decided a long weekend away could be a nice remedy. As we drove away, the boys smiled and waved once more, then turned and ran back into their grandparents' brick house, each boy pulling the other one back to get in front, eager to get started on whatever awesome grandparent-led activity awaited them.

I sighed and brushed away a tear from my flushed cheek. I would miss my babies desperately, but I knew I needed a respite from the trials of motherhood, away from Nashville, and away from my husband. Meeting up with girlfriends of mine from my old high school (Class of '91—go, Falcons!) would be just the thing I needed to erase my boredom and sour mood. Weekends away always seemed to refresh my mind and soul, allowing me to come back rejuvenated and appreciative of the wonderful things I had in my life. Lately, though, weekends away hadn't been enough to shake away the funk. I wanted even more time away, more space, more freedom, and I felt terrible about it. I struggled regularly with my selfishness.

I glanced sideways at my husband of 9 years and studied his face while he looked ahead at the sparse Nashville interstate traffic. Jimmy was a fine-looking man and I'd learned to appreciate that fact. Most men in their 30s tend to give up, get fat and bald, and not take care of themselves, but not Jimmy. Not only did he still have all of his dark, wavy hair but his regular ice hockey games and workouts at the gym kept him healthy and in shape. He'd managed to get better looking with age, and even though we'd had trouble recently with our emotional connections, I was still very attracted to him physically. He noticed me staring and glanced at me with his big brown eyes and blinked his long dark eye lashes.

"What?" he asked defensively.

"Nothing," I answered in a sigh. Like I said, we'd been having some trouble communicating lately. Mostly my fault, I presumed. Now in my mid-thirties with two very independent children, I had been struggling lately with my identity, my purpose, my direction in life. All my lifetime goals had been achieved in my eyes. From birth, women set out to achieve certain goals—graduate, job, marriage, children. Once all of this has happened, where does one go? I'd been measuring myself by the little things my children had achieved—eating with a spoon, walking, reading—and I'd tried to fit into the June Cleaver role and feel good about a clean house every day, but I couldn't measure myself by laundry and groceries anymore. It made me feel bad about myself. I often turned inward during these times and couldn't express to anyone that, even with a great husband and family, I felt like a loser. Jimmy interrupted my thoughts.

"You worried about what they're gonna think of you?" He was referring to my friends whom I was going to be meeting up with in D.C.

"I guess," I responded, sighing once again. "You think they'll make fun of my Southern accent?" We'd moved to Nashville from D.C. three years earlier. As much as I'd tried not to, I had picked up a definite drawl, and I was sure my girlfriends would notice.

"Nah. Who cares?" said Jimmy gruffly. "And stop worrying about what they'll think of you and if you'll have fun." He knew me so well, my husband. Although I was very outgoing, I tended to obsess on meetings like this. "Zoe," said my handsome husband, "you're in great shape from all that Zumber dancing or whatever it is you do, you're blonde and pretty, and you've got a nice rack. I'd pull this truck over and do you right now if you said I could!" Jimmy ended his little joke with a smug chuckle. Jimmy always thought his jokes were hilarious. I smiled mildly.

"Thanks, but we have to be at the airport in 15 minutes. Do you think the kids will be okay?" Jimmy seemed annoyed at my question.

"Of course—your parents will have them while I'm at work and I'll get them when I get home." Jimmy was an IT consultant and his current project kept him busy building technology infrastructure systems at a nearby hospital. He'd been thrilled lately with the work he'd been doing and I was proud of him, but I was jealous too. I also wanted something to be passionate about, and I was hoping this trip to D.C. would help me find some inspiration. To help me remember what my passions used to be before I became a wife and mother.

We arrived at the Nashville International Airport and pulled up to the Southwest sidewalk kiosk. Jimmy hopped out of the truck and went around to the back to get my bag out. I slowly got out of the passenger side and stood quietly watching him. He walked over to me and grabbed me in a big bear hug and gave me a loud smooch on the lips.

"You'll be fine once you get on the plane. Go, have a nice time, and behave yourself, you sexy thing," he said cheerfully as he patted me on the behind. We broke our embrace and said our love-yous, and I waved as Jimmy got back into the car and drove away. I sighed deeply once again, feeling that guilt that a mother and wife feels for doing something for herself. There were some days where all I could think about was getting away, and now that I'd finally gotten what I wanted, I wasn't so sure it was such a good idea anymore.

I turned in my bag at the counter, got my boarding pass, and wandered around the airport looking at people and roaming through stores, trying to keep my mind off of my family whom I was leaving behind in Nashville. Before long, I made my way to the gate, boarded my plane, and off I went. Jimmy was right—I was finally able to relax once on the plane. I stared out the window and allowed myself to enjoy the silence and solitude. My thoughts began to wander as I retraced the last several months to remember exactly I had gotten to the point where I was going to leave Nashville and head to DC for a weekend with girls I hadn't seen in over 15 years.

It all started with Facebook. I made one of those profiles, added a few personal details and some pictures of myself and the family. Before I knew it, I was looking at a list of people I might know and they were looking at me. Very quickly, I was put in touch with far-away family members, old professors, and even classmates from way back when I had a different last name. I enjoyed making these connections and sharing a smile or a nice note with people I never thought I'd see again. I often wondered if my closest girlfriends from high school would end up on Facebook. It wasn't really my thing to be on there—I don't like to spend lots of time on the computer and prefer to be in touch in person—so I simply figured they would be the same. But it wasn't long before my first real close friend from the past popped up. Holly Spencer's tiny picture and name appeared on my screen one day and I jumped at the chance to add her as a friend to see how she was doing, still living in Washington DC. Almost immediately she accepted me and we began talking and catching up. Soon after came Tricia Salmons (now in New York City), Allie Kasmir (somewhere in Colorado), and Skylar Stewart (also in DC). These girls were my true sisters growing up in the small suburban town of Severna Park, Maryland, and to be in touch with them again gave me butterflies. The Falcon Five was what we called ourselves back then, after the Severna Park Senior High mascot. It was so surreal that the Falcon Five were catching up again, on Facebook of all places.

We all began to trade messages, pictures, new stories, and old memories. We found out what happened after college; who was married, engaged, or single; who had kids; who was doing what for work; where we all lived. We started to care about each other again, to reconnect in a significant way I'd not thought possible using what I'd always seen as cold technology. Suddenly, posting a status update that I'd had a bad morning sparked several concerned responses from my longtime friends. I started to feel a bit more like myself again.

As a stay-at-home mom of two boys, I knew lonely very well, particularly now that one boy was in kindergarten and the other was in preschool 4 days a week. When my sons were younger, it was easy to devote myself tirelessly to their care. My days were exhausting and never-ending, but they were busy and full as each new day meant new challenges and work for me. Try as I might, I never felt fulfilled, but the job was so demanding and busy I didn't have the time to stop and reflect on it until now. I was proud of my sons and cherished their independence. I wasn't one of those moms who coddle their children to reinforce their own self worth. I wanted my sons to be secure and know how to handle the world around them. But while their independence and self reliance served them well I found myself increasingly disconnected from my purpose in life. What was I going to do now? What was I supposed to be doing? Poor Jimmy watched helplessly as I dragged around aimlessly, complaining I had no purpose. I was down a lot—I'm sure it was depression—and I was always careful to keep it from my boys, but I didn't keep it from Jimmy. He'd been asking me where his funny, sexy wife had gone, and while I still was her, I felt different. We'd been pulling apart the more my void grew because I couldn't say why things were bad—I just knew they were and that he couldn't fix them. There were a lot of silent nights watching television lately. A lot of time spent talking to each other about anything but what needed to be talked about.

Facebook didn't fill the void I was feeling, but it helped me evade it. My old friends and I developed a virtual support system, checking in regularly with one another. Ever the leader of our small group, I suggested a weekend together: no kids, no work, no men—just us getting together again. "Let's get the Falcon Five together again," I'd written on everyone's profile pages. After few days of emailing and planning, we decided to meet in Washington DC as middle ground for everyone.

When was the last time we were all five together? Was it our graduation? I shuddered when I remembered our graduation, and the weeks that followed it. It was a memory I had worked many years to leave behind. I wondered if they still thought about it as I often did.

The pilot's voice came over the loudspeaker, breaking my thoughts, and announced we'd be on the ground soon. Within a few minutes, we landed, bouncing gently on the tarmac, and pulled into our gate with ease. I was so excited I practically ran to baggage claim and bounced impatiently watching the mostly black bags riding slowly around the conveyor belt. Finally, I spotted mine—a shiny leopard print pink Prada bag—and I grabbed it and almost skipped out the door to grab a cab. I skip-walked past the airport newsstand and failed to see the *Baltimore Sun*'s small headline that read "Mentally ill convicted murderer escapes Crownsville Mental Hospital. Police have no leads."

Chapter 5: Together Again

The Falcon Five had decided to meet for dinner at 7:00 PM at Old Ebbitt Grill on 15th Street on the Friday night of my arrival. I chose a simple black dress for the occasion—a fitted, satiny, spaghetti strap number that cut in at the waist and then went just to my knees. It was a favorite of mine and I rarely had an opportunity to wear it. I wasn't a skinny little waif of a girl, but I was definitely in good shape from cardio exercise almost every day (what else was there for me to do?). But still, I've always been a woman with more curves than straight lines, and my nice bust and magical Jennifer Lopez booty attracted men and women from far and wide. I would wear this show-off-my-curves dress with my colorful high heeled Louis Vuitton shoes. I also carried my black Prada clutch and had a simple diamond bracelet, tear-drop diamond necklace, and small diamond earrings to match. Maybe I wasn't such a simple fashionista after all. I definitely knew how to lose the t-shirt and jeans and dress up when the occasion called for it—I just rarely had an occasion that called for it anymore.

I felt sexy—even stunning—and it showed. The doormen at the Mandarin Oriental Hotel tripped over themselves rushing to get me a cab to the restaurant. I smiled and winked at the winner— as a married woman in my 30's, I'll take a compliment like that any day. Per usual, I arrived early to the restaurant getting there a full half hour before our agreed upon time. Generally, I liked to get places early and park at the bar—it gives me a chance to have a glass of wine and check out the scene. It would also gave me time to think about things the girls and I might talk about and ways to keep the conversation going if things got awkward. Even though I was feeling feisty in my sexy black dress, I was still nervous and unsure about how things would unfold.

The cab dropped me at the restaurant and I paid, tipped generously, and stepped out onto the street. A couple with two kids who looked very similar in ages to my own walked by on the street.

I noticed the look on the mother's tired face as the children fought back and forth, yelling "Mine! Mine!"

Her eyes looked far away as she told them in a mild voice, "Please, stop you two." The children barely noticed her and went on battling, their father oblivious as he chatted away in a very important business voice on his iPhone. The mother sighed deeply and looked away from her unruly children and our eyes met. She studied me from my freshly washed, dried and styled honey blonde hair, my expertly applied make up, the sparkly diamond earrings and necklace, satiny black fitted dress, matching clutch purse and designer shoes. She looked down at her own clothes as she absentmindedly tried to fix her messy hair that had fallen half out of her pony tail. She was dressed in gray sweats and tennis shoes and carried a big, worn diaper bag. This mother clearly didn't need a diaper bag as her kids were of the age to use the toilet, but I suspected it was just force of habit to grab the biggest bag she had when on an outing with the family. She looked back at me again with an envious spark in her eye and then shrugged her shoulders, sighed once again and looked down, dejected. I tried to convey to her with my sympathetic smile that I very rarely dressed up in my trendy clothes or jewelry, that I knew first-hand about the messy pony tail, the absent working husband, and the rotten fighting children. I wanted her to know that I might have looked perfectly put together, but inside I was crumbling and had been for some time. I wanted her to understand that while I looked together, I was really just like her. I also knew that feeling deep down of wanting the best for her children and the great sacrifice it took every single day to give them that. I'd sighed that exasperated sigh just like her almost every day and I knew the feeling of wanting to detach and let them all take care of themselves. But I was also well aware of the terrible guilt that came with feeling such terrible things. A mother exists to love, nurture, and protect her children—how dare she think of running away sometimes?

I was also painfully aware of the deep and true love a mother has for her children and family and of the battle within her as she tries to balance the family with her own life. Any loving mother will lay down her life for her family, but should she live her life that way? Is there ever a fair balance? When is it okay to breathe?

The sweats-clad woman fussed at the children once more and shuffled away, turning back once more to meet my gaze and offer a small, sad smile. I smiled back, but inside I was screaming to her that I understood her and that it would be okay, that it had to be okay. I found myself watching the children, feeling sad that mine weren't close. Even though there was a struggle within me, it was a labor of love that I wouldn't give up for anything. As much as taking a nice break was necessary, it never filled the hole that was created by being away from my sons, my loves. My soul would forever be connected to them. I had tears in my eyes as I thought about them, though I hadn't even been gone for a whole day yet! I could see now that I had desperately needed this break. And a drink. I turned away from watching my sad self walk away and took my dressed-to-the- nines self into the restaurant and went straight to the bar and ordered a nice glass of a California wine country cabernet.

After a few minutes, the bartender wandered by checking on my glass. I could feel him thinking about chatting me up until he spotted the wedding ring. That doesn't always deter interested men, but it seemed to do the trick for now—I was happy when he busied himself cleaning glasses and chatting with other patrons about the game.

I checked my watch—6:55 PM. They would all be arriving soon. I wondered who would arrive first tonight and who would be last. Tricia definitely would be running in at the last possible second under great duress. I can't remember a time growing up when she wasn't running to something or somewhere as if her life depended on it. She could make just walking from one room to the next a huge deal, moving amid in a flurry of wild movements and loud sighs. I imagined that Holly would arrive precisely at 7:00 because she was never early and never late—a rule follower to an annoying degree. We used to tease Holly that she had the body of a Hooters girl with a brain of a nuclear physicist. Then there was Skylar. Skylar, a high school English teacher, was the quietest of our group but the funniest, though in an Eeyore kind of way. Slow-moving, methodical, and definitely passive aggressive, Skylar controlled the world around her by digging in her heels and waiting. Her turtle-like qualities drove the rest of us bananas, except Allie. Allie was the mother hen in our group. She was the one who would watch over us when we got into mischief in high school. She was the person you could call at 3AM for a ride home so your parents wouldn't find out that you weren't where you said you were. Sure, she was irritated beyond belief, but she would never let a friend down. It was Allie who checked on me every week after the big accident our senior year. And it was Allie who I expected to walk through that door at any moment.

I sat silently, contemplating my role in our group when the bartender approached again.

He uncrossed his arms from across his chest and placed them on the bar as he leaned in "Want a refill, beautiful?" he said. I nodded yes and watched him pour another glass.

"You're from Montreal?" I asked suddenly. The bartender looked surprised.

"How'd you know that?" he asked. I had no idea how I knew; I just knew. I'd grown accustomed to knowing things about people before they said them. Jimmy always said I was a psychic, but I really just always felt I was just seeing things that were right in front of everyone else that no one else noticed. My ability to read people often made me an object of desire for men, as they had never met anyone who could understand them like I could.

"Your accent," I said, demurely. Maybe I'd get a free glass of wine out of this. At 35, getting a younger bartender to cover your glass of wine always felt like a great accomplishment.

"You like my accent, eh?" he responded. He reached over and grabbed my hand and kissed it. "The French like to kiss zee hands, yes?" he said faking a ridiculous French accent. Just as I was about to tell him where to go, I felt a tap on my shoulder. Black-haired Allie was standing next to me.

"Some things never change do they, Zoe?" she laughed as she glanced curiously at the bartender still holding my hand. I snatched my hand away and grabbed her.

"Zut alors! Bon-freaking-jour, Allie!!!!" We hugged tightly and pulled back to look at each other. Allie looked young for 35—perhaps it was her small stature. At only 5-foot-1, she could barely reach the barstools. She also still had round cheeks, full lips, and sparkly dark eyes. Allie wore her black wavy hair down to her shoulders and she always knew how to dress for her figure. For as tiny as she was, she was built very voluptuously. Always a little embarrassed by her large chest, she tended to dress in dark colors. Tonight she was wearing a black velvet v-neck long-sleeved shirt, crisp white pants, and the tallest high heels a person could wear. Even with those high heels, she barely made it past my shoulder.

"How do you keep getting more adorable?" I asked her incredulously.

"Oh, please, little miss blondie," she responded, looking me over and smiling. "Somehow you managed to get even sexier in your old age."

"I wasn't exactly what you'd call sexy in high school," I reminded her lightly.

"True, we were so young and inexperienced then, yes?" she replied "But I definitely saw the future of what you were capable of!" I followed Allie over to the hostess "Table for 5, use the name Lewis, please" I said. "Others will be trickling in so just send them our way, okay?" The hostess nodded and showed us to our table near the window.

"How are you?" I asked excitedly. Since we'd been in touch on Facebook I knew that Allie was a married yoga instructor with two kids.

"I'm good. Flight was good, but even better is D.C. Who do you think will show up next?" As if right on cue, over walked the stunningly beautiful, nerdy-to-a-fault Holly. 'May I join you ladies?" she asked politely. Allie and I jumped up quickly to embrace her and to ooh and aah over how fantastic she looked. She still had her long straight white blonde hair, fair skin and blue eyes. She couldn't look more German or Swedish but was born in Fairfax, Virginia and was American through and through. Per usual Holly was dressed in clothes that accented her figure but did not announce it. She wore a fitted gray ruffled button-down top and a black pencil skirt. On her feet were a pair of shiny red heels - a hint that she wasn't *that* buttoned up, in fact she was known for letting loose but only at her discretion, never for anyone else.

"How's your writer fiancé?" I asked "Last update you posted was that he's on his way home from some secret location?"

"Oh yeah so secret" she responded rolling her eyes "He was in Vegas with a few of his wilder buddies and they had the time of their lives not following any rules" she said. "Back home to me and it's not so much fun being hung-over while I insist we go on our Monday morning 5-mile run!"

"He can sweat it out" said Allie "Get rid of the poison."

"Speaking of poison," I said "Shall we order a bottle of wine? What's everyone having tonight?"

We busied ourselves with the wine menu trying to determine what the other girls might want when in came Tricia, like a hurricane. Her light brown hair was disheveled and she had several bags that were swinging all around her.

"Lewis table please!!" she said loudly to the hostess "L E W I S" she spelled a little too slowly "Lewis. Like Lewis and Clark, Ray Lewis, Lewis Black. LEWIS." We watched as Tricia tapped her heels and sighed deeply at the hostess. "Really? This is hard? Here let me see the sheet" Tricia jogged around to the hostess stand and sighed loudly as she found the name. "There! Right there! I haven't got all day, show me the table!" Allie, Holly and I stood as Tricia came rushing over to the table. "Girls girls girls, can you believe that idiot hostess? Goodness Holly you look like a Barbie doll, Allie a nymph and Zoe a nympho!" her words came out in a rush "This was such a lovely idea, Zoe! Don't I look like a zillion bucks? Botox ladies, each and every one of you should be looking into it right now this second." She stood with her hand on her jutted out hip allowing us to get a look at her outfit which looked to be quite designer and quite expensive. Despite the chilly fall weather Tricia wore a sleeveless brown, green and black silky paisley top that tied around the back of her neck and that left her back bare. She had on a black leather mini skirt and black cork platform shoes. She was tall, five foot nine, with shoulder-length brown hair that she wore with a pin on one side. Skinny arms and legs and a short waist. We used to tease her that she looked like Olive Oil from the Popeye cartoons.

"Hey Olive" I said "Sit down and have a glass and let one of us get a word in edgewise, okay?" Tricia/Olive grinned and plopped herself down.

"Where the hell is Turtle?" she asked looking around "Shocking that she's not on time tonight."

Allie looked concerned "I texted her about 20 minutes ago and she said she was on her way." "Have you lost your mind?" I asked Allie. "When has Skylar ever been on time, ever?"

I looked around the table at my chatting friends. They were smiling, laughing, clinking glasses and *sparkling*. The void in my chest was unnoticeable as I sat there with them reliving our old times.

"Raise your hand if you slept with Matt Croker" said Tricia suddenly. "Not you Zoe, your hand is a given!"

"Hey!" I retorted "I actually didn't sleep with many boys way back then. I was more of a kissing bandit in those days." Tricia pondered this for a moment before responding "Really, Tim Carney?" The table burst out laughing as everyone was then reminded of an evening a 16-year-old me spent with an older, college-age boy.

"He said I had gentle hands" I said joining in the fun.

"What does that even mean?" said Holly. "Would you have normally just punched him in the face?"

"I don't think she used her hands on his face, Holly" said Allie pointedly.

"Enough!" I said loudly "I have enough dirt on each and every one of you that is just as bad if not worse than my gentle hands so I'd zip it if I were you!" Then I raised my glass for a toast "Wait, Skylar's not here yet!" said Holly.

"If we waited on Skylar it could be hours before we toast" said Tricia "Go on Zoe."

I raised my glass again and said "Here's to the girl who dresses in black she always looks neat she never looks slack...and when she kisses she kisses so sweet...makes a thing stand that never had feet!" We all said the last line together and put our glasses in for the toast when something strange happened. My hand got very hot, and as I looked around the table the girls also seemed to notice their hands holding the glasses. Our eyes were bright - almost glowing, actually - and we looked around at one another with our mouths agape at what we were seeing.

Tricia spoke first "What is happening?" she said wildly.

"Is there something wrong with our wine glasses?" asked Holly. Allie wanted to know if we were feeling our hands as hot as she was. We confirmed that we were. Just then the waiter interrupted our trance by asking if we were ready to order. We abruptly pulled our hands back and I smiled brightly at the waiter and asked if he could please just give us a few minutes. He seemed a little stunned by my attentiveness but walked away anyway promising to come back in a bit.

"Well that was odd" said Tricia.
"I'm sure it was just the lighting in the room" Holly responded "Reflections and such, no big deal." Even so, we decided to forego the toasting again until Skylar showed up. Where was Skylar?
"Who's got Facebook on their phone?" I asked coming up with a silly idea. "Let's update our status' to read something like 'In DC at old Ebbits grill with the gals waiting as always for the Turtle. That will irritate the daylights out of her." Everyone but Allie busied themselves for a few minutes typing into various cell phones, blackberries, and iPhones.
"You guys are mean" said Allie. "I refuse to participate. I looked down at my phone that usually had such great reception and was frustrated to see it had elected to turn itself off. Sighing, I looked around the table at the others who were silently cursing their own phones that had also not been working properly.
"Must be the location" I said to no one in particular "We can try later."

Back came the waiter to take our orders.
"I'll have the linguine with white clam sauce," I began. "And the girl to my left will have the cranberry chicken; the girl to her left will have the steak, medium rare please and a side of green beans; the blonde will have the pork tenderloin and Olive Oil over there will have the French onion soup to start and the chicken Caesar salad." I finished by ordering us a fresh bottle of wine and gave the waiter a special wink as a thanks. The waiter thanked me and walked away to place our orders. I was suddenly aware that the table was silent and all eyes were on me. Their mouths were open wide and they blinked slowly at me and then at each other.
Tricia spoke first "Dude," she began "What the...? How did you know?" I looked blankly at them answering,

"How did I know what?"

"What we wanted to eat" answered Allie never taking her eyes off of me.

Holly added, "I was going to get spaghetti but then changed my mind right as he walked over. How did you do that?" It was beginning to dawn on me.

"Didn't you tell me what you wanted?" I asked. "You did! You whispered to me what you wanted, I was just repeating it back to the waiter." They shook their heads slowly.

"No, Zoe" said Allie. "No one said anything about food at all."

"Really?" I asked. "Are you sure?" They all nodded in agreement.

"You just knew it, Blondie" said Tricia.

"Ha Ha" I said "What is this, April Fools? Punked? Not buying it," I said trying to deflect their weird stares and open mouths. "Well I hope I got it right because I'm sure to never be that precise again, right?" I joked.

Allie responded "Yes, well, I'm sure it could be just a coincidence, right gals? I mean we have known each other like sisters for 20 years." Allie's comment seemed to relax the group and although no one forgot the ordering incident we decided to move on to discuss more important things like what brand shoes Tricia was wearing.

It was now 7:45 and Skylar still hadn't shown up. As I listened to the girls chatter—we'd moved on to very important topics like had anyone heard that high school hottie Tom Park had been going bald, like Dr. Phil bald?—I felt an undertone of constant worried feeling buzzing around me, a concern for Skylar's whereabouts. She was always late, but never this late. Something felt very wrong about her not being there yet. But I pushed the thought away. I was on a roll tonight with weirdness and was not about to freak everyone out with my newest thoughts.

Allie spoke "I'm going to call Skylar. She's never this late." She got out her iPhone and began to press on the tiny screen slowly at first but then faster and with more frustration. "This silly thing," she said with her teeth clenched "I paid a zillion dollars for it and it's not working! It's like it's been struck by lightning or something!" She turned the phone off and back on again.

"I'll call Skylar," offered Holly.

"No darn it" answered Allie clutching the phone tightly in her hand "I will make this work!" As if on cue, when Allie said the word "work" the phone simply shattered into pieces. It didn't make a loud sound, more of a crunching and the pieces were teeny tiny scattered all over the table where she sat. For the second time tonight, we were all dumbfounded.

"Allie?" Holly said softly "Are you okay? Did you hurt your hand?" Allie slowly opened her hand.

"It's a little cut up but nothing bad" she answered. "My iPhone. It's ruined." Our waiter appeared with our food and noticed the plastic mess in front of Allie.

"Let me scrape that off for you, miss" he said professionally.

I answered back to him absently "Oh it was her iPhone, thanks." He looked at me questioningly as did the rest of the table.

"Didn't you ask…?" I said. "It appears I've done it again," I murmured quietly. The waiter scooped the contents of Allie's damaged phone into a little plastic bag and left it next to her plate in the event that possibly the phone people could either fix or replace it for her. Then he and a bus boy distributed our food, filled our wine and water glasses and hurried off. No one spoke for a while as we picked at our food and shoved it around our plates.

Holly spoke first "Someone should really call Skylar, I'm getting concerned." Tricia picked up her phone and suddenly threw it back down onto the table "Son of a bitch!" she yelped "It shocked me!"

"Try mine" said Holly curiously as she slid her phone over to Tricia. Tricia grabbed impatiently at the phone, which promptly lit up with a blue spark, causing her to cuss and hurl the phone back to Holly. I followed suit and handed Tricia my cell phone. This caused us both to feel a charge—but it wasn't the phone that was shocking us. The shock seemed to travel from Tricia's hand, through the phone into my hand tossing the phone up a few inches. It landed in my lap and felt very warm.

"What is this an iPhone throwing competition?" she said sarcastically.

"Let me try something else."

Tricia called the waiter over to the table but I spoke before she could "Excuse me" I said batting my eyes at him "Do you happen to have one of those chefs gloves? The thick black rubber kind?" The waiter said he would have to check.

"It would be fantastic," I said "if you could bring one out to us?" Without questioning me, he scurried off and came back quickly with the glove. We thanked him and shoed him away to see if this rubber glove would do the trick. Tricia slowly put on the glove murmuring to herself that this was ridiculous, why on earth couldn't she touch a fucking cell phone without a shock racing through it. The glove worked. Tricia was able to pick up the phone without the electric shock, but with the heavy glove, she was unable to dial Skylar.

We stared at each other.

"I guess I'm next?" Holly asked.

"Everyone's got something weird going on tonight except for me" she stated.

"Maybe you'll get married and have kids" snorted Tricia. Everyone at the table laughed and that eased our tension a little bit. Tricia and Holly had always been in a silent competition for everything. Boys, grades, popularity were just a few of the things that they'd battled over way back when. Now it seems the new battle is the family battle. Since Allie and I were already married with children the competition was now over who would get married first and who would end up the old maid. It seemed so funny to me that Tricia and Holly were in such a *hurry* to have what I routinely took for granted. A nice husband, a big house, a healthy family was something I had that they wanted. Being single and living in the big city, traveling the world like they did - that appealed to me. They were exciting. I was *boring*. Of course I loved my husband and children dearly and would not trade them for anything. But to live my life existing only for them was difficult and now that my children were older I found myself not having anything but time to live for and time isn't a nurturing entity. Living with time was lonely and I craved to live life in a more exciting way. I just didn't know how.

"Ass," said Holly as she looked away from Tricia "At least I'm engaged."

"Yeah for the last 4 years" responded Tricia.

"How come you guys never fight with Skylar about this stuff?" I asked.

"Because Skylar never slept with my boyfriends," retorted Holly.

"Oh I slept with your boyfriends? Hey pot, meet kettle," barked Tricia.

Allie stepped in "Gals, come on. Let's be friends and enjoy the evening shall we? Tell me Holly, how was France the last time you were there?" Holly lit up at the question and began telling a narrative of her last trip to France. She was a chemist of all things—the most beautiful chemist ever in the whole world of chemistry. I chuckled as I thought of what those French nerds must have thought when she walked in the door. No doubt they were expecting to flirt and chat her up but Holly was not a game player and not a flirt. Serious to a fault, she was a hard worker and being silly was not in her nature. I always thought it was interesting how Holly and her fiance had found each other. She was only science and he was only art. I listened as she described the latest compound they'd been working on. Some sort of genetic code breaker of sorts. They'd had a lot of trouble finding ways to test this compound as it was volatile and testing on humans simply was not an option.

"And on that note," Holly said suddenly "I have to use the loo, excuse me ladies." She hopped up and walked off to the restroom her long blonde hair swinging behind her as she stepped. The waiter returned for the rubber glove.

As Tricia handed it over to him her cell phone rang. Forgetting her electrical issues she picked it up "Hello?" she said casually. We all noticed that the phone did not cause a shock. Tricia smiled "Yes this is Tricia" she said sweetly. "Oh good lawd, Steve I'm out to dinner can't this wait?" Tricia was a big time publicist in NYC and nothing ever waited when you were a big time publicist. She waved her hand at us to motion that she would be a second. She didn't leave the table but turned her back and spoke in annoyed hushed tones to Steve, her assistant.

"Zoe, what's she thinking?" said Allie quietly. I closed my eyes.

"I don't know? That Steve should get a life? It's 9:30 on a Friday night for chrissakes." We laughed and I was relieved that I didn't know a damn thing Tricia was thinking. For a brief moment, we relaxed. Then everything happened very quickly. Holly walked back from the bathroom and my head exploded "*if that jack ass thinks he's gonna fire me over this…"* I thought I heard Tricia say. A second later the phone shot out of Tricia's hand in a blue flash and landed in Allie's lap.

"I won't touch it!" she said, wide eyed. "I don't want to break it!" No one moved or said a word as we all looked over at Holly. She looked just as surprised as we were when she held up Allie's formerly damaged cell phone. It was totally reassembled as if Allie had never shattered it in the first place.

I was the first to speak. "You know what?" I said "Let's just get this check, head back to my room at our hotel, get a few bottles of wine or champagne or straight tequila and figure this thing out, yes?" No one spoke and they exchanged knowing glances to each other as if I didn't know what they were thinking. I continued "Testing me are you, gals?" I smiled. "I can see in my head that you all are game for my hotel drinking plan and no Tricia I don't have any weed, you're on your own."

Tricia snorted "Like I was thinking about weed…" she trailed off. We all exchanged glances and talked small talk while we paid the check.

"What about Skylar?" said Allie once again.

"We'll call her from the hotel—I'll use the regular phone," answered Holly. Off we went, the Falcon Five minus one, back to my hotel. Room 1098 at the Mandarin Oriental Hotel was in for a treat tonight.

Chapter 6: Nikki Sixx

The cab ride from the restaurant to the hotel was just minutes but it felt like hours. We sat quietly as it seemed like every chance we moved or talked something strange would happen to us. We arrived at the hotel and Tricia moved to put her hand on the metal car door handle to let herself out but thought better of it and allowed the doorman to do so.

"Finally," she breathed impatiently "I gotta wait all freakin day?" I paused for a second trying to figure out if she'd said that out loud or if it just appeared in my head and I determined that she had in fact stated that out loud and it made me relax some. Perhaps this was just one odd night of strange happenings. *Probably some sort of rancid wine.* I heard Holly say. Or did I? She had gotten out of the cab already and was near the door. Did I hear her or did I feel what she said? I scooted out of the cab ready to go ask her when I actually did hear Allie apologizing profusely to the taxi driver.

"Oh jeez I'm sorry, so so sorry sir," she said quickly. "I must have grabbed too hard. This must be an old cab!" In Allie's tiny hand was the outside door handle from the taxi. Holly strode back from the hotel door, took the handle from Allie and promptly pushed it back into place with a snap.

"There!" she said shakily "All fixed." Holly looked at me pleadingly "Can we go in now Z? I really need some of that tequila." I nodded vigorously and guided my friends into the hotel and into the elevator (Tricia was careful not to touch the buttons) and up to suite 1098. I slid in the key card and we were inside.

"Hey big spender!!" Tricia said animatedly "I though my room was nice but damn!" I smiled and explained that we'd accrued many hotel points over the years and I thought staying at the Mandarin Oriental Hotel in D.C. would be a great place to start using them. We all dropped our purses on the floor—it was a mini designer bag showcase, Gucci, Prada, Louis Vuitton and Versace - and slid off our shoes (another showcase) and padded around in our bare feet. I went straight to the phone and dialed room service. I ordered five bottles of red wine (Shiraz, Allie's favorite), one bottle of champagne, one bottle of tequila and some chocolate covered strawberries and other assorted fruit. I didn't know about the rest of them but I figured it was safe to assume that this was definitely a chocolate emergency for us. It's not every day that you discover you can do tricks with your mind. Tricia ran around the place shouting oohs and ahhs at the tan marble floors, the lush couches, the stunning view of the Potomac and of course the huge walk-in closet. "Thank God you have a walk-in closet ," she stated matter-of-factly "A girl has to have a place for her Jimmy Choos."

I held my hand over the mouthpiece of the phone and said to Tricia in a mock serious tone "You ain't kiddin. I flew with them in my carry on, no way am I going to risk them being lost by the airline." Holly and Allie had parked themselves on the plush red couch, talking softly about the taxi door handle and how really it was probably just a coincidence that it broke and Holly fixed it. I could feel everyone thinking that they were worried about Skylar. *Skylar Skylar Skylar.* She was definitely a slow mover and always late but she wasn't inconsiderate and she would never miss a party, especially one with us. I finished my call with the room service and promptly dialed Skylar's number. It rang a few times and went to voicemail.

"Where the hell are you, Turtle?" I asked. "Give us a call or a text please and let us know you're not lying in a ditch somewhere, okay?" I hung up the phone and happily answered the room service knock at the door. In came a beautiful table on wheels covered in white linen. It was pushed by a very handsome, young college-aged man. He was very thin and sported long, black hair that he kept in his face, covering up beautiful blue eyes.

"Yet another reason to stay at this hotel," said Tricia eyeing our room service waiter.

Seemingly embarrassed, the waiter busied himself setting up the drinks on the table.

Holly laughed and addressed the kid directly "Don't mind her, she just got out of prison. It's been a while, if you know what I mean."

Tricia eyed Holly for a moment and retorted "Oh yes," she said looking at the waiter's name tag that read 'Christian.' "Christian, allow me to introduce to you my prison bitch. She wasn't actually in prison with me but she is definitely a bitch."

Christian looked around at us with shifty eyes and before he could speak I answered him, "It's my room, I'll take the receipt, do you have a pen?"

Christian pulled a long, brown pencil out from behind his ear and spoke so softly we had to lean in to hear him "Here you go," was all he said. But I could hear something else from him—if I could just quiet the girls in the room I could figure out what he was thinking. *he's hot.. Easy targets. Who uses a pencil anymore? See em said it would be easy. I really need a drink. No pot! Sucks. Be patient, not now. Did I really fix that? Did I really break it?* There was so much noise in my mind that I couldn't clearly delineate what Christian could have been referring to in his thoughts—I figured perhaps that Christian thought Tricia or Holly might be easy to get into the sack. I smiled knowingly at him and as I walked him to the door I told him if he was working the late shift that it was very likely we'd be ordering some room service at about 2AM and we'd just love it if he could make another appearance. I walked back down the hallway to our cozy sitting room and we discussed how Christian the room service waiter looked a little like Motley Crüe's Nikki Sixx, who was hotter in the Crüe's heyday Nikki Sixx or Tommy Lee (two votes for Tommy and two for Nikki—tie) and whether tequila or champagne would be a good way to start our evening. General consensus was tequila— we all did a shot to the Falcon Five sans Turtle—and the night began.

Allie started the discussion. "Alrighty gals, this has been one weird night and I think it's time we just get it all out on the table here. I will go first. It appears at times I am super strong." She stopped as suddenly as she started, clearly unsure of where to go with her speech. She glanced at me saying "Zoe, you go. What's your weird thing?" I took a deep breath and answered

"Well Allie and gals—I'm not really sure how to explain this—but I can feel what you're thinking. I can almost hear it." I felt ridiculous saying this and like Allie I just stopped abruptly and turned to the next in line, Tricia. She looked at each of us and spoke "Evidently, I'm electric or something," she said in a clipped tone. We all turned to Holly for the last announcement.

"I fix," stated Holly matter-of-factly as if fixing broken iPhones was something she'd gone to college for.

"Fantastic," I said sarcastically "More wine. I need more wine." I got up to pour the wine and promptly tripped over Tricia's long legs and fell right into the table that fell into the hotel's very fancy plasma television, cracking it. We paused and slowly all turned to look at Holly.

"What?"she said sharply. "I'm not sure I can just command myself to fix it ladies, I'm not MacGyver."

"You might save me one helluva terrible hotel bill if you could, you know," I said hopefully.

"Come on, hotshot," added Tricia "You fixed it so my prom date went home with you junior year, I'm sure you can fix this."

Holly rolled her eyes "We've been over this ten million times, you said yourself you didn't like him and could I help that he thought blondes have more fun?" Tricia coughed and leaned over to pick up a chocolate strawberry as she began to chatter.

"Who ever said that you were blonde? To be fair he was a big nerd just like you…" she replied, ready to go on. Allie waved her hand to quiet Tricia and pointed at Holly who was staring at the broken television intently. I could feel the air in the room getting thick and Holly looked different. Her eyes glowed brightly as she sat in front of the damaged set and quickly her hands flew into action. I wasn't sure if I could even really see anything happening at all. Holly's head was cocked to the left, her jaw line set and steady and her lips a thin line except for her tongue that was poking out ever so slightly on the right side. That was all I could see - all any of us could see - for her hands were a blur. A tornado of colors swirled around in front of her as she worked. No one made a sound, including Holly. She reassembled the broken set in silence—no sound from her and no sound from her work—as if she was working in some space-time continuum. In seconds, she was done. She sat back with a great big sigh and straightened her head, tossing her blonde hair to the side. Her eyes returned to their normal bright blue and she turned and smiled us.

"Done," she said. "I don't know what I just did and I couldn't teach a class on it to save my life but for what it's worth I fixed it. Oh, and Tricia, you know what they say about sleeping with nerds, right?" Tricia looked up waiting for the answer "They know just what keys to press, if you know what I mean!" Tricia picked up a pillow and hurled it across the room but Holly ducked.

"You had sex with Matt Miller? My prom date?!? Slut!" she said laughing.

Holly responded "Takes one to know one."

"Gals, please," I said decisively "You're both sluts, okay?" Suddenly I was hit square in the face by two red paisley pillows. I tried to throw them back but even though Tricia and Holly didn't move to duck, I missed.

"Guys, look!" Allie said interrupting our pillow fight. She leaned over to the television and flipped it on. "It works," she whispered as the images flashed brightly on the screen. "Nice work!" cheered Tricia. Not to be outdone, Tricia announced she would be the next to practice her "weird thing" but first she had to pee so could someone please open another bottle of wine and everyone get out their cell phones to see what she could do with them. We watched her stagger off (the tequila was catching up to us for sure) and we obliged, taking our phones out and laying them on the thick glass table in front of us. As soon as Tricia was out of sight, they all buzzed at the same time.

"I got a txt," I said picking up my phone. "From Turtle!" Before anyone spoke I added "We all have the same text, yes?" Everyone smiled and nodded. I was happy I didn't have to display my "weird thing" like the rest of them did, it just sort of existed in my head and was quite easy to demonstrate. I clicked on the text message and up popped a picture of Skylar with the following message. Falcons i had 2 wrk late, will call 2morrow xo turtle. The Falcon Four were quiet for a minute as we looked at the text and the picture.

"Huh," said Allie.

Holly added, "Rude?"

"Look at the picture she sent," I said. The picture was a typical text picture a little out of focus and I could barely make out where she was.

"Since when does an English teacher have to work late on short notice?" I continued. Skylar looked tired in the shot, her dark blonde hair was pulled back in a loose pony tail and her make-up looked smeared, as if she'd been rubbing her eyes.. Something looked odd about the picture but I couldn't quite put my finger on it—besides the voices in the room (in my head) started getting really loud again. Suddenly the phones started cutting in and out as Tricia returned to the room.

"Damn it, Trixie," I said to Tricia, calling her a nickname from our past, "You're messing up our phones again, can you turn yourself off, please?" Tricia stopped in her tracks and knitted her eyebrows thoughtfully.

"Well I'm sure that I don't know if I can do that or not," she said "Let's see…" She sat down and slumped against the wall behind her. A hum of voices came across the room and I was inundated with thoughts from the girls. *What's she doing? I'm getting drunk. Where is Skylar? I wonder if I can fix our phones. Chocolate is making me fat. Where is Skylar. I have to pee. I feel fat. This is scary. I wish Nikki Sixx would come back.*
I screamed to them "Stop it!! Stop it! I cannot think - your voices are too loud!" I, too, slumped down next to Tricia to try to get myself under control. Tricia's head was up now, sitting on her knees as she hugged them to her chest. Her eyes were bright and glowing—much like Holly's had been when she worked on the television set. She held

her palms a few inches apart and took a deep breath and let it out slowly. Between her hands a little blue bolt of electricity was rushing back and forth. At first it had a mind of its own, pushing back and forth rapidly and wildly. As Tricia's eyes grew even brighter the electricity began to pulse. As I watched I realized it was a regular rhythm of a heartbeat. Bum bum. Bum bum. Bum bum. Tricia sat up suddenly and threw her hand in the direction of the television.

"Duck!!" I yelled and the girls all hit the floor and covered their heads in a gasp. The blue light shot out of her hand and smashed into the plasma TV, breaking it (again) and along the way our cell phones all buzzed loudly and then were quiet. The blue light suddenly came out of the television and flew back into Tricia's hands and was gone.

"I guess it's like an electric boomerang," she said softly. "When I close my hand and stop my mind from thinking about it, it stays put." Tricia looked around sheepishly "Sorry about your iPhones I was trying for the TV. Maybe Holly can fix 'em up." Allie and Holly got out of their protective positions and chuckled. All three girls moved back to the couches, grabbed their wine, and chugged. I could not move. Their voices were overwhelming my mind and the sound was deafening.

"How do you control it??" I asked loudly between clenched teeth. "Help."

Allie repeated what Tricia had just said "Tricia said, close your mind, Zoe. Try to stop it." I sat there with my head spinning and the constant noise of thoughts and feelings rushed around me, making me feel nauseous. Suddenly, their thoughts came in a rush.

Come on Zoe I likethesecolorsymore tequilai'm sadiatetoomuchatdinner

"It's like being in a noisy city with taxis and airplanes and people talking all over—I have to work very hard to turn down the buzz to make out the individual sounds!" I explained breathlessly. Everyone nodded in understanding and smiled. *herturn*I *guess it's my turnherturn.* I shook my head trying to delineate who was saying what. I turned to Allie and spoke "Yep. Your turn. Why don't you pick up this couch for me?" I motioned to the couch that had Tricia and Holly lounging on it. Slowly Allie approached the couch. She bent over and put her hands under it and tried to lift.

"Ug!" she grunted. Nothing. The couch didn't budge.

"Try pushing it!" said Tricia. Allie put her shoulder up against the side of the couch and pushed.

"Unn!" she moaned. Nothing.

"I can't do this!" said Allie angrily. "Why can everyone else do their weird thing and I CAN'T?" as she said the last two words she pounded her fist on the couch, breaking off the side of it and sending it crashing to the floor. This movement also caused Tricia - who was closest to the side that was demolished - to jump into Holly's lap in surprise.

"Get off me you big baby," said Holly rolling her eyes.

"Don't act like you didn't enjoy it," retorted Tricia quickly.

She then spoke to Allie directly "Al, you're like an angry two year old!" she said laughing.

Allie laughed too. "My weird thing is that I throw temper tantrums and break things," she said.

Holly countered, "At least your's has a purpose—you are strong! Zoe can hear our minds, Tricia can send blue bolts around the room. What the hell can I do? I put televisions back together. Call me cable guy. Worst superhero power ever," she pouted. We all turned our heads to Holly and I spoke.

"Superhero power?" I repeated in a high pitched voice. "Is that what we've got going on here? Why us? Why now?"

"I do not know the answer to that one," replied Holly, and she suddenly shut us out as her eyes grew bright and her hands flew to work on the television. "There," she said seconds later. "The plasma television is fixed once again—let's try to keep it that way." With that she flipped it on and the end of the ten o'clock news with Maureen Bunyan came on.

"OMG, I haven't seen Maureen Bunyan in years," I said. "She looks the exact same, even in high def." Tricia studied the news anchor.

"I don't like her hair. She looks like Rhianna's Mom." We chuckled and Holly reached over to turn the TV back off when I stopped her.

"Wait, what's she talking about Crownsville for?" Maureen Bunyan, anchor of the 10 PM news, was talking about an escaped mental patient that goes by the name of Charles Mitchell. The Falcon Four sat silently listening to each word out of her mouth.

"Mitchell escaped today from Crownsville Psychiatric Hospital. Police believe he had assistance from a hospital employee, Chris Jeffreys, who has also been missing since this morning. Mitchell suffers from severe delusions and is extremely dangerous. Anyone with any information regarding Charles Mitchell or Chris Jeffreys should contact the state police at 444-0009." Holly slowly pressed the off button on the television and we sat in utter silence. I was the first to speak and my voice trembled as I said "Charles Mitchell. Remember?"

Chapter 7: Skills Practice

"Of course we remember," Holly said softly. "I still have the pencils he left at my feet," she continued. I remembered that a bloody pencil had also been left at the scene where the deck collapsed and asked the girls about it.

"Ewww, remember how it was stuck in Jeff Sharp's leg?," Allie whispered. "He was confused because he wasn't on the deck when it collapsed but somehow it stabbed him when he was trying to help people get up."

"You know, I heard Charles stabbed a guy with a pencil when he first got committed," said Tricia whispering even lower, "My Dad's friend was a medical director there and he told my Dad that Charles went nutso when he found out we graduated and didn't die like he'd wanted us to." I studied the faces of my friends, my sisters.

"We all know that we shouldn't have walked out of the hospital that night," I said in a low voice. "We were all injured. We were all hurt badly. Charles injected us with something—we all know that. Why didn't we die like Todd?"

Holly answered quietly "I have been thinking about that for years," she said. Holly continued, "As you all remember, due to the hospital error, we were all accidentally injected with water moccasin snake venom antidote." She went on "Now ordinarily that wouldn't make a difference either way since we hadn't been bitten. In 30 to 40 minutes or so the antidote would just have been absorbed into our blood stream and moved on its merry way." Holly paused twisting a few strands of hair around her finger before she continued. "But Charles Mitchell had something bad in those needles they found. Whatever it was killed Todd Hemar. My guess is whatever he developed to kill us was met with the snake venom antidote and instead of killing us off it allowed us to develop these "weird things" we've got going on tonight." I picked up the tequila and began pouring more shots at the girls unspoken requests. Allie began chopping up more limes. Tricia looked confused "If that's the case, Holly," she murmured then why haven't I been running around shooting blue lights out of my hands all of these years? Why hasn't Allie broken her damn husband in half in a fight of rage?"

Holly stopped twisting her hair, sat up straight and looked directly at Tricia "Look I can only theorize okay? But I have always had a knack for fixing things. Maybe not like I can now, but I have always had this affinity for it."

"I have always been really intuitive," I added. "Just not to this extent."

Tricia laughed. "You know, I have always been prone to picking up shocks from things like the carpet or even just turning a light switch on."

Allie chimed in gently. "I am a yoga instructor extraordinaire," she said. "I have always been the tiniest teacher yet the strongest anywhere I have ever studied."

Holly the scientist took all of this information in and responded in a hushed tone. "Well then, it seems to me that all of these abilities have been dormant within us," she said. "And now that we are together they are at their strongest. Charles Mitchell's poison, the antivenin and our internal reactions to that combination came together at the same time. We were never all together at the same time after that night."

"Now that we are they are at their strongest!" I said excitedly.

"Shhh!" said Tricia whispering again.

"Why are we whispering, Trix?" I asked.

She giggled drunkenly "I dunno. It just seemed like the right time to be using our secret telling voices."

Holly spoke again in her most serious scientist voice "But Skylar isn't here. So I am theorizing that when she is here our powers will be at their strongest."

Tricia snorted. "Our powers. That's right, we're superheroes!" She lifted her shot glass "To superheroes who carry Prada bags and wear Christian Louboutin shoes!" We lifted our shot glasses, each rim touching the one next to it. We were getting used to our eyes becoming bright when we did this, and the air around us crackling.

"Weirdest superheroes ever," I added sarcastically "What are we gonna do, punch, fix, electrocute and think our way to protecting innocent people everywhere?" Allie responded "Sure, why not? As long as we look good doing it."

Tricia yelled "Does that mean we get to buy a new outfit?"

"Of course, Tricia," I said. "Now, down the hatch!" We swallowed the bitter tequila and shoved the limes into our mouths. This was shaping up to be one interesting girls' weekend, I thought.

The girls and I spent the next few hours worrying about Skylar, practicing our new-found skills and finishing off the five bottles of wine and fruit I'd ordered. Tricia learned that if she was on the balcony, and was close enough to still hear our voices, that she could send a blue shock through glass to the hotel phone inside. This was unfortunate for me as I was on the phone calling room service when she launched her electric boomerang. My hair stood straight up on end for a full 10 seconds and I had burns on my hands and feet. I stomped out to the balcony to tell her to get it under control, but she was laughing so hard (as were the rest of those traitors) that I couldn't stay mad. I decided to get her back and when she snuck off to talk to her boyfriend Tate, I announced to the girls every detail that she was feeling and thinking. Even though I still had all of their noisy thoughts in my head I could pick out bits and pieces from hers and his. And to be honest, some of it I could just hear through the door. I knew I had a long way to go before I was going to be able to control this thing. Evidently, in addition to be an enthusiastic lover, Tate was quite well endowed and their last love-making session had left Tricia with a bit of a limp the following morning. She'd explained at work she'd just twisted her ankle but she and Tate had some talking to do about how they were going to work things out for next time. An important public relations executive simply cannot be limping around at work the day after each salacious encounter with her youthful boyfriend. When Tricia came out of the bedroom after her chat we were all sitting there nonchalantly with bananas between our legs and a strawberry on either side. When I got up to get her another glass of wine, I limped. In fact, we all limped for the next hour. Tricia took it like a champ, however, and was smart enough to turn her attention to Holly to see how she could deflect the joke to her.

"At least I have something big enough to ride," she said snidely.

Holly shot back "Your boss must love having his highest paid flack hobbling around like an invalid. I'd say teach Tate that patience is a virtue but we both know you're not very virtuous."

I interjected and reminded Holly that she wasn't exactly a nun and if anyone would lose the slut battle it would likely be her. Tricia smiled triumphantly at me for coming to her defense and I also reminded Tricia that it was me that told everyone about Tate's, um, appendage in the first place.

Allie was quite happy with her power. Tiny and youthful looking, she was rarely taken seriously in her daily life. She was always getting pushed out of the way in busy crowds, overlooked in long lines, ignored while trying to get anything - from a cab or someone's attention. It was something she was accustomed to but not ever happy about. When Holly refused to move from her newly claimed spot on the couch (that had previously been Allies minutes earlier) Allie simply furrowed her brow and lifted Holly up and dropped her not so gently onto the floor. Holly landed ungracefully in a heap of arms and legs and accidently kicked the plasma television once more and breaking it once again.

"Fix it, fix it!" we chanted unceremoniously the words slurring together. Holly looked perplexed and thoughtful as she pondered what to do with the TV.

"Hey make something else," I suggested.

"I bet you could make one hell of a vibrator out of that thing," added Tricia drunkenly. Holly paused, her eyes bright with excitement "I am going to make something I saw on one of Dave's silly video games once." Dave, Holly's writer boyfriend, often spent his downtime playing video games. This was one of the reasons they had not yet tied the knot. Holly just wasn't sure that she wanted to marry an oversized child, no matter how talented a writer he was. "He has this zombie game where they kill all of these wandering dead people," she said. "They use all of these ridiculous totally preposterous weapons, things I just know no one could really build..." and with that she trailed off and we watched as she turned her back to us, cocked her head to the side, stuck her tongue out ever so slightly and began to work. Seconds later she turned to face us with a big hunk of metal in her hands. It was black and silver, with a huge rectangular handle connected to the television cord the other end was a long, cylndrical snout.

"Um that is the biggest vibrator I have ever seen," said Tricia.

Holly sighed "It's not a vibrator, you bimbo," she said. "It's a plasma gun!" Holly continued "I took the plasma from the converter and it can heat up from the electricity created when I plug it in!!" She ran to the wall and shoved the black plug hurriedly into the electrical socket. I heard *time to try this baby out* and I screamed to my friends "GET ON THE FLOOR!!" and threw myself under the table. Everyone followed suit and fell to the floor. "Oh relax! It's not gonna do a thing," she said "Probably just gonna make a fizzle noise and peter out..." she trailed off as she fumbled with a little metal piece that must have been the trigger. She proceeded to push the little metal piece forward and waited. "Any second now, it should shoot," she said softly. Suddenly there was a loud click and my sisters and I squealed and grabbed each other's hands in fear. We waited for the next big sonic boom, but nothing happened. "Well shoot," said Holly. Saying "shoot" was the closest she'd ever get to swearing. She preferred to find other words to express herself as she viewed swearing as crass and unprofessional. "Let me fool with this little doohickey here..." she mumbled.

"Doohickey is a scientific term, Dr. Dork?" asked Tricia from her crouched position under the table. Holly smiled suddenly and pulled the little metal trigger backwards and then let it go. In that second Holly's new toy—a plasma gun—sent a white light whooshing across the room and left a nice round hole of fire in the door. "Much quieter than I'd anticipated," said Holly to no one in particular "Different from that zombie game plasma guns. Someone make a note of that, please."

Allie's head popped up "Fire!" she squeaked and she ran to kitchenette returning with the fire extinguisher. She sprayed the fiery hole in the door while Holly studied it closely. "Clean shot, right through," she muttered with obvious satisfaction.

Tricia got up slowly from her crunched up position and walked to the door "That's gonna cost you lots of hotel miles," she said darkly.

"Way to go Dr. Destructo," she said to Holly "You made your first weapon." Holly couldn't have been more thrilled.

"Don't be jealous, Trixie," she said flippantly "Not my fault my power is cooler than yours." Tricia grinned and shot out a blue light at Holly's feet causing her to jump up onto the couch.

"Watch it!" Holly warned "That's a sixty five dollar pedicure you're about to fry!"

"Have to be sure your feet look good when they're up in the air, eh?" I got up off the floor and reached up to give Holly a hand down.

"Alright you two," I said "Let's use our powers for good okay? Destroying overpriced pedicures just seems like a major crime to me."

Chapter 8: He's Got Invisibility

"When is the food getting here?" groaned a tipsy Tricia. "I'm starving!" Just before Tricia had made my hair stand on its tippy toes I had ordered some late night snacks from room service and even requested the cute room service waiter Christian-Nikki Sixx look-a-like to bring them to us.

"I think he's close," I said "I can hear a man in my head and he's nervous about something."

"Probably wondering if Trixie's gonna have her pants down when he walks in" slurred Holly.

"He wishes," snapped Tricia. "Me want food."

"Well he's probably in the elevator now," I said "And I gotta run to the potty, so you're on your own until I return okay?" I asked. I looked at my friends as they lounged on the couch ignoring me "Are you listening?" I asked loudly.

"No but you are," barked back Tricia "Go pee, we can handle it," said Allie sweetly.

I walked off to the luxurious bathroom in my luxurious suite at the Mandarin Oriental Hotel in Washington D.C. Just this morning I was an ordinary housewife from Nashville, Tennessee. One dinner with the girls and I could hear peoples' thoughts, saw a woman make a plasma gun out of a television, had an electrical hair moment and saw the tiniest girl I know destroy a couch with her fist. I turned on the sink water and stared in the mirror in disbelief. Who was I, really? Despite all of the distractions the evening had brought I still missed my boys, so I was definitely a mother. But I missed all three of them—I was definitely still Jimmy's wife. In the midst of all our discoveries this evening I couldn't shake the feeling that this would be so much more amazing if Jimmy were here to share it with me. I knew that he would accept my stories about tonight's events and not question them. The more I was away from him, even in this short amount of time, the more I realized how much of a champion he was for me. On my darkest of days it was Jimmy who would lift me out of the doldrums and tell me I could be anything, that I could do anything. Only now was I realizing that he might be right, perhaps this new-found power was something he sensed in me all along. I felt the urge to call him to tell him all about what was going on with me, with my friends, with the new forces working within us. But I didn't call. Since I'd shut off so completely from him these past few months I found it harder and harder to get back. I couldn't remember how to approach him. Trying to open up would make me feel weak and vulnerable. I'd built such high walls around myself that I couldn't break through them to get to him. I wouldn't call, not tonight. I just wasn't ready. I heard the knock at the door—I'd been so focused on thinking about Jimmy that I'd completely turned off the voices in the living room—I shook my head as if to reorganize my thoughts and began to "listen" as I splashed cool water on my face. My head snapped up as I heard a man's thoughts *SEE EM…saidtoinject…itintomyleg…rightbeforeIgo…isomeoneatthedoor…myhairisamess…if eelfat* Quickly I turned and my wet hands fumbled to get the bathroom door open. "Girls?" I said loudly "Girls! Don't let Nikki Sixx in until I get to you okay? I thought I heard something." Quickly, I grabbed a towel from the sink and used it to twist open the handle. I ran out into the living room just as Christian was coming in. *Damn he's hot. Tommy Lee has nothing on this kid. I'm hungry. Think my husband would mind if I just grabbed his bottom.* That last one was Allie! I stared at her in disbelief "Allie, really?" I said. She looked at me realizing she was busted and shrugged her shoulders. "It looks nice," she said unabashedly. I struggled to find the voice I wanted to hear and stared long and hard at our handsome hotel waiter as he slowly pushed the cart into the room with his right hand and kept his left hand in his pocket. The buzz of their voices in my head was loud but I could make out something faint. *glorious…foodLetme…inladiesihope…weorderedfrenchfrieslet…her rip.*

"Guys," I said timidly and way too quietly "Something isn't right, he's up to something bad. I couldn't get the words out to explain what was happening, there were still so many of their thoughts in my mind, competing with his. *Get them. What's she talking about? Hurt who? How? Piece of cake..* I turned to Christian "What are you up to?" I asked fiercely "I know you're not here just to bring us food."

Christian looked around at each of us, his eyes darting from face to face in confusion "How did you…" he started to say. I shook my head trying to clear the loud buzzing from my mind.

See…em…saidthismigh…thappenwhat…is…zoedoinghope…thisdoesn'tmess…upsnackti me He pulled out his left hand and brandished a small black-handled knife.

"You all need to come with me," he said impatiently. "Come quietly and I won't hurt you. Give me trouble and you'll be sorry."

Tricia smiled and addressed Christian "Oooh! Me first! But only if you promise to stab me" she said reaching towards him. He took a step backward and waved the knife at her. As soon as the metal blade was close to her she cupped her hands together and threw a small blue spark at the shiny silver blade. It missed the blade and it found a new spot, Christian's cell phone, that was in his shirt pocket. The phone flashed brightly as it flew out of his pocket and onto the floor where it buzzed once and lay still. The spark bounced back up from the phone and Tricia caught it expertly, as if she'd been doing this for years. *Whatisgoingon…yaytricia…see em…saidthismight…happenwhatdo…Idonow*

"See who??" I said angrily. Suddenly, Christian staggered backwards as if he'd been hit by something hard in the chest. I looked to the girls questioningly to see if they'd caused his backwards stumble, Tricia responded to my glance "Don't look at us, he just started that one on his own!" Holly gasped "Look!" she said pointing back at Christian. He was standing with his hands over his chest wild eyed and breathing heavily.

Whatis…wrong…iamchanging…what…ishedoing "What are you doing, Christian?" I shouted. No sooner had the words come out of my mouth when I saw what Christian was referring to. Little by little Christian started to *fade*. His hair disappeared first, eyebrows, eye lashes and then his skin followed. It paled and then peeled off in scales that vanished as they fell off of his body, leaving nothing in their place—just blank airspace. Right before our eyes, Christian was becoming invisible. His fingernails slid off and fell into the invisible skin pile, his shirt was suddenly hanging in thin air. *Ohthatisgross…getclothesoff…ifeelsick*

"He said something about his clothes I think!" I roared at my frozen in place friends "He's disappearing! We won't be able to fight him if we can't see him!" But by the time I'd finished my sentence our Nikki Sixx look-a-like had stripped clean and he had completely disappeared.

Holly, Tricia, Allie and I moved to stand side by side in a circle. *Whores!*

"Zoe," whispered Holly "What is he saying?"

"He just called us whores," I replied.

Tricia snorted "How did he know about Holly?" snorted Tricia.

Holly replied sharply "Ahem, glass houses."

Soscarediam…scarediwil…lblow…onhersoscared…whereis…he I felt a soft burst of air on my left ear.

"He's right next to me," I said nervously "He just blew on my ear." I froze and tried in vain to spot him, to see any sort of movement of his body.

"Well he's barking up the wrong tree," said Tricia, "I'm right here, handsome. Come leave a little kiss on me," she said teasingly. *Tricia…no…nicelegs…besafe*

"Oooh, I guess he forewent the kiss on the face and grabbed my legs instead," Tricia said, but this time she was not sounding so brave.

"I thought I heard 'nice legs'?" I said absentmindedly as I searched for his frame.

"Nice legs?" said Holly noisily causing us all to jump "I have nice legs. She has skinny bones and knobby knees." Tricia did not argue and we all turned to watch Holly.

Comeget…meWhores…besafe I felt a breath near my face.

"He's over here," I said "I swear I heard the word whores." The girls looked around indignantly.

"Well I never…" began Tricia in mocking tone. A man's voice spoke from my right, very close to where Allie was standing.

"Ladies, I have orders to bring you all to my boss. Please come willingly or I will have to kill you here and now."

Allie responded "Yes, of course. We will come willingly. Can you tell me, sir, who your master is?" Tricia, Holly and I looked at Allie oddly. Why would she say the word master? Christian answered in an annoyed tone from the same place next to Allie "I have no master. In fact, now that I can..." As he spoke, Allie's arm came out like a flash and punched hard into the invisible air next to her. As her fist connected with Christian's unseen body, a loud grunt emanated from him and his concealed figure slammed into the wall behind him leaving a huge hole in the dry wall and sending a painting crashing on top of his suddenly -- unbeknownst to him -- very visible head. He jumped up and stumbled to the right and disappeared again. *Hurt.* Before I could tell the girls what Christian was thinking Holly grabbed us and whispered "He doesn't know we can see him when he's been impaired! We have to keep wounding him to see him! Allie, play like you're hurt—play it up!" Without questioning Holly, Allie began fussing loudly over her hand.

"My hand, girls, my hand! What was I thinking? I'm too small to fight a man, I think I punched right into the wall! Has anyone see or heard from him? Oh god oh god!!" she wailed. *Bzzzzz* My head vibrated with the noise as I tried to listen to him *iwill...smashhim...imhurt...badiwill...shoot...him*

"He's back," I said. "I think he's hurt I am sorry girls I am terrible at this," I added. Allie slumped over feigning pain.

"Oh my hand," she cried.. *comeonsucker...notthatone...fallforit*

"I don't know what he is saying!" I cried. My eyes scanned the room looking for anything that would show me where he might be as I watched my friends do the same. "Maybe he said fall for it?" I couldn't believe how bad I was at using my power. *Keeptryingzoe...iwant...themin...dreader...zoedont...giveup* "You guys, it's..." I struggled to get the words out before he could get to me but it was too late. My neck felt as if it was in a vise and Christian threw me forward so that I fell onto my knees. I could barely breathe but I knew that if I fought too hard that the girls wouldn't have a clear shot at Christian. I needed to struggle just enough to survive while they mounted an attack. Mount an attack? I thought wildly, Can they even do that? I clawed halfheartedly at the unseen hands around my throat. *Whatdowedo...iwillsavehershe...willsuffer...movenow* "Zoe!" Allie had stopped moaning long enough to say "Are you alright?" All I could do was look at her. There was no room to breathe, let alone talk. Lightning shot across the room and hit the invisible choke hold on my neck, releasing me. I fell to the floor and rolled towards Allie and we all turned to see Christians angry face in full view along with his burned hand. A white flash blazed across the room and hit Christian in the shoulder knocking him backwards. Holly had her plasma gun and was looking to aim it once again at our waiter. Christian's entire face and naked body sans hair were in full view now and he was now aware of his predicament. Holly, flanked by Tricia on one side and Allie and me on the other stepped gingerly toward Christian as he flickered in and out of view. Allie spoke "What are you doing here, man?" she said casually.

Tellus...wewin...see em...see emyoulose

"Who said we win?" I asked her not waiting for an answer.

"Z, what's he thinking?" she said still staring at him. "He keeps saying something like see em, see em, over and over but I can't be sure," I said slowly. Leaning close to his face I spoke. "Christian you look like a broken Christmas light," I said. "You're never gonna get out of here, so just relax your mind and let me see inside." Christian scooted backward on his elbows. His shoulder and hand were burned, his chest deeply bruised and he was trying hard to breathe. I could see him looking around for anything to defend himself. "Hey Christian you need to invent some invisible clothes next time around," said Tricia chuckling "I guess fighting superhero chicks causes major shrinkage?" Holly chimed in "Yeah Christian, to be perfectly honest I could have gone without seeing … it. This is so awkward." We all exchanged glances—this was actually kind of fun. But we were new to this superhero business and we relaxed way too soon.

Heissoskinny...menneverhavehips...imgone...penisisnt...thatsmall Christian had inched over to his pile of clothes and while we were snickering and breathing a sigh of relief, he'd grabbed a tiny syringe that had fallen out of his pants pocket.

Callcopsfixhotelimgonetiehimupimgone

"He keeps thinking…" I said. Suddenly Christian jumped up, stabbed himself in the leg and made for the door. As he ran, he went clear. Holly responded by shooting several zaps of white light into that space, hitting him only once and allowing us to see his pasty white derriere as he ran out the door.

"Shoot," she said in her nerdy swear as she fiddled with the trigger. Allie ran to the door and slammed it closed and locked it. We all stood there in utter shock at what just happened while listening to Holly click the trigger back and forth.

"I never did get a chance to pee," I said finally. This broke our trance and we looked around at each other, wide eyed.

"Dude, go now. I bet the hotel is going to send up some major muscle after all that noise just went down" said Tricia. I suggested to them that they try cleaning up some of the shot and wine glasses before our newest guests arrived and I finally went back to the bathroom to relieve myself. As I walked back into the living room I was once again taken aback by the scene that unfolded in front of me. At the mention of the hotel sending staff up, my friends pushed aside the cleaning and waiter duties I had suggested and displayed their top priority at the moment: themselves. They'd each grabbed their stylish purses and shuffled through them searching for their tinted, bee sting for extra pouty lips, Mac lip gloss. They took turns using the hallway and bedroom mirrors as they fixed foundation, combed out their hair and complained loudly of the unfairness of wrinkles. Next step for my superhero friends was to find their shoes and put them on. After all, I thought, you can't look like you've just wrestled with an invisible waiter when the staff arrives. What would they think? Vanity can be an ugly thing, I snickered to myself. Not to be outdone and just as vain as the lot of them, I too, touched up my make-up, fixed my hair and put on my heels. These women were beautiful, sharp, successful women even before they'd made their powerful discoveries, and I was one of them. Time to act like it, I thought smiling.

It was going to be a long night. In the midst of all the drinking, discovering and practicing powers, Charles Mitchell's escape and foiling the Nikki Sixx look-a-like, we'd forgotten about the last Falcon of the Falcon Five, who'd mysteriously not been able to make it tonight. Skylar had some big-time explaining to do when we caught up with her tomorrow I thought, as I answered the knock at the door. If she could get a word in edgewise, that is.

Chapter 9: Food and Revelation

I awoke to the sound of my cell phone playing ACDCs Back in Black. I had added that cell ringtone recently and it made me feel so bad ass when it rang. I found it especially funny when it rang at inappropriate places like church or my son's school. Particularly in Nashville, Tennessee -- the Bible Belt -- this was funny to me. People pray before soccer games in the Bible Belt. They pray before meetings, they pray at the gym. I took a spinning class once where the instructor yelled a prayer over the loud music as we hit a particularly difficult climb in the routine. As a result I always got a little kick out of wearing my Lynyrd Skynyrd skull shirt or having iconoclastic Back in Black by ACDC as my cell phone ring. I don't know if it ever bothered a single person but it certainly amused me. "Back in black!" my phone shrieked but by the time I reached over to the table to get it, it had turned off. Sighing and stretching I rolled onto my back and stared at the ceiling trying to remember last night's unbelievable events: The dinner, the powers, (powers?) the after-party, practicing our skills (powers), the battle with an unusually evil waiter, and then the fact that the hotel manager was so taken with us flirting with him that he said he'd cover that silly hole and pay for the broken painting (Holly had reassembled the plasma TV as well as our cell phones - back to their former selves). It surely helped that we insisted with wide innocent eyes, soft breathy voices and lots of cleavage that the entire thing happened before we got there and we saw a very shady, long-black-haired bus boy leaving the room just as we arrived. That dumb manager agreed to cover all of it as long as we promised he could buy us a drink the next night. All that money and we were all going to get a free drink out of this? I love having boobs. I pushed my thoughts of the pushover manager out of my mind as I remembered one element that had been missing from the entire crazy scene. Skylar. I reached out for my phone again and flipped it open, scrolling to the text message she'd sent all of us last night. It seemed so long ago. I studied the picture closely. Her face was so close to the phone camera that you couldn't make out a room behind her. Just her hair - her very messy hair that last night I thought had been in a ponytail was actually pulled back in a Japanese kabuki style with pencils sticking out of it - and her tired face. I could barely make out that her eyes were green and her mouth was set in a small fake tight lipped smile. I thought, "What English teacher works that late?" Why hadn't she called any of us? The more I considered the details of her not showing up the more worried I became. I decided to get up and get the day going, get the rest of the girls up and figure out what happened last night and to find Skylar. I snapped the phone closed and sat up only to promptly lay right back down on my big, luxurious bed. My head hurt and my mouth was dry and I never got a chance to sleep in at home. I stretched out my arms and legs and sighed – wincing a little at my throbbing head. My superhero girlfriends would have to wait. Sleeping in, having a hotel room to myself and not having a worry in the world was a rare decadent treat for me. I was going to take full advantage. I fell back to sleep in seconds. I dreamed of Skylar running.

A little while later my phone started blasting it's angry rock anthem again and I shook my head to wake myself up to answer it.

It was Tricia "Jesus, you and Allie are impossible to get out of bed!" she said.

I blinked slowly, my voice hoarse and dry, as I answered "Hey, jackass that's cuz we never sleep in ever. Little people called children run in at 6:30 in the morning and insist that we feed them."

Tricia was quiet for a moment and she responded in a rare emotional way "Yeah, your life sucks. You have babies who love you unconditionally. Must be rough."

Startled, I tried to stammer out an apology but Tricia cut me off.

"Never mind," she said. *You have no idea how good you have it.* That thought came through loud and clear. I wondered briefly if it was because it was just the two of us and no other thinkers close by. "Meet us downstairs for breakfast in an hour!" she ended cheerfully and hung up. I rolled over onto my back, thinking about what Tricia had said out loud and in her mind. Sure, I had people who loved me, but so did she. And she could sleep in. And travel whenever she wanted, to anywhere. And she had this great job and could kiss anyone she wanted. She could go to Italy and learn Italian. The last thing I learned that was new was that Publix brand canned green beans were 30 cents cheaper than the name brand. Her life was amazing, I thought to myself. Mine was stale. But yet her comments struck a chord in me. Would she want to be tied down to my Ground Hog Day life? Same thing, day in and day out? As I sat up and threw my feet over the side of my huge bed I made a mental note to ask her more about this later. I had other things to think about currently. Important things, like did I remember my razor and what outfit would I wear to breakfast. I knew we'd be doing some walking so I decided that comfort would need to play a role in my outfit choices for the day. I decided on my Lucky brand tight blue jeans and my light purple Free People cotton shirt with velvet flower designs on the sleeves. I would wear my black Van tennis shoes that of course that match my black leather jacket. I'd look absolutely cute and casual, I thought as I flounced off to the shower.

I jumped out of the shower squeaky clean and put on the hotel robe. I needed to call Jimmy and check on the family. I sat on the straight-back red cushioned chair and dialed home. Jimmy answered.

"Hey, it's Mommy!" I heard him say excitedly. Immediately, pangs of guilt stabbed me harshly. He was excited to hear from me, my babies were too. "Hey, I'm going to put Pierce on first okay Zoe?" he said excitedly.

"Of course," I answered anxious to hear my baby's voice.

"Mommy?" came a tiny 4 year-old-voice. "Hi Pierce!" I said practically screaming. "Mommy rode on an airplane yesterday!" It was quiet for a moment and Pierce said "Mommy? Where ARE you?" My child does not know where his mother is; I am by far the all-time worst mother in the history of mothers.

"Baby, I'm in Washington. Remember Mommy was going to a boring grown-up meeting?" I said meekly.

He responded "Mommy? When are you coming home?" Toddler 2, Mommy 0.

"Piercey, Mommy will be home in a few days, I promise okay? Are you being good for Daddy?"

"Max took my storm trooper," he stated matter of factly.

"Well it's nice to share, but be sure he gives it back to you honey, okay?" Pierce was not happy with that answer "Max! Share it back with me!" he yelled at Max, who was nearby. "Pierce? Pierce," I said "Honey, Mommy is going to bring you back a present okay? Something you will love." That got his attention: Pierce 2, Mommy 1.

"Okay Mommy, I love you. I miss you a lot," he said in his sweet little baby voice. Ouch. I really am the worst mother in the universe. They should just make me a shirt that reads "This woman is a terrible, terrible mother."

I struggled not to cry as I answered "I love you too, sweetie, more than anything in the world." The phone suddenly sounded as if it was going through the motions of many little hands who were likely fighting over it. Next was Max.

"Hi, Mommy, bye Mommy" said my 6-year-old. I sighed deeply as Max wasn't one to talk on the phone anyway and now he was also probably mad at me for being away. I was a snake. A low down dirty snake.

Jimmy spoke "Zoe? You still there?"

I sighed even deeper than I just had "Yes."

He laughed "Oh please, they're fine. Excuse me, we are having a guys weekend. We are going to barbeque and watch star wars and play sports!"

I waited for him to finish and I added "Does that mean someday you'll add to that list drink beer, fart, and watch Spike TV?"

Jimmy laughed again and said "Duh. How are things going? Is anyone fat?" For the first time during the conversation I smiled.

"Not one of us," I answered triumphantly. "We all look pretty damn fabulous. Some of us more than others," I added. Jimmy wanted to know who.

"Obviously the ones who haven't yet had children still have flatter tummies and higher breasts," I said.

"Your breasts are amazing," he answered.

"Gross, Jimmy," I said "Can we have one conversation ever that doesn't include talking about my boobs?"

"Nope," Jimmy replied quickly "So is it fun? What's been going on?"

I hesitated for a moment and took a deep breath "Well, here's the thing," I began.

"Wait a sec," Jimmy interrupted "Boys! We do not push each other's faces into the floor!" I shook my head. Wasn't this always this case at home? Anytime I tried to say anything, anytime Jimmy tried to listen and vice versa, weren't we always interrupted by our darling children. If they weren't fighting they were doing something adorable.

Something like a hand-made puppet show from the back of the couch. It was that sort of thing that absolutely begged our attention to be turned only to them. And once our attention was off of each other, it very rarely came back. Besides, who can compete with a 4- and 6- year old's puppet show?

"Hey Jimmy," I said loudly to overcome the sounds of kids crying and Daddy yelling at them "I gotta go get breakfast with the girls."

"Oh okay," he said sounding a little dejected. "Love you. Say hi to everyone."

"I will," I answered. "You too." Lately we had been so far apart emotionally we hardly even said the "I" in "I love you." Somehow it was easier and safer to just casually say "love you." I had definitely been perpetuating the terrible habit because for me just adding that extra "I" made me feel vulnerable. I don't know if Jimmy even noticed but it was just another way for me to avoid my feelings. That the statement 'love you' was really just a comfortable rut we had fallen into. But it wasn't true, I thought. I did love him and them deeply and seriously. I loved them completely, no matter how miserable I had been feeling. I knew I needed to unlock my heart again and let him back in. Particularly now that I was a superhero. I just hoped he loved me enough to understand that what I was going to share with him wasn't anything he'd ever dream of hearing.

I managed to get myself down to the breakfast at Café Mozu, the swanky breakfast place where we were all meeting, 10 minutes shy of our meeting time. Of course I was the first one there and I knew exactly who would be showing up and when. I told the hostess that I was waiting for other people to show and I sat down to wait on a bench nearby. As I waited I flipped open my cell phone and texted Skylar asking her if she was up yet and asked if she wanted to meet us for breakfast. I knew as I hit send that she had probably already received three other messages just like mine already this morning but I still had to try. I snapped the phone shut and decided to see if I could use my power on the people around me, without the girls nearby. There was always a hum surrounding me when there were lots of people around. I'd just always assumed that this was a general noise level of everything at once becoming one sound. But now I listened to it differently. It wasn't a hum as much as it was many whispers of consonants coming together. I could hear s' and t's and d's and f's. The sounds of r's and l's and n's were also a part of this whisper sound cluster. I shook my head as if to clear out the clutter and I tried to decipher individual words and sounds from the whispers.

The sound I heard jarred me out of my concentration and scared the living daylights out of me "Hi!" dark-haired Allie said gleefully and shrilly. I jumped out of my seat blinking at her.

"Good lord," I growled at her "You scared the living crap out of me!"

Allie laughed and said "Good lord?" she asked "Someone's been spending a lot of time in the bible belt." She reached out to give me a hug greeting and I smiled and hugged back. Allie looked adorable as usual wearing a simple black fuzzy Chanel sweater and jeans.

"Don't look at my shoes," she added sheepishly. "They're Dr. Scholl's dance brand." I glanced at her feet. "I'm just not capable of running around in high heels all day long!" she said apologetically.

I rolled my eyes at her and said "Al, really, they're cute shoes. And comfort is so important. I'm wearing Vans for chrissakes!" I deliberately added the 'chrissakes' to try to redeem myself for the "good lord" comment I'd made previously. She grinned at me and then pointed over my shoulder at Tricia, who had come running out of lobby elevator at top speed in what looked to be patent leather 5-inch heels. She skidded to a stop in front of us, looking rushed and bewildered in her white tank top with a white button-down shirt as a jacket and BCBG smocked leggings. She also looked about ten feet tall.

"Jesus," I said deliberately in Allie's direction "What's up Shaquille O'Neill?"

Tricia looked down from her tower of height and heels and said sarcastically "Cute."

I looked up at Tricia in mock amazement and said "Not only are you as tall as the Washington Monument, but you're here exactly on time!"

"Yeah, what gives bean pole?" chimed in Allie. An answer from a statuesque blonde came from behind Tricia's towering figure.

"I stole her watch and reset it so she'd think she was late and would then arrive precisely on time," said a very pleased Holly. "Although I'm actually rather sad I missed her running late in those ridiculous shoes," she added, staring at Tricia's monster high heeled shoes. Of course Holly was dressed for the occasion in smart 7 for all Mankind flared jeans, Tod's lace-up black shoes and a baby blue Banana Republic long sleeved high v-neck t-shirt.

Tricia looked lazily in Holly's direction and answered "Oh, it is dress like a shrew day? I didn't check the calendar."

"Evidently it's dress like your favorite 80s pop star, Pat Benatar," Holly retorted. I had had enough of this banter for the moment and told them so.

"Food," I said simply. Allie nodded and spoke to the hostess who'd returned and was staring opened mouth at Tricia who was standing quite naturally on her stilts and enjoying every second of the attention. *I feel so sad.* I whirled around looking from girlfriend to girlfriend trying to figure out where I'd heard that and how I'd heard it through the general room hum. It came through so clearly. The hostess had approached us at this point so I figured maybe this was something I just happened to pick up from her.

We followed the hostess to the table and scooted ourselves into the booth when I noticed Tricia's face. It was streaked with tears.

"Trix?" I asked cautiously "Don't tell me you're crying because your toes hurt in those shoes." At the mention of Tricia crying all eyes at the table turned to her with concern. Tricia covered her face and laid her forehead down on the table, sighed deeply and said nothing. I realized it was Tricia I had heard a few seconds ago and it was Tricia I was hearing now.

"Trixie," I said gently "I can hear you." Tricia looked up at me her eyes smeared with black mascara.

"Yeah, great," she said sarcastically. "So you know how jealous I am?" she asked looking at Allie and me one at a time.

Allie responded saying "Well I don't, what is going on?"

Tricia sighed deeply again and with her lip trembling and her voice shaking she began to tell us. "You know I'm the same age as you two. And what do I have to show for it?" she said. "I have no husband, no children, no family close by. I live in the big city and run around like I'm 20 years old but I'm not."

"But you're engaged!" Allie interrupted.

I joined in adding "And you've got this great job where you meet celebrities and you have total freedom to do whatever you want whenever you want!" These arguments sent Tricia into a new round of tears.

"I know! I know this!" she answered angrily. "And it makes me feel worse to know that I have these things but that I don't appreciate them. And I want more. I want children. I want a home, not a stupid apartment. I want what you have," she said looking me right in the eyes. I was totally taken aback at this. How could Tricia, the high-powered public relations professional, want what I have? I'm a stay-at-home Mom for chrissakes. (Take that, bible belt!).

"I feel exactly the same way, Tricia," said Holly softly. "I travel around the world for work but what do I come home to? The same thing day in and day out." Holly went on saying "I come home, Dave and I have dinner. Then we go home and watch a movie. I take a bath, I go to bed. Next day I get up again and go to work. Then I come home. It's like Ground Hog Day. I hate it." My chin was on the floor. Holly too? And how it is that Holly and Tricia were echoing exactly my feelings about my own life, if we led such different lives? I decided to tell them what I'd been feeling.

"You guys sound just like me. Like, verbatim - exactly my thoughts," I said. "The difference is I thought that you having a job and time for yourself would make your lives better and more fulfilled!" I went on, "I have little kids, I'm home in my dumb house every day. I do dishes, laundry, wipe noses and teach math facts. I cook dinners and pick up dry cleaning. Talk about Ground Hog Day!" I said crossly "This is the life you want? All this time, I wanted what you had."

Allie chimed in saying quietly "Oh my god, Zoe, have you been as depressed as I have? Why didn't you tell me?"

I sat for a second considering this and I responded "Because you seemed so happy! All of you did. No one said anything about what was below the surface."

Tricia spoke "You have no idea what you have, Zoe, Allie," she said miserably. "Children change every day! You don't have to work with silly celebrities who aren't doing a whole lot to make the world a better place. You get to make the world a better place, through what you teach them!"

I laughed and looked at Allie "Yeah I teach them that if they hit their brother with a light saber one more time that Mommy is going to run screaming down the road in a fit of rage."

Allie smiled "Or that putting a green bean up your nose means a trip to the emergency room." Holly and Tricia exchanged glances and I could see that they didn't quite see that we could possibly be feeling as they do.

"Look guys," I said "I have nothing for me. I have lived the last six years with no career, no goals, no plans. When the kids were younger, I was all about them. But now they are older and more independent. I have sat for days on end crying as I fold the laundry for the umpteenth time, angry that I have to clean the kitchen counter for the tenth time that hour, feeling terrible for wanting to run away from what I created, but not knowing how to change it. It's not all hugs and birthday parties," I said tearing up, "And up until this very second, I didn't know anyone else in the world felt this way."

Allie reached over and squeezed my hand. "I get it," she said. "And the guilt for not loving every second of your life makes it ten times worse."

Tricia and Holly nodded "How is it we're all feeling this way," asked Tricia "If we have such different experiences?"

Holly answered "Well, I am thinking of it as a stages of our life kind of thing," she said. "We're all in our mid thirties trying to achieve our goals and maintain a level of happiness." "Since I've achieved many career goals I feel like now I need to achieve more with Dave, or to start working on the family goals. Maybe really it's a simple as figuring out new goals and finding ways to achieve them."

I nodded vigorously "You're right!" I said "And I have achieved the beginning of the family goal, so now I need to find new family and personal goals!" I said excitedly, well aware that I deliberately left husband/relationship goals out of that sentence. I wasn't ready to tackle that one. We all nodded to each other.

Tricia wiped her tears and said "But what if we can't? What if I can't think of goals or don't know how to get what I want?"

"Just realizing that we can find a way out of it is the beginning, Tricia," I said reaching out to hold her hand. "One thing at a time. I, for one, had no idea you could be depressed in your situation. I thought truly I was the only one. I am so relieved to know that not only am I not alone, but that you suckers are down in this pit with me."

Tricia smiled at that, responding, "At least I'm the prettiest one in the pit."

Holly snorted and rolled her eyes saying "I'll let that one slide given that you just cried like a pre-adolescent." We all smiled and the low mood at the table began to lift.

"Promise me this though," I said looking at each of them "Please let's not pretend we didn't have this conversation. Can we please just be honest and not hide if we're sad or down? No one gets to judge the other right?"

Allie nodded "Absolutely, I was keeping quiet because no one else said anything. Just like you Z, I thought I was the only one."

Tricia added "You'll be sorry you ever told me to tell you how I feel."

Holly laughed saying "I already am. Let's eat. Zoe, you want to order for everyone today?"

"Definitely," I replied "I need to practice anyhow. Hey, by the way Trixie, I'm really beginning to feel like I know Tate on a whole new level now. Sheesh." Tricia giggled saying "Oops, sorry. Back to the menu."

We ordered the food, and the subject of the table turned to the unbelievable encounter we'd had the night before. Everyone was thrilled at how we had all been able to use our fledgling powers to chase Christian away.

"But what was he doing there?" Holly had asked.

"He didn't want to rob us, he wanted us to go with him," said Tricia. "Z, could you pick anything up from him at all?" I told the girls that while I still needed to practice on hearing specific voices in a room full of frightened female voices that I was sure that I heard Christian thinking "see em" repeatedly. I told them I heard him thinking it a few different times during the fight.

"I think the "em" in "see em" is whoever sent him to kidnap us," I said.

"Why is anyone sending someone to kidnap us?" asked Allie who was visibly shaken.

"I don't know, Al" I answered solemnly "But we need to figure this out because whoever it is will come back for us now that they know we have powers. I cannot shake the feeling that last night was only the beginning." We sat in silence for a moment, considering this as we sipped our coffees.

"Maybe someone knows we have powers," said Holly thoughtfully. "I mean, what are the mathematical odds that we would all find out we have powers and then encounter another person who can…" she lowered her voice "Turn invisible?" Holly continued "It is obvious that whoever it is knows about us and our powers."

I looked at the faces at the table and said "Why would anyone care if I can read minds? Or that Allie is strong? And how do they know?"

Holly replied "Well that is something we're going to have to figure out, Zoe, somebody sent that waiter to get us—that I know for sure."

Allie leaned forward looking at Holly and said "Do you think Skylar is in danger?" Certainly, Skylar was just home in bed asleep and hadn't gotten our messages yet, right? Holly shrugged her shoulders and replied "It is likely she has some kind of power given the four of us all have manifested powers from what happened with the venom and Charles Mitchell's death compound."

Tricia spoke up saying gravely "If she was alone, she would have been no match for Christian. Allie, could you call her one more time?"

We had all been trying to call Skylar all morning to no avail. It wasn't unusual for her to turn her phone off when she was sleeping, however, and we hoped that this was just one of those instances. *Is Skylar like us? Could she have a power to defend herself?* I looked up, not bothering to figure out who was thinking that and just went ahead and answered, "I have no idea if Skylar has powers like us, but I think it's time we make a trip over to her place to get her out of bed and find out." *Oh god I hope she's in bed asleep.* "Me too," I said to the girls, "Me too."

Chapter 10: Skylar's Place

Skylar lived over in the Glover Park neighborhood, just north of Georgetown. I remember her telling me that even though her place was small it was a prime D.C. living location: walking distance to the national cathedral, ten-minute drive to the Kennedy

Center and 15 minutes to the White House or national mall. Not to mention she was right around the corner from Wisconsin Avenue's many bars, shops and restaurants. As we approached her place I found myself longing for the city life that she lived. I imagined her walking to a bar with friends at happy hour, picking up dinner at the Fresh Fields on the way back to her apartment. She had a modest place that she shared with her on-again off-again musician boyfriend, Myles. He was her on-again boyfriend because he was a handsome, gentle guitarist. He was her off-again boyfriend for the same reasons. There wasn't a whole lot more to Myles except music (and pot) and Skylar had struggled for the past few years trying to figure out if his laid-back ways were what she really wanted and needed in a future husband and father. Currently, they were off again and Myles had been on tour across the country with his band. The girls and I hopped into a cab and headed over to her place. We arrived at 193 Camden Place, paid the cabby, got out stood side by side staring up at the tall brick building in front of us. As we stood I noticed several tenants walking in and out of the front doors to the complex.

"Uh oh," I said looking at my friends "They all seem to be using a security code and," I said squinting my eyes," "I can see a security camera focused right on the door so we can't just run in after someone else, damn it!"
Tricia laughed and punched me lightly in the arm "Hey ding dong," she said "We're freaking superheroes. I think we can manage a security lock."
"Is there an intercom?" asked Allie.
"Doesn't matter," I answered, "Skylar's not there." It dawned on me that what Tricia had said about us being superheros was right. I could probably stand over there and try to listen to thoughts as a tenant typed in his number. Or Allie could break it open. Or Tricia could zap it. I supposed if we were really in a bind, Holly could build another plasma gun and shoot it open, but that seemed like overkill at that point. Since my power of listening would cause the least damage to the door, we decided to go that route. The first time I tried we all walked up there together, lounging very obviously by the door trying to act nonchalant. The others were all so nervous no one else could get a thought in edgewise and I could only make out from the tenant that he thought we were acting oddly. The second time I just brought Tricia with me—I figured her ridiculous clown

outfit would distract the tenant so that he or she would have to think about the number clearly as they typed it in. Unfortunately, the next tenant who was at the door was a gay man who was so taken by her height and absolute fabulousness that not only did he forget his code, he ended up in a 15 minute conversation with her about her outfit and the courage she had to pull it off. *At her age.* I didn't tell Tricia that part. I could only imagine the damage a statement like that would do to her ego. On our third attempt we got a little smarter and I approached the door while the girls sat on a nearby bench each one pretending to talk on her cell phone. I knew they were all calling Skylar, just one more time, to see if this time she would wake up and let us in. But she did not. I stood at the door pretending to search in vain for something in my purse when the female tenant approached. I listened to her along with anyone within a 15 feet radius. *My feet are killing me. What the hell am I going to be for Halloween? The G'town street party is in 2 nights and I've got nothing to wear! 8982. Maybe a German beer wench. Has to be sexy and cool.* As she disappeared into the building elevator, I motioned for my cell phone talking friends to join me.

"8982," I said "Holly, remember that in case we need it again."

"Got it," she answered firmly. I leaned over to the pad and typed in the numbers. With a buzz and a click, the lock opened and we were in.

While I walked very casually over to the elevator my best friends in the world did not. It was as if they thought all eyes were on them (and in fact they were, given the way they were acting) and that we'd be thrown out if anyone guessed we were up to no good. They laughed loudly and awkwardly saying such gems as "This old lobby hasn't changed in the entire five years I've been living here!" and "I wonder who the tenant will be in the apartment next to mine? I hope they won't mind me practicing my violin!" I pressed the up button for the elevator and turned back to them with disdain in my eyes as they acted like complete idiots. They were walking over to me but very casually, swinging their arms slowly and almost marching in place. Each expression was an overdone smile with raised eye-brows as they each feigned interest in what the other one was saying. When the actors were close enough to me I whispered to them to knock off the theatrical displays and act normal. They all looked surprised at my comments and sheepishly complied. The elevator door opened and we all got on.

I was the first to speak "Hey no one was winning any Oscars back there," I said irritably. "I might not be too up-to-date on my superhero behavior but I certainly don't remember Superman acting all obvious that he could fly when he worked at that newspaper!"

"Clark Kent," said Allie.

I turned to face her with my eyebrows knitted "What?" I said.

"Clark Kent," she said again. "You said Superman worked at the newspaper, but he was Clark Kent when he was at his day job."

I raised my eyebrows and said, "Semantics."

Holly interjected "Actually, you both have good points. If we are to be acting like superheroes we should try to follow the pre-set comic book story—man by day, no one knows hero by night so they don't dissect him in the name of science sort of thing."

"I don't care what superhero story we follow, Holly," I said annoyed "But what you guys just did was embarrassing."

Holly replied "Given that we are all in a new situation and most of us…" she glanced quickly at Tricia "Have not snuck into other people's apartment buildings before, I think it is to be expected that we will make some mistakes."

I nodded, saying "Yes, I suppose we're all new at this." I thought for a second about what Holly had said previously about the pre-set hero model and added "If we are to follow the superhero comic book story then doesn't that mean we should have outfits?" The girls all turned to me with a look of surprise on their faces.

"You mean like costumes? Like batman?" said Allie.

"Or like Wonder Woman!" said Tricia.

Holly replied darkly "I would rather die ten times than dress up like Wonder Woman. Besides, perhaps we should start by pressing the button for Skylar's floor first? We've been standing in this elevator on the ground floor for quite some time, ladies."

Embarrassed I leaned over to press the number 12 saying "The acting must have thrown me off my game, my apologies. Here we go." We rode up to the 12th floor in silence, exited quietly, made our way to door 1218 and stopped in front of it.

The door to apartment 1218 looked like any other door in the hallway – weathered and gray. The numbers on it were a faded gold and the little black peep hole underneath them looked foggy at best. I went to knock on the door but Allie stopped me.

"Zoe," she said urgently "Look down." I looked down suddenly noticing the newspapers. I bent down and picked them up while the others watched with wide eyes.

"There are two papers here," I muttered. "Today's and…"

Tricia stepped forward aggressively grabbing at the papers in my hand "And what?" she said forcefully.

"And yesterday's," I said. The stale air in the hallway was suddenly hard to breathe as we realized that Skylar hadn't been there in her apartment for at least two days.

"Maybe she was just lazy and didn't pick up the papers?" said Allie hopefully. But we all knew this was not like Skylar. She was a neat freak and would never have left a pile of anything anywhere especially not in her hallway in her building.

"We need to get inside," said Holly. "Even if by some random turn of events she went out of town and didn't tell us and all of this is just a silly scary coincidence, we still need to get in there." We all nodded in agreement.

I turned to face them saying "We used my power to get us in the building, which one of you wants to take this task?" Holly, Tricia and Allie each promptly pointed a finger at the other one.

"Not it!" said Tricia.

"Not it!" said Holly.

"I guess that leaves me," said Allie. "I guess you'll fix it after, Holls?" she said.

"Absolutely," said Holly smiling. Allie looked awkward and unsure as she approached the door. *Go…amnotmad…skylarwhereareyou.* I closed my eyes as I heard their thoughts trying to decipher them. Once again, I couldn't be sure but I thought Allie was having issues with not being angry enough to break the lock.

"Allie," I said goading her "Take your little tiny hands and do something with them for once in your life."

Allie looked at me hurt, "Ouch," she said.

Tricia joined in singing "Remember that song we used to sing?? Short people got no reason to..."

"Enough!" said Allie. "I don't need you to give me any more reason to be pissed," she said angrily. "Someone might be hurting Skylar, that's enough for me."

Allie bent over the knob, placed a petite hand on it knob and turned. While normally a locked doorknob would stop on the half turn, this doorknob did not. Allie simply and powerfully kept turning the knob until it broke off into her hand with a muffled clunk. Then she quickly put her small finger into the hole to the back of inside knob and pushed it through. She stood up, put her strong and tiny hand in the open hole and pulled the door open. Eight pairs of eyes peered in cautiously, not sure what they were looking for.

Skylar's apartment looked just as I'd pictured it. Muted shades of blues, oranges and reds covered the couches and instead of a coffee table she had antique suitcases stacked underneath a rectangle cut of glass.

"Wow, that's not so kid friendly," muttered Allie motioning to the sharp edges of the table. The living room had lots of unique artwork on the walls and there was also an eclectic mix of figurines and statues of different sizes scattered around. She had more things in one room than I would have dared but her creative mind and gift for utilizing space made it work beautifully. There was much detail to see but nothing felt cluttered or claustrophobic.

"Skye?" I called out tentatively.

"If she was here, she would have heard us breaking the door," Tricia noted.

Holly appeared from the room at the right of the living room saying, "No one in the bedroom and I just checked out the bathroom," she said seriously. "And I don't think she's been here today and likely wasn't last night. The tub and sink are dry, toothbrush is not damp – if she'd been here this morning they would have been for sure." I shook my head in disbelief and walked in to Skylar's bedroom to see for myself. Like the living room, Skylar's bedroom had an arty comfortable feel. Her off-white comforter and pillows looked to be made from organic cotton, as did the reddish orange blanket that lay folded at the end of her bed. Just as Holly had said, the bed was made and her room was neat and organized as if no one had set foot in there – at least not recently. I walked slowly back into the living room to the murmur of my friends' thoughts of worry and fear. I suggested we all to sit down on the couch and floor pillows and talk—we needed a plan.

"Tricia," I began "Are you able to control your electricity enough to use your cell phone?"

She nodded proudly "I've gotten quite good at controlling it! Sometimes I still mess up sometimes but I've gotten much better."

I sat down in the oversized chair and leaned forward with my hands on my knees and looked at the girls very seriously. "We need to figure out what is going on here. Allie, I think you should try to get in touch with Myles. I know he's on tour and they're not even together but maybe he's heard from her." Allie nodded in agreement. "Next," I said "We need to walk around her place slowly and carefully to look for anything and everything that might point to where she is. Look for plane ticket stubs or any kind of mail or receipts." Holly was already on her feet looking carefully at some papers that were scattered on the table next to the couch. She flipped Allie a book that said "phonebook" on the cover and mouthed, 'Myles's number' and pointed to it. "Trix, can you get to Facebook on your phone?" Tricia nodded. "Okay, well hop on there and check your mail and check her profile page. Then we can all take turns with our own e-mail on Facebook to see if she's communicated anything at all. We must see if there is anything that we missed." I paused for a second, and then said, "I'm going to look at her text one more time. Something about it has been bothering me. Maybe I can it figure out." Tricia typed quietly on her phone, Allie flipped through the pages of the phonebook and then walked out of the room as she dialed. Holly walked slowly through each room methodically looking at everything. I flipped open my phone and stared at Skylar's picture. Skylar was not the smiliest person on the planet so it was not unusual to see her mouth set in a line, but there was something different about her eyes that looked strange to me. They were open fairly wide and staring with a quiet urgency out at me. And her hair—Skylar rarely if ever wore her hair back—was tied up in several long pencils and looked a mess. It was so unlike her to be out in public looking like a mess. As she did in the photo.

"Shit," said Tricia. "Shit, shit, shit." We all turned curiously to look at Tricia.

"What?" I said.

"She has changed her status, in fact she changed it last night," she replied, shaken.

"Well what does it say?" Allie blurted immediately.

Holly leaned over the table and grabbed Tricia's phone away from her and stared at the small screen saying "It ... says ... I am a little **pencil** in the hand of a writing God who is sending a love letter to the world."

"Cut and paste that," I said "And Google the crap out of it so we can figure out where that came from.

"Yes master," she replied.

"What time was it updated?" I asked.

Holly squinted her eyes and moved the phone closer to her face and then back out replying "Looks to be about 15 hours ago." No one spoke as we all rewound time in our minds to figure out what exact time that would have been posted.

"That means she would have written that at about 6:00 p.m. yesterday, right?" Allie asked the room.

Holly nodded and I spoke saying "Just before dinner."

I looked back down at her picture on my phone thinking about what her message could have meant. "She has these big pencils in her hair, you know," I said holding the phone up so they could see the photo.

"She looks retarded with those in her hair," said Tricia.

"I know," I replied "So not like her to wear her hair like this. And it's pencils. And her status is a saying about pencils.

"Maybe she was just trying something new? Thought it was funny and posted about it?" Allie asked.

"Or maybe," I replied "She was trying to tell us something. I think it's almost spelled out — "

"I googled it," Holly interrupted "It's a quote from Mother Theresa. I'm not clear on why she would post anything religious since she's about as God fearing as Tricia."

Tricia turned to Holly and shot back with "If you walked into a church right now you'd be struck by lightning."

Holly laughed and replied "At least I'd get in the door. More than I can say for you."

"Neither one of you would fare well in church," said Allie diffusing their battle "I think we should call that one even." I leaned back in the chair, closed my eyes and opened my mind to hear what my friends were thinking. *I have to pee. Christian made Zoe sign with a pencil not a pen. There's a pencil on this table. In first grade I stabbed my hand with a pencil and it left lead spot on my hand. Pencils.* Once again I shook my head as if to organize their thoughts along with mine. I had trouble hearing everything at once but I definitely heard something important.

I sat straight up and spoke hurriedly "Christian made me sign with a pencil?"

Holly answered looking at me strangely "I will never get used to you being in my thoughts," she said.

"Nevermind that!" I said "Why do you remember that he made me sign with a pencil?"

"Well," she replied "I remember being surprised that it wasn't just a digital keypad form for payment. And then when it wasn't that, I was confused at why he'd have a pencil to sign something with his tip on it."

"Cuz he could just erase it and put in his own tip, right?" Tricia said knowingly. "I mean, I would have totally done that," she said smiling.

"So…" I said drawing it out. I knew where this was going and I was pretty sure they did too. I just knew none of us was willing to say it. "Pencils for the tab, pencils in her hair..." I said.

Tricia interrupted "In her messy-ass hair."

I gave her an annoyed look and went on "She writes pencils on her status…"

Holly spoke "Look at this," she said "Here on this table where there was a PENCIL by the way. It's a flier from the cathedral." Skylar was a big patron of the National Cathedral. Since it was within walking distance she would take walks over there and spend time in the wooden gazebo on the grounds and paint or grade papers. I got up from my seat and walked over to where Holly was standing by the table.

"Um, I know you guys probably don't want to consider the totally obvious here but…" I began.

She interrupted me handing me the flier saying "It's got the gazebo on it, see? And look, she circled part of it—in pencil." The flier was a full page with black old-world font text on it and in the middle was a picture of the gazebo. "National Cathedral is renovating its beloved gazebo" was at the top of the sheet. "World-renowned architect Kevin Jameson has graciously agreed to donate his artisan talents in wood to redesign and rebuild the gazebo. Come to the grand re-opening of the National Cathedral Gazebo November, 1st 2009. Refreshments will be served." We passed the flier around silently each of us studying it closely.

"I guess she was planning on attending this," said Tricia.

"You know she loves that gazebo," said Allie, ever the sensitive one. "I bet she's been out of sorts with it being under construction and a big wooden mess."

I nodded feeling frustrated that the flier seemed like a dead end. "So the gazebo is getting fixed – big deal," I said. "Can we talk about the friggin enormous elephant in the room here?"

"Well," replied Holly ignoring me, "Sometimes the simplest theory is the best. Let's talk about what we know."

I answered her "We know we have powers accidentally given to us by a nuts kid who tried to kill us in high school."

Allie followed the tangent of my statement with her own saying "We also know that he just escaped from the hospital. Oh and we know that a waiter who made Zoe sign the receipt in pencil could turn invisible."

Holly turned to Tricia who said "We know that Skylar's been gone since last night and she was having a major bad hair day so she stuck pencils in it. And we also know that she wrote pencils on her status on Facebook."

"So," stated Holly directly "Where does this lead us?" No one wanted to say it.

I looked around slowly at my friends "Look, I don't want to say it either," I said with rising panic. "But I will. Pencils, girls, Charles Mitchell's weird signature at the deck and when he killed Todd and when he tried to kill us." I went on saying "Christian was thinking "see em" over and over again last night. I thought he was trying to throw me off by thinking something so repetitively, so that I couldn't follow his other thoughts." I looked down at my hands and then back up at them again "But now I know, and I know that you know, "see em" is actually "C M" or everybody's favorite escaped mental patient Charles Mitchell. He's practically stamping his name on our foreheads it's so obvious. And now, somehow, he's gotten out and it appears he sent Christian to us. Christian is working for him and … " I couldn't finish the sentence.

Allie did instead, saying "And they have Skylar."

"I think that's clearly correct," said Holly in her scientific tone. "And remember falcons, I think it's very likely that Skylar also has a super power. Whether it's manifested without us being near her remains to be seen, I think Charles has her and he's going to use her to get to us."

My head was swimming with their thoughts. I closed my eyes tightly and sighed deeply "But why?" I said with exasperation. "Why is he out to get us? Why was he out to get us then? I was never anything but nice to that kid."

Tricia responded "Remember when we tried to stop him from getting that major beat down from Todd the Hammer?"

I nodded replying, "Yeah, that guy was such a prick," adding sarcastically a bible belt saying that southerners use when they bad mouth someone but don't want to be responsible for it: "Bless his heart." "He was such a prick, bless his heart," I said.

Allie ignored me. "Charles wouldn't listen, do you remember that? He just stood there looking at us with those scary blank eyes." I remembered that night so clearly. Todd had been drinking and was looking for a fight. We were all so disgusted with him—he'd been grabbing at us, calling us sluts when we rebuffed him—he'd made Skylar a big target of his that night. He'd grabbed her and pushed her into a wall, but Allie stepped in and pulled her away —which is ironic because she was the smallest.

"I remember trying to leave," said Tricia "Why did we stay as long as we did when he was being so horrible?"

"Because," I said "We saw him looking out the window, we saw him spot Charles approaching and we saw him get that fraternity paddle out."

"Yes," said Allie. "Remember, Zoe, you and I ran to the door first to tell Charles to leave?"

I nodded "But he wouldn't go! Why wouldn't he go?" I remembered watching Todd drag
Charles like a rag doll into the street.

"I ran back in the house to get one of the other guys to help Charles, but no one would go
up against big, stupid Hammer," I said to them, "so I called the police."

"Yes," said Holly "that was the right thing to do." I faced her and said accusingly
"But we left. We left Charles in the street being attacked by Todd. That was not the
right thing to do."

When Holly replied to me her words were chosen carefully. "Zoe," she said "We were
young. We were scared. Todd was a violent bully. We tried to stop Charles from being
there. We tried to stop Todd from hurting him."

"But..." I said.

"Z," Tricia added "We stood in that doorway and screamed for Todd to stop and it made
him even more angry. We called the cops. There was no standing up to Todd and no
helping Charles at that point."

Allie spoke saying "We did what we thought was right. We tried to control it and when
we couldn't we called the grown-ups and took off. There was no telling what Hammer
would have done to us if we'd stayed." I knew they were right but still I couldn't
understand why Charles would be after us now, after all this time, especially since we
had never done anything to him, and I said so.

"Who knows," responded Allie. "But what matters is not why. What matters is what
we're going to do to get Skylar back."

I put my face in my hands and tried to focus on actually thinking my own
thoughts and not theirs. They were so noisy! "Ladies," I said sharply "I am having
trouble focusing on thinking when you are all prattling in your heads. It's driving me
crazy."

Tricia flopped down on the couch mockingly saying "Oh pardon US for thinking," she
said. "Hey, believe me, I'd be much happier not knowing that Tate has a heartshaped
birthmark on his inner thigh." I replied.

Tricia blushed but didn't have much of a comeback because it was true "Christ, you're
like the mind police," she mumbled.

Abruptly, Holly slammed her hand down on the coffee table. "Hello?" she said furiously "Skylar is in trouble and you two are bantering back and forth as if we're at a flipping happy hour!" She stood up and strode briskly out of the room and into Skylar's tiny kitchen.

Tricia and I looked at each other reproachfully "I didn't mean to…" Tricia said. Allie patted each of us on the knee and motioned for us to follow her to the kitchen. Holly was standing with her forehead on the fridge, eyes squeezed shut and arms crossed tightly around her body.

"Holly," I began softly.

"Shut up! Just shut up okay?" she replied in a teary voice.

"Are you…crying?" asked Tricia. Tricia looked at me, pointed at Holly's back and mouthed "I have never seen her cry before!"

Holly whirled around to face the three of us. "Skylar is in real danger and we have no idea what we're going to do or how we're going to get her back! You two are joking around like it's not a big deal! It IS a big deal!"

Allie reached out to touch Holly's shoulder "I know exactly what you're feeling." Tricia nodded "Me too, guys," she said "I don't know how to handle this. What the hell are we doing?" Looking at my crying sniveling friends in the kitchen, I began to feel infuriated.

"Well, I don't feel that way!" I said sharply jarring them back into reality. "Sitting here crying and complaining isn't going to get us anywhere."

Holly's eyes blazed "Have you lost your mind?" she asked "This is real! We could all get hurt!" I returned her gaze calmly.

"Last I checked we were superheroes, not whining babies. For whatever reason we have powers that regular people don't have. And I don't know why and I don't completely understand how, but I know what I can do, and what each and every one of you can do. And it's special. It's better than special, it's a phenomenon. Charles having Skylar is real, but this miraculous and powerful synergy we have together is just as real, and it's what will get her back!" I turned and stomped out of the kitchen, my own anger bringing me close to tears. As I stood in the living room with my back to the kitchen I could hear the girls walking up behind me.

"You're absolutely correct," said Holly "We are a phenomenon that I'm not even sure science could fully explain. I suppose I need to get used to this status." I turned to face her and smiled, holding out my arms to hug her. She came to me and we held each other for a brief moment and pulled back.

"Your joking around just set me off," she said.

This was not the first time I have been told to keep the joking to a minimum during sensitive times. Many times during my life I found humor where it shouldn't be found. Funerals, emergency rooms -- anything emotional that affected me deeply -- I generally coped by using sarcasm as a defense. Even in my marriage I used humor to deflect what I was really feeling; saying something funny to avoid the real pain I was feeling inside.

"I know I tend to be too silly in tense situations," I said.

Tricia put her arms around us. "I definitely do," she said. Allie walked over and put her arms around Tricia's arms so we were all in a big embrace.

"Bear with me, okay?" I said "I don't know how to handle this but I do know if we don't laugh and tease our way though it we might as well give up now."

Holly smiled and nodded in understanding. "I get it. I will lighten up as much as is possible for me to do."

Tricia snorted teasingly, "So ... not at all?" The closeness of our embrace had set our eyes aglow in the white bright light.

Allie asked, "Can we back up?" "I'm afraid if we stay too long like this something will happen to our eyes."

"That's definitely something we should experiment with in the future," replied Holly, ever the scientist.

Tricia said, "In the interest of lightening up the mood I must announce that I have the absolute worst song in my head right now! 'We don't have to take our clothes off, to have a good time, oh no.'"

"Tricia," I groaned "That is the worst song of all time!"

Allie turned to Tricia "What are you singing?" she asked. Tricia responded singing loudly and very off key "Na na na na na na NA NA, we don't have to take our clothes off, to have a good time..." Allie nodded her head along with the song and then I heard the end of the song from her thoughts "oh no."

"Ha," I said grinning at her "I can hear you singing in my head."

As soon as I spoke, I glanced back over at Tricia. "Don't you dare," I said. "I know you're gonna try to get everyone to sing in their heads, which will then be in my head. Knock it off."

Holly laughed, saying, "Well Zoe, you wanted humor, so now you're getting it." Suddenly my mind was taken over by a chorus of "we don't have to take our clothes off, to have a good time, oh no. We can dance and party, all night. And drink some cherry wine, uh huh!"

"STOP," I demanded. Relentlessly, they kept on counting 1, 2, 3 to each other before beginning again. There was only silence in the room but the song played over and over in my head as if I was listening to them in concert. As they sang in my thoughts, my friends even stepped and spun to the music in their minds. Suddenly, I heard another voice over the din. It was a man's voice and it was very low but getting louder. *This is all going according to HIS plan.* The song the girls were thinking was creating a backdrop of sorts—they were the traffic noise in the street and I was able to make out his thoughts very clearly over it, just like hearing someone talking next to me on the street. *Dumb whores don't even know I'm here.* I looked up in terror—we were not alone. The girls stopped singing when they saw my expression and back came their thoughts, loud and confusing.

"SING!" I commanded them "Keep the song going! Just trust me!"

They all look at each other skeptically but the fear in my eyes compelled them to do as I asked. Their mind vocals started "we don't have to take our, clothes off" and quickly dissolved into a bland hum. Above the purr of their background music I could hear him clearly again. *I'm going to knock this pencil to the floor.* I turned to stare at the table, my eyes wide in horror as I watched the pencil roll softly to the side of the table and drop to the floor. The singing stopped and their thoughts returned.

"Christian is here, near the table!" I shouted.

Tricia's hand moved fast, and she threw her electric weapon in the air where I had pointed. In a flash we could see Christian as he tried to run but got hit and in another blink he was back to being invisible. She threw it again, trying to guess which direction he might have moved in but it was in vain. The blue shock returned to her hand and we all looked around in silence, trying to discern where Christian might be hiding.

"I know this is going to sound ridiculous, but I need you guys to think that song again. Do it," I said forcefully.

"Worst song ever," said Tricia.

"That's what you get with your little revenge wars, Tricia," replied Holly.

"Sing it!" I shouted.

Suddenly I heard a different song in my head "all the old paintings in the room they do the sand dance, don't ya know," and Tricia whispered to the girls "I'm thinking Walk Like an Egyptian - you guys know it?" The girls all nodded, counted their 1, 2, 3 and off they went in my head with another one of the worst songs ever in the world. I didn't have time to complain, however, because Christian was close and I needed to hear his plan. *Was just checking in ladies. So glad to hear you're on the right path. I wanted to leave you this little gift from Skylar to let you know she's alive. For now. Call the cops and we kill her.* "Can you hear him?" Tricia said abruptly. "Walk like an Egyptian" stopped in mid chorus and I was brought back into my thoughts and theirs again.

"He's gone," I said. "He said he left something of hers, so we would know she was with them and she was alive. Look around." We ran around the room searching the space, desperate for anything that would show us that she was okay.

"Oh God," I heard Allie say. "I think I've found it." She was sitting on the couch holding a small picture frame in her lap. She lifted it up and turned it to face us. "Do you remember when this photo was taken?" she said looking nauseous. We leaned in closely and saw a picture of us from high school. I stared in disbelief at the photo. It was all of us standing on a very high, wooden deck and we were leaning on the railing talking to each other and smiling, totally unaware that our picture was being taken from the ground below us. The silver frame had the words "The Falcon Five" engraved across the bottom.

"Oh God, the deck," I said softly my eyes filling with tears. Tricia reached over me and grabbed the frame to get a closer look at the picture. As she did, a piece of paper fell off the back of it. Holly picked it up and slowly opened it, her expression pained.

"Girls," she began sounding very alarmed "This is a note from Skylar." We stood up in silence and stared at Holly. "Falcon Five, it says" she began. "This is a picture that he took as he watched us at the party," it read. "Probably an hour or so before the deck fell. He is very angry that we did not die in the hospital. I'm going to tell you not to come find me, but I know you will. He wants you to know this will be the end. Bring me a light for my last cigarette, okay? Love you guys. Turtle." We sat in silence, stunned. This was all becoming too real for me. Wasn't it just this morning I talked with my sons and husband? Wasn't it just this morning that I was all too happy to sleep in and felt entitled to do so? Now all I wanted was to rewind the days and get back to when life was simple and Skylar was safe. But it was entirely too late for any of that. I had become something new and a friend of mine was in grave danger. There was something about the note from Skylar that I didn't understand.

"She quit smoking right after high school," I said after a few minutes of quiet.

"She probably just started!" said Tricia.

"I don't think so," said Holly. "I think she's trying to tell us something. Maybe she knows something about him that we don't."

Allie nodded her head to Holly saying "I agree and we should bring her matches when we see her, at worst we light her cigarette. At best we use it against him."

I stood up and motioned for them to come with me. "I need to know if he is still here, guys," I said.

"Oh crap, don't tell me we have to think-sing again?" asked Tricia with her eyebrows raised.

"I need more practice to be able to tune your thoughts out and bring others in," I answered sincerely.

"But for right now, you're horrible singing in my head helps me delineate new thoughts. Hop to it!" I said smiling. Tricia nodded, rolled her eyes and counted 1, 2, 3 "Walk like an Egyptian, walk like an Egyptian" came rolling through my mind and my friends began dancing ridiculously around to no music, high fiving to the invisible rhythm and shaking lots of booty. I closed my eyes to listen but heard nothing except neighbors nearby who evidently had plans to attend the Georgetown Halloween Festival on M street. This Halloween festival was a huge Georgetown tradition complete with the closing of M Street for costume wearers only (no costumes meant no festival) and lots of drinking and wild behavior. Locals came from all parts of the city to see the famed Drag Queen Race that always started somewhere around seven p.m. and lasted about a half hour. If you haven't seen the race you haven't celebrated Halloween, thought the neighbor.

"Oh my God!" I said holding my hands over my ears in mock fear.

"What??" they said in unison looking terrified.

"Your singing sucks," I answered smiling wryly. My friends exhaled collectively and gave me dirty looks.

"I should shock you for that," said a perturbed Tricia.

"What did you hear, if anything?" asked Allie. I explained to them that I'd heard the neighbor making plans for this coming Halloween in Georgetown and we all laughed as we remembered the Drag Queen races.

"I think Tricia should run this year," said Holly looking at Tricia "You could definitely pass for a queen in those ridiculous shoes."

"Girl are you kidding me?" Tricia sniffed "I would kick some major ass in that race. Those queens wouldn't know what hit them."

Allie turned away from Tricia and Holly as they bickered back and forth about whether t was fair for a woman to race in a drag queen race. She looked at me and said, "What do we do now, Zoe? We can't go to the police. We have no idea where she is."

I nodded and chewed on my thumb answering,"I've been thinking about that. Facebook was updated last night, and from the status that was posted I am pretty sure that Skylar didn't write it. I think he wrote it." Holly and Tricia quieted down to listen to me talking. I went on "So if we could trace the Facebook trail to the computer that it came from, maybe we could find them."

Holly nodded vigorously "Yes! I was thinking the same thing, but how?" I reminded the girls that my husband was an information technology professional.

"Oh that's right!" responded Tricia enthusiastically "Call that boy!" I looked down at the floor continued to chew my thumb.

"What is it Zoe?" said Allie concerned. I sighed deeply and replied in a low voice "Remember how we were all bonding earlier over being depressed in our lives?" Everyone nodded slowly waiting patiently for me to continue. "Well I am too, you know. And I know I've been married to Jimmy and we've got two great kids and all ... but ... " I paused, not knowing how to tell them that I hadn't really spoken to my darling husband in months. That I couldn't bear to tell him that I was unhappy, how on earth could I tell him I was a superhero who needed his help no questions asked. "Things aren't that great between us," I said finally. "We talk very superficially, very unemotionally. We talk about the kids. He knows I've been down but I haven't told him what that means."

Allie nodded and spoke "Boy, I hear that," she said. "I have been the same way with Kevin. I try to be the wife and to cook and clean and be a mommy for the kids but when I'm unhappy with that he takes it so personally. So I say nothing."

I looked at her with wide eyes "Really?" I said "You sound exactly like me!"

"Yes," Allie answered.

She turned to Tricia and Holly saying "Marriage is hard, ladies. And kids make it harder."

Allie turned back to me and took the hand that I wasn't chewing on and said "But it's Jimmy. It's Jimmy! The same guy saw your insides when you got a c-section and still is hot for you."

Holly joined in, "And did he or did he not buy you a second engagement ring when you didn't like the first one?" I looked at them, my eyes brimming with tears, the guilt for not appreciating what I had overwhelming me.

"And," said Tricia beginning the same way Holly did, "Did he or did he not tell you to come see us this weekend and have a good time?"

I nodded vigorously, saying in a tearful voice "I know all of this, guys, I know it. I just don't know how to get back to him to let him in again."

"I know it's hard," said Allie "Believe me I know, but you get back very simply by just going back! Just start to let him in again." I knew we needed Jimmy's help to trace the computer. I also knew that if I didn't do this that we could lose Skylar. But more importantly to me at that moment, I knew that this might be a path to find him again, to find us. All I had to do was pick up the phone and talk to him.

"By the way, y'all" I said smiling "Since you're singing his praises, you should know he also graciously offered to be the videographer should we decide to have a topless pillow fight that ends in a make out session."

Holly wrinkled her nose and replied "Men are gross. Call him."

Tricia added "Girls making out is so 90s!" she said emphatically.

"Oh right because you definitely haven't done it," smirked Holly.

"You wish I was kissing you right now, Dr Prude," retorted Tricia.

"I'd rather be Dr. Prude than Miss Herpes USA," was the response.

"Call him, Zoe!" interrupted Allie as she handed me my phone.

"Oh my friggin goodness, fine! But here's the deal, I'm calling him to ask for help but I am not telling him about this whole superhero thing," I said irritably. How could I start on the path back to Jimmy with an absurd, totally unbelievable story about super powers? I would call for his help, but I wouldn't let him in on this secret. It was just not the appropriate time. "Who knew you were all going to be my personal marriage counselors," I waved them out of the room. "A little privacy, please?" I demanded.

Jimmy picked up after the first ring. "Hi!" he said enthusiastically. "How's it going?" I wasn't sure how to begin this unusual request so I just blurted it out.

"Jimmy, I need you to trace a computer for me." He waited silently for me to go on.

"Skylar supposedly posted on Facebook last night but we think someone else posted on her profile from a different computer and we need to know where this computer is. Can you do that?"

Jimmy answered slowly "Well," he said "I am pretty sure I can run a triangular digital trace program on it. It really shouldn't be an issue to figure out the address, but why not just ask Skylar yourself?"

I ignored his last question and responded "Great! What do you need to get started? Can you hack her profile page to get her password and information? When will you run the program? How soon can we get an address?"

"Wait, Zoe," Jimmy said sternly. "What is this all about? Why would anyone do this? Why do you need to know where the computer is?"

I closed my eyes tight and wrinkled up my nose before answering "Um," I began not so eloquently "Look, I can't tell you right now, okay?"

Jimmy replied sarcastically "Oh well when you put it that way, no problem." Tricia had walked back into the room giving me a tentative thumbs up with a questioning look on her face. I shook my head no at her.

"Jimmy," I began firmly "I need your help. I can't get into why yet but I need to you trust me. Can you do this for me with no questions asked?"

Jimmy snorted. "No! You keep too many secrets. I never know what you're thinking anymore, and I'm sick of it!"

I was taken aback by Jimmy's response. Something seemed to have snapped inside my normally accommodating husband. Had my long-term lack of communication pushed him to the edge? This was going to be far more difficult that I'd thought.

"Hon, I know I've not been the most forthcoming about lots of things over the past few months."

Jimmy interrupted darkly "You think?"

I ignored him and went on, "And I want to change that and I will. But I can't do that right now over the phone all the way in DC. I need you to just do this for me and I will give you a blow job every Monday night for a month when I get back," I said hoping that would lighten the mood.

"Hilarious," he answered scathingly "I'm mad at you, Zoe, for a lot of things. And this is the last straw, I mean it." My eyes lit up as I knew he was caving in. "I will do this, but when you get back we have some major talking to do," Jimmy said very seriously.

"I know," I said "Thank you, thank you! You're doing the right thing, I swear," I said insistently.

"Let me hop on Facebook and hack her page," Jimmy said in his business voice. "That will take about an hour. Then I'll run the triangular trace and see if I can find the address of whoever is messing around with it, okay? Probably another few hours if I can get your parents to watch the boys while I work."

I jumped up and down in excitement "Yay! You won't regret this Jimmy, I promise I'll let you in on this and other things when I get back!"

I heard Jimmy take a deep breath and let it out slowly. "Yeah, yeah," he said knowingly. "I'll call you back in a few hours."

"Great!" I replied.

"Oh and Zoe?" Jimmy said "When this is all said and done you're definitely on the hook for that blow job offer." And with that, he hung up leaving me to consider just exactly what Mondays were going to be like at my house for a little while. I called for the girls to come join me and I explained what Jimmy was going to have to do and how long it would take him.

"By the way," Allie said to the room "I can't get ahold of Myles. I think that's probably a dead end anyhow since he's touring."

"Does Myles have a Facebook page?" I wondered. "Maybe he's updating his status and we can find him just in case he may have heard from her."

"I'll check it," said Tricia "I've been looking at my page since Zoe was on her call. We waited as she went to the Facebook home page to check for the latest status updates.

"Whoa," she said abruptly. "What?" I asked, concerned at her demeanor.

"Is Myles okay?" Tricia looked slowly up from her iPhone.

"Oh yeah, he's fantastic," she said "He's in Seattle playing the Moore Theatre."

"So what's up?" asked Allie looking pointedly at Tricia.

"Skylar's status has been updated again," she said anxiously. I froze in place and said, "I don't want to know. But tell me. What does it say?" Tricia took a deep breath in and let it out slowly saying "It says, Skylar Stewart is heading down to the Halloween Festival in Georgetown tomorrow! I'll be dressed as Mother Theresa!"

Chapter 11: Costume Shop

We Tricia read Skylar's new status over and over again as we tried to make heads or tails of it. We thought maybe Jimmy had hacked into her profile and posted that as a test to see if it worked. One quick text to him ruled that out as Jimmy hadn't even gotten the kids to my parent's house let alone had a chance to begin breaking into her Facebook page. When that was ruled out we knew we'd have to face the fact that we didn't know if it was Skylar or Charles who was communicating with us, and that we'd have to attend the Georgetown Halloween festival to find out what was going on.

"I think someone should reply to the status," said Holly. She continued saying "We should set a meeting place and tell her what time we'll be meeting her."

I didn't understand why and told her so.

"Simply because we should have some sort of trail in case something should happen to one or all of us." As much as we didn't want to admit it what we were planning on doing was dangerous.

"We can't call the police," I said to the girls as I heard their thoughts. "And even if we did, what could they do? As far as I know we are the only people in the world who can battle an invisible man."

I stood up and walked over to Holly and said "Go reply to her status that we'll meet her at the corner of M and Wisconsin by the bank. Even if the others bail, I'm with you."

Tricia rolled her eyes "I'm with you too. Holy dramatic moment." Allie had been quiet for a long time. I knew, like me, that she was thinking of her darling babies and her unsuspecting husband. I knew that this was a huge risk that we were all taking. But I think the whole time we'd been living through our groundhog days waiting for this moment. That we now had a purpose bigger than we'd ever anticipated and that it was time to live out our destinies, together.

"I know, Al," I said, looking deep into her eyes. "You don't have to do this, you don't have to join us." Allie looked up from her long stare at the floor.

"Zoe, all you can do is hear thoughts and Holly can't do a thing without a weapon. You need me. This is our destiny." I felt relief flood through me. Tricia, Holly and I ran over to her and we all hugged, giving our eyes that brightness that we were becoming accustomed to.

"Holly your eyes are blinding me," joked Tricia.

"Well, stop snuggling with me then," answered Holly.

Allie and I smiled at them as Allie spoke "I think the girls are getting hungry, don't you Zoe? They're grouchy." Suddenly I was aware that it was late in the afternoon and we hadn't eaten since breakfast. "Let's get out of here and go grab some pasta!" I said excitedly. "You guys remember Enzios on Wisconsin? "I haven't been there in years."

We broke our tight embraces and the dazzle drained from our eyes. We headed out the door. Holly stopped briefly and, in seconds, repaired the broken knob.

We arrived at the restaurant minutes later. It seemed like a betrayal of sorts to be out, trying to eat a meal when we didn't know where Skylar was or who she was with or even if she was okay. I heard whispers of my fellow hero's thoughts and I made a half concerted effort to assuage them.

"We have to eat," I began "And like I said earlier I'm going to have to have a little humor to get through this. So let's try to suck it up and enjoy what we can because we have a huge task ahead of us." My friends didn't even blink at the fact that I knew their thoughts.

They nodded and Allie put her hand on my back and patted me in understanding. "Let's go see Antionette," she said softly.

Enzios was a very rare treat in Washington D.C. the land of famous chefs and their fancy restaurants. A cleaned-up hole in the wall with only six metal tables covered in white tablecloths, Enzios was a mom and pop delight with a menu of homemade breads, pastas, sauces and desserts. The restaurant's general manager, head waitress, bartender and bus person was Antoinette Enzio, a rotund, loud-mouthed woman who seemed to be a New York city Italian in every sense of the stereotype.

Antionette was known for standing in the middle of the restaurant and loudly yelling at diners to "Shut up and listen I'ma gonna tell ya the specials. I'm only sayin' 'em once, so you better listen!" If you didn't already know her she could intimidate you into silence. I'd seen many a customer get hollered at by her for being too quiet. Conversely, I'd also seen Antoinette lash out at patrons who were too loud—if she wasn't included in on the conversation that is. She would regard everyone with suspicious eyes upon meeting them but was quickly won over by handsome men and friendly women alike if they offered a smile in their greeting. Being on Antoinette's good side meant copious amounts of free house Chianti and extra garlic bread. She would sit at the tables with her favorite customers, boisterously telling them her funny stories from the day. She was a true Italian delight who reveled in running an intimate Italian restaurant in the middle of a big city. I was thrilled to have a chance to see her again as were my friends. We all wondered if she would remember us after all this time. I'd moved to Nashville three years prior, Holly lived nearby but hadn't been there in years. Tricia and Allie's last memory of Enzio's was from when they'd graduated from college before they moved away from where we grew up.

We walked in and stared nervously around the room. There was only one open table.

Antoinette was sitting behind the counter her head bent over a paper and a calculator when she hollered without looking up "Come in, sit!" We knew that she was not happy when diners dawdled so we moved quickly to our seats at the one remaining table. We sat down, shuffled around our menus, and waited for her to approach. Antoinette looked up and saw that we were seated and she picked up the water pitcher to bring it to us. "Water?" she said simply. I looked up at her to make eye contact and I smiled. At first Antoinette looked blankly at me but then the realization of who I was dawned on her. "Well hello!" she said practically screaming as she slapped me hard on the back. She surveyed the table suspiciously. "I remember you!" she said to Holly. Her eyes moved to Allie "Still a tiny thing ain't ya?" Antoinette's eyes stopped on Tricia and she pursed her lips saying "Hm."

Tricia sat up and smiled very big saying "I'm Tricia! It's been many years Antoinette. You look stunning."

Antoinette regarded Tricia carefully, replying only, "Trouble." That one word cracked us all up, including Tricia, and significantly lightened Antoinette's grouchiness.

She grinned and hollered "Wine!" as her next statement and she waddled off to get it. Soon, wine was served, specials were screamed and we settled in to our meals and discussion.

"So," said Tricia in between bites of veal parmesan and sips of wine "The festival is tomorrow and we can't go if we don't have costumes."

Holly snorted at this "I refuse to wear a costume," she said "I'm 35 years old and am far beyond any sort of costume silliness."

I was always a huge fan of Halloween so I was thrilled at the prospect of dressing up and I said so. "Pierce is going to be Darth Vader. Maybe I could be him too. The kid would love it."

Allie frowned as she considered this. "I don't want to be anything from Star Wars."

Tricia jumped in "Well what if we picked a different movie to choose characters from?" Holly dropped her fork on her plate loudly and said angrily "Ladies, let me repeat myself. I absolutely will not be caught dead in any sort of costume. They will just have to allow me into the festival costume free."

Tricia rolled her eyes replying "Hey Dr. Buzzkill, it's a Halloween festival. You won't get in without an outfit. Rules is rules," "Maybe you can go as a wet blanket!" she added laughing. "Or a party pooper," I said grinning. Allie shook her finger at us telling us to knock it off while Holly pouted.

"Look, Holly," began Allie "You're going to have to be something." Allie selected a few strong female figures in history to assuage Holly's apprehension, to no avail. "How about Juliette? Or how about Joan of Arc?"

"How about no?" Holly retorted, crossing her arms defiantly. "I'm sure that I can get in without a costume."

Allie did not give up "Holly, it's a Halloween festival," she began "And we have to get into it to figure out where Skylar is. You know as well as the rest of us entrance is prohibited if one does not wear a costume." Holly looked at Allie as if she were a defeated child being scolded. Allie continued "Skylar needs us."

Holly sighed deeply. "You had to play the Skylar card, eh?" she said sadly. "Under one condition. I refuse to be anything fictional and ridiculous. It is simply beneath me." We all smiled at each other having achieved a victory over the very uptight Holly. It had been many years since we'd been together for a Halloween and the more I thought about it I couldn't remember Holly ever dressing up.

"Joan of Arc costume it is!" I said triumphantly as Holly sighed.

"If I must dress in a costume for this then that is a suitable idea," she answered.

Antoinette thundered over and refilled our wine. "I heard you talking about costumes," she yelled at us. We nodded and she went on, saying, "Costume shop on 215 M St. closes in 2 hours. Who wants dessert?"

One and a half hours and 3 bottles of wine later our tummies were filled to the brim and our minds were a little fuzzy. We all gave Antoinette big hugs, even Tricia, who Antoinette had forgiven once she saw the tip on the receipt. The girls and I stumbled out the door into the chilly night air and hailed a cab.

"To 215 M, please," said Allie to the driver. Holly pursed her lips in quiet disappointment as we went on our way to the costume shop that Antoinette had told us about. Tricia, Allie and I talked quietly about what kinds of Halloween costumes we thought might be available to us at the shop. All I knew was that I didn't want to be something slutty. Over the years Halloween costumes for women had been relegated to making up their own or sexy ones. Sexy nurse and sexy maid were all we had back in the 80s when I was growing up. Since I wasn't old enough to be sexy I was forced to be creative in my costume and not rely on being a sex-pot for the festivities. One year I was Cyndi Lauper; another time I was the girl from Flashdance. I made my own 80s style sweatshirt for that one by cutting off the sleeves and using them as leg warmers. As someone who is as far from being Martha Stewart as she can be, that was an accomplishment I was quite proud of. But nowadays costumes for women had become plentiful and every one of them was sexy in some way. Sexy fireman, sexy alien, sexy cop, sexy taxi driver were among the many choices. I was always so disappointed that these were the choices for girls today. I was looking forward to getting to the costume shop and finding out what we were going to be for our Halloween rescue. When I mentioned that I didn't think we should be any of those standard sexy costumes Tricia reacted as if I'd just said she was fat.

"Excuse me?" she said her voice rising "But Halloween is all about being sexy!" I opened my mouth to protest but she shushed me and went on "Look ladies, I'll be damned if I'm going to this shop and am going to be dressing up like some ugly goblin. Halloween is a great time to go as a hooker to show off how hot we are!"

Holly looked pained "I am NOT going to be a hooker!" she moaned.

Tricia went on as if Holly hadn't spoken "I for one am going to find the sexiest costume out there. The very last thing I want to do is dress as some frumpy old pumpkin!" Our cab driver snickered quietly and for a moment I could hear him thinking that Tricia already looked a lot like a hooker in her current outfit. His thought made me smile to myself as cab pulled up to our stop.

"Look Tricia," I said "Just be something so we can get in to the festival, okay? Who cares about your boobs? Not the gays, that's for sure." We slid out of the seats and stood side-by-side, facing the costume shop, preparing ourselves for our next challenge: the outfits. The shop was sandwiched between and Urban Outfitters and an Irish pub called The Guards. It had one sidewalk-to-roof rectangle-shaped, filthy window in the front that was covered by a dingy brown curtain. The old sign above the door read Georgetown Costumes and the hours posted on the dirty glass door underneath reminded us that we had little time to waste.

"Shit, we only have 30 minutes!" Tricia exclaimed.

Allie gave her a dark look "Oh boy, potty mouth."

I looked at Allie "Allie, you've been hanging out with little kids too long. It's okay to say Shit. See? Shit, shit, shit shit. You should try it."

Allie smiled "I'm afraid if I do I'll never stop." I turned to face my friends "You ready to do this?" They all nodded except Holly who looked away annoyed. We walked up to the door of the Georgetown Costume shop and went in.

It appeared that the Georgetown Costume shop used to be a dry cleaner. The counter was long and dingy white and behind it was a large purple velvet curtain that hung from wall to wall, ceiling to floor. There was no one behind the desk but there was a small push-button bell that Tricia began pounding on impatiently.

"Hello??" she brayed rudely. From behind the curtain came the store clerk. A thin, boyish-looking woman appeared, she was in her late 20s, with short brown hair styled in a faux hawk. She wore a loose, white t-shirt with the sleeves rolled up and a pack of cigarettes trapped in one of them, tight black skinny jeans and green converse shoes. On her arm was a rainbow tattoo and she had many piercings in her ears. She regarded us curiously with her eyebrows raised and her eyes settled on Tricia who was tapping her index finger loudly on the counter.

"Can I help you ladies?" she said in a deep voice. I smiled brightly to counterbalance Tricia's rudeness, a habit I'd picked up over the years.

"Yes... Toni" I said glancing at her name tag. "We need four Halloween costumes for the festival tomorrow." Toni's eyes slowly looked me up and down and I felt almost naked in front of her.

She laughed and replied saying "We have nothing left of the newer costumes, but there's a big trunk in the back with old stuff you can look through, though." Our faces fell as we looked at each other. We hadn't considered that there might not be any costumes left and now we were going to have to scramble to piece together disguises. Toni approached me and patted me on the back. "Don't look so sad, cutie," she said gruffly. "I'll take care of you." For a minute I heard Toni's thoughts loud and clear and what I heard made me blush furiously. I straightened up and winked at my friends. I would gladly take one for the team and get hit on by the clerk if it would get us costumes for the festival. Tricia, who was visibly irritated at not being the chosen one for Toni's affections, tried to flirt her way into Toni's heart.

"Anyone ever tell you that you look like Zac Efron?" Toni turned slowly to Tricia and her eyes praised Tricia's tall lean figure.

"You're tall," she grumbled.

"And you're brilliant," Tricia said flippantly.

"What I meant was, there are very few costumes left in the bin for your height." Toni turned to Holly, bypassing her face entirely and staring directly at Holly's ample chest. Holly rolled her eyes "What?"

Toni made a low whistle sound with her lips before replying "Not much back there for those big cans either." Holly glared at her. To make peace, Allie quickly moved forward to try to keep Toni from undressing us with her eyes.

"Toni," she said in a motherly tone "You're obviously a professional in this business and we are going to need your help picking costumes. We are in a terrible hurry. Can you be a dear and help us?" Toni turned her stare to Allie and smiled a genuine smile.

"I will gladly help you ladies," she said. She turned her appraising eyes back to me and took my hand in hers. "Follow me."

As Toni stepped back behind the curtain pulling me with her I turned to my friends with a beckoning stare. They came closely behind me beyond the purple velvet. Behind the curtain were a vast array of empty plastic costume cases hung up on hangers. There were a few colorful scarves and belts that hung on the walls or were laying on the floor. Random old-fashioned shoes strewn about with the empty bags on the floor. The room had the stench of mold and dust. There was a large full-length mirror on the right wall and the left wall had more purple curtains that were presumably makeshift changing rooms. Along the back wall was a long counter top and a mirror. Sitting on the grungy white surface were mannequin heads that displayed the few wigs that were left. Underneath the counter top was a large red, black and gold trunk marked "Used." Toni let go of my hand to pull the heavy trunk out from under the counter top.

"The leftovers," she said reaching in and swirling them around. All of us leaned over the box and peered in curiously.

Tricia stood up and announced that she didn't need to use the box because she'd seen enough things hanging around the room that she could make her costume with. Off she went in a flurry of arms, legs and scarves as she gathered her things. While Allie, Toni and I looked in the box I noticed Holly off to the side with her arms crossed over her chest.

"Holly," I said "Come pick something out, you don't have a choice." Holly shook her head stubbornly.

"I'm going to look for some Groucho Marx glasses with the mustache and fake nose," she replied. "That is a costume I can deal with."

Toni looked at Holly and said "Don't have those anymore, jugs." Holly whirled around to face Toni.

"Excuse me, Toni" she spit Toni's name out with venom, "but I would think in this day and age where women are expected to be taken seriously for their intelligence and not their bodies, that another woman…" she gave great emphasis to the word "woman" and gave Toni a hard look up and down before she went on, "… would be respectful of that!" Toni grinned and looked Holly straight in the breasts.

"Take it while you can get it, Sweetie," Toni replied. "They're not always going to be that perky." Holly pursed her lips together and stalked off to the other side of the room and whipped out her iPhone and began typing furiously.

"There's not a lot to choose from here that's gonna fit those fun pillows," Toni called after her. "You had better pick something before it's all gone!" Holly turned around and uncharacteristically flipped Toni the bird.

Toni chuckled and turned to me "She's stunning when she's angry," she said. "What can I get you into today, Baby?" she asked me in her gruff voice.

I reached into the trunk deciding I would be whatever I pulled out first. I grabbed a long white, sparkly fabric and without looking at it I dragged it into the changing rooms with Toni close behind. "Toni," I said "Privacy, please." Toni feigned shock and surprise. "What do you mean?" she replied her voice meeting a higher register now "It's just us girls, right?" I rolled my eyes at her. Toni continued in her artificial voice saying, "Oh, just because I'm gay doesn't mean I'm hitting on you! I just thought you might need help zipping up the old Elvis there!" At the word Elvis my heart soared! I had selected an Elvis costume! I didn't have to be a sexy nurse! Ignoring Toni's perverted thoughts and expressions I stripped down to my bra and panties and quickly put on the sparkly, satin jumpsuit. I waited expectantly for Toni to zip me up but she just stood there staring at me. "Give me a minute," she grumbled "That was hot." Suddenly she was close behind me and I could feel the warmth of her body behind mine.

"Toni, zip me up" I said firmly. Toni paused and sighed deeply and I felt the zipper pull and slide up my spine. Her head appeared next to mine in the mirror "Perfect fit, Baby! It fits great right here" and she promptly patted me on the rear. I barely noticed her. I was thrilled. I couldn't believe an actual Elvis costume was in that trunk! Toni had said that it was because it was a girl's Elvis costume and there weren't many girls -- or gays for that matter -- who wanted to be him so they retired it to the trunk.

"I need shoes," I told her "And a wig."

"No problem." Toni disappeared and returned with a nasty Elvis wig that I shook violently to release it of dust and other creatures. I placed it on my head and it fell lopsided and stayed there. I tied the sparkly belt around my waist and stood on my toes to simulate tall boots. Toni had also returned with a pair of bluish, chunky winter boots and handed them to me.

"That's all we got in your size." I put on the blue moon boots and figured they would have to do.

"What's Allie doing?" I asked Toni "Why don't you go pat her ass?"

Toni grinned. "She's in the other dressing room and your tall friend is in the third one. Jugs is sitting in a chair pouting."

"You know," I said slowly "You really shouldn't call her that. She's a highly regarded scientist who has an IQ of 200"

Toni looked me straight in the eyes "She's got huge tits for a nerd." Realizing that Toni had no interest in changing her sleazy ways I smiled and agreed.

"Yes, she does."

Toni patted me on the back "Hey maybe you and I could get a drink sometime?" I shook my head and once more rolled my eyes at Toni before walking out into the costume room. I stood proudly in my improvised Elvis persona, absolutely thrilled that I wasn't a sexy French maid. Allie, Tricia and Holly turned to stare at me and burst into hysterical laughter.

"That is wretched," Holly said and turned back to her iPhone.

"You look fine," said Allie shooting Holly a look. "Well, actually you look, ahem, unusual." I couldn't believe they didn't like my new outfit.

"I am Elvis you haters, and this costume is awesome!" I shouted. I tried to jog to the full length mirror but my long pants got in the way and I promptly tripped and fell, sending my nasty wig flying across the room. At this, the entire room, including the grouchy Holly, erupted into major laughter. We laughed so hard our voices (even Toni's) got high pitched and then non-existent as we fought to breathe. I laughed until I cried with the tears streaming down my face carrying mascara along with them. I laughed until my stomach muscles ached and my throat hurt. I rolled back and forth on the floor clutching my stomach and holding my legs together so that I wouldn't pee. I couldn't remember the last time I had laughed this hard. I thought briefly that in my darkness over the past few months that I'd forgotten to really just open up and laugh. And this was hilarious. And it felt spectacular. It was a cathartic release of tension that had built up.

We finally collapsed in deep breath and the let out of "ahhh" but we did it all at the same time which started us laughing all over again. When we finally quieted down the thoughts of what was to come came back to us and we got back to work.

I finally stood up and brushed off my Elvis costume and turned to face my friends. For the first time, I noticed Allie and Tricia were dressed in costumes. I looked incredulously at Allie "Are you…" I stopped.

"Yes, I am a ladybug," she said miserably. "Toni only had one costume that fit me," she said "And it was this child's ladybug costume." Toni explained that for a while they tried to carry children's costumes in the store, but only adults came in for costumes. So they sold most of what they had and threw the ladybug in the trunk just in case a child came in.

"At least your costume is all brand new! And you have all the pieces to it," I said, motioning to my blue moon boots.

"Fantastic," Allie replied sarcastically as she fixed the red and black antennae hat on her head. Tricia stepped around Allie to get to the mirror and I was able to see her "costume." Tricia had managed to make a costume out of the hodgepodge costume leftovers that were laying around the room. She wore a belt on which she'd fastened different scarves to that acted as a teeny tiny, very revealing mini skirt. On her legs were fishnet stockings with huge holes in them and on her feet she'd managed to find enormous platform heels that were 8 inches high. On top, Tricia was sporting her lacey white bra and a dusty yellow boa that had seen better days.

"I guess you're a hooker," I said flatly to her.

"Why yes!" she replied happily "The perfect girl's costume. I'm dressed up but I look sexy as hell."

She stared at my Elvis costume "Which is more than I can say for you." "I don't need to dress like a hooker for Halloween to have men …" -- I glanced lovingly at Toni -- "or women want me!"

Tricia huffed and suddenly Holly spoke "I think that boa has one feather," she said softly. Toni and the girls all turned to face Holly who was regarding us with a very sour expression.

"It's time for you, Holly Dolly," Allie said sweetly. "Come on," she continued "It's for Skylar." Holly rose up out of the chair and stomped over to the trunk.

"There is only one costume left!" she said sharply, turning to face Toni. Toni smirked "Actually that's the only one you can wear, Melons. All of our other costumes have been rented out and anything else we have left would not fit those funbags." Holly stared icily at Toni.

"Well," she said briskly "I suppose I do not have a choice. I will wear whatever this thing is!" Briefly, I could hear Holly's thoughts of "this is for Skylar. I can do this for Skylar. It's only Halloween." Holly walked into the third dressing room and we all looked at each other with wide eyes, wondering what she would be. Suddenly we heard a shriek coming from the third dressing room. Alarmed, Tricia, Allie and I ran to the dressing room and threw open the velvet curtain, ready to fight. What we found was not a bad guy but Holly dressed in a Wonder Woman costume and looking absolutely furious about it.

"This," she said through clenched teeth "Has got to be a joke. Where is that store clerk?" Toni appeared and grinned a huge grin "You look hot, Jugsy!" she exclaimed, raking her eyes over Holly's very visible cleavage. If looks could kill, Holly would have murdered Toni on the spot. She walked over to Toni and put her face so close to Toni's that their noses were almost touching.

"You listen here you little dirtbag punk, I will not be wearing this abhorrent costume out in public do you understand me?" she reached up to Toni's shirt and grabbed the top of it. "You will go into that trunk and find me something I can wear that is decent and respectable or so help me God, I will…" She stopped and Toni jumped in saying, "We might have a Hooters girl costume you could wear."

"UGH!" Holly exclaimed whirling around and stomping back into the dressing room. Trying desperately to hide our laughter, the ladybug, the hooker and Elvis stood by the closed curtain and coaxed Holly out.

"We all look dumb," I started saying.

"Speak for yourself!" barked Tricia flinging her sparsely feathered boa around.

Allie looked at Holly and said "This isn't about you, it's about Skylar."

We all nodded our heads in agreement "Relax and have a little fun with it," I said "You kind of are Wonder Woman in a way."

Holly looked up at me and smiled feebly. "Thanks," she said simply. "These boots are the wrong color," she said looking at Toni. Holly put the dingy greenish boots on and the one bracelet that was left and looked in the mirror. Toni walked by the opening and threw in a huge pink beehive wig.

"Need hair," she croaked. Together we all walked to the long mirror on the wall above the counter top. In the mirror facing us was sideways-wigged, long-pants Elvis, pink-haired, green-boots-wearing Wonder Woman, a hooker with a sparsely feathered boa and a darling adult ladybug. It was difficult not to laugh and incipient chuckling turned into all-out roaring laughter as we pointed out each other's ridiculousness. Our fun was cut short when I got a buzz from my cell phone. I walked over to my Prada bag and pulled it out to see who was texting me. It was Jimmy. The text said "I've got the address you wanted. Call me." I looked at the Falcon Four in all our gloriousness and said, "It's time to get back to work, Falcons. Let's roll."

To Toni's delight, we changed back into our regular clothing. She made catcalls and whistled at me the entire time. "Costumes due back day after Halloween," she said as she took our money. Toni charged everyone but me for their costumes but since the costumes were such a mess the others only had to pay a few bucks.

"I can't believe you'd even want these horrific things back," Holly growled at Toni. Toni sighed "Oh kitten," she said smirking "I just want to see this one again," she pointed at me.

"I'm married with two kids, Toni," I replied.

Toni grinned mischievously and leaned in so close I could smell some sort of men's cologne on her "Never stopped me before. I just need 10 minutes alone with ya." Allie stepped in between us and reached out the shake Toni's hand.

"Toni," she said earnestly "Thank you for your time and costumes. I will be sure we return them to you right on time!" Toni stepped back and for a brief moment the noise cleared and I could hear her thinking *is this ladybug for real?*

I smiled at Toni and said "Oh yes, this is how she is all the time. The other girls are already out the door, we've got to go!" I walked out chuckling at Toni's confused expression. Tricia had already hailed a cab and was patting loudly on the seat next to her and yelling at me to hurry it up.

I hopped in the cab and we went back to our hotel. On the way it was decided that we'd all get in to our respective rooms, check messages and call husbands and children or boyfriends and then meet promptly in my suite to discuss what Jimmy had found and our game plan for the next day. When I arrived in my suite, I was anxious to talk to my sons. I had not heard their little voices since that morning, and going from all the time to barely any of the time was a big change for me. I dialed them up and Jimmy answered almost immediately.

"I have the address you wanted," he said. I wasn't ready for that just yet. For just a few minutes I wanted to be a wife and a mommy and not a hearer of thoughts.

"Jimmy can we just cool it on that stuff for now?" I said sighing. "I'm sick of this superhero stuff. I just want to talk to Max and Pierce for a minute." There was silence on the other end of the phone and then he spoke.

"What superhero stuff?" he asked curiously. I hadn't even realized that I had almost let our secret slip.

"What did I say?" I said not very convincingly. "We had some wine at dinner I must be saying silly things." Jimmy didn't buy my lame excuse for one second.

"Really?" he said doubtfully "You had some wine with your girlfriends so you randomly let loose a sentence about superheroes?" I pondered for a split second whether it was time to just confess and let him know what we were doing, but I just couldn't. So many months had gone by with us barely talking to each other about anything under the surface. I had so much to say, but I was holding back. How on earth would he accept this?

"Hon," I said lovingly "Ease up. I told you I will tell you soon okay? This is not a conversation for the phone. My phone clicked for a second and I could hear Jimmy moving the phone to check the caller ID to see who was calling. I concentrated to hear what he was thinking. *Jen the hottie from work. Best not to tell Zoe yet.* Best not to tell me what? I wondered.

"Who is beeping in?"I asked.

"Wrong number," Jimmy answered softly. My heart began pounding and I tried desperately to get back into his mind but suddenly I heard two more little voices and they all drowned each other out.

"Is that Mommy?" I heard Max say excitedly.

"Yes it is!" said Jimmy, "Would you like to talk to her?" Jimmy put Max on the phone and then Pierce. We talked for the longest time about their days. Spongebob, Transformers and evidently their Dad let them have a brownie each for breakfast. I delighted in each story they told me, realizing how I never appreciated it when it was right in front of me the entire time. And now that I might soon be risking my life made it even more poignant. I loved and missed them with every thread of my being. We finished our talk and Jimmy got back on the phone.

"I have some work I have to do," he said still angry at me for withholding. "I will send you an e-mail with the address." I was so confused. Why was Jen from work calling? Why would he hide it? I wanted to ask Jimmy. I wanted to reach out and tell him everything I was going through and beg him to forgive me for disconnecting.

"Jimmy," I began.

"What?" he said sounding a little hopeful.

"Love you," I said lamely and hung up the phone.

The knock at the door and the noise in my head alerted me to the fact that the girls had arrived. They came in the room in a rush chatting loudly to each other about the conversations they'd had with family and loved ones. Each one of them was wearing her pajamas. Tricia was sporting a light pink satin nightie that had faux fur trim. Allie was wearing a neck to floor worn nightgown and Holly was wearing light blue satin pants and button--down top. Each girl had her nighttime hair look as well. Holly had her hair up and glasses on, Allie's hair was pulled back in a headband and Tricia had pigtails. I welcomed them in, told them to make themselves at home and ran to my suitcase to find my pajamas. I pulled out one of my other favorite t-shirts, a black cotton tee with a white pirate skull on it. The skull head was holding a knife in his teeth and the shirt says "Pirates do it dangerously" I pulled it on and grabbed my black cotton cropped pants. I twisted my hair into a rubber band, pulling it back into a loose bun, and grabbed my small framed reading glasses. When I walked out I found my friends already lounging on the couches and chair. Someone had poured a bottle of wine and a glass was waiting for me. Everyone sat up when I walked in and looked at me expectantly. For a few seconds they stared at me and I stared at them.

Finally I said "What?"

"Dumbass," said Tricia "What did Jimmy say?"

I laughed "Oh yeah!" I replied "You guys were so quiet I was thinking that I must have looked really fat and you were going to have an intervention." I sat down and opened up my cell phone to check my e-mail. Up popped an e-mail from Jimmy that said, "Zoe- the address was 3101 Wisconsin Ave NW, Washington DC 20016. I have a lot of work to do so I won't be able to talk anymore tonight. Talk to you in the morning. Jimmy." I noticed there was no "Love you," on that e-mail and it hurt. I kept that from my friends and announced to them the address. Holly was busy typing the address into her iPhone.

"Trixie," she said looking over at Tricia who was laying on pillows on the couch. "Do you have that flier you found in Skylar's apartment?"

Tricia thought for a moment and said "Not on me, why?" We all sat forward as we waited for Holly's answer.

"Because that's the address of the National Cathedral in DC." "Skylar's favorite place to write!" said Allie.

"And the place that was on the flier we found in her apartment" I said slowly.

"Whoever posted on her Facebook did it from the Cathedral," said Holly.

"But why would we have to meet them at the Halloween festival?" said Allie. The room was silent as we pondered this.

"I can only theorize," Holly began "But perhaps Skylar just happened to have the flier in her apartment because she is already an avid Cathedral goer, but Charles wouldn't have anticipated that. And he probably didn't expect that we could trace the Facebook posting." She went on "And Georgetown is merely blocks from the Cathedral."

"So...?" said Tricia.

"So it is likely that we are meant to be captured in an area where there is lots of chaos and strange things going on and perhaps be brought to the cathedral." She continued, "He clearly thinks we can be brought down easily."

I interjected "No one would notice us doing anything out of the ordinary during the festival. We will fight!"

Allie interrupted "But why the Cathedral? What is significant about that?"

"I don't know," Holly answered shaking her head slowly. "I just can't figure that one out."

"Worst. Nerd. Ever," stated Tricia. "His crazy mom was a religious nutcase, remember ladies?" she said. "Maybe that has something to do with it."

"It doesn't really matter why it is significant at this point," replied Holly seriously. "We have to go on what we know. Someone write this down." Allie grabbed a pad of paper and a pen from the nearby table.

"We know he has her," I said. "We know she said to bring her a light for her cigarette," added Tricia. We waited while Allie scribbled.

"We know we have to meet at the festival," said Holly.

"And we know we might end up at the Cathedral," I said. "Why not just go right to the Cathedral," I asked the room. Holly knitted her brows together and scratched her chin. "Because he won't just be waiting for us out in the open. It is quite likely that he has her hidden and himself hidden. If we were lucky enough to find them he might kill her on the spot if he's rushed. We must go to Georgetown."

Our eyes were wide. "Kill her?" Allie exclaimed in a high soft voice.

"He's proven he can kill," Holly answered. "We must be prepared for the worst." We nodded in agreement.

"Then let's get started, shall we?" I said. "We're going to have to locate some plasma TVs and maybe some other things that Holly can make into weapons and maybe even shields."

Tricia spoke up at this "I might have a guy who knows a guy, I'm not sure how much it will cost us though." Suddenly the room was quiet and Allie and Tricia looked very seriously at Holly and me.

"What?" I said looking at them strangely.

"Look Z…and Holls," Allie began. "You guys don't have powers that can protect you like Tricia and I do."

"Yeah," said Tricia "So your weapons are important, but you're vulnerable otherwise." I didn't understand where they were going with this.

"And?"

Allie answered saying "Tricia will protect you and I will protect Holly."

"I don't' need any protection!" answered Holly indignantly. "My weapons are flawless!"

"Look Dr. Flawless," Tricia said looking annoyed at Holly. "Your weapons are the bomb—pun intended—but our powers are going to protect you better than you can protect yourself. Shut it up and rely on me to keep you safe."

Allie looked at me with her big brown eyes. "Let us protect you." Holly and I exchanged knowing glances.

"Fine," I said "But I'm still going to fight like nobody's business."

"As am I," said Holly.

"You guys are regular AmToddan Gladiators," Tricia said sarcastically to both of us.

"I'm gonna go call my guy who knows a guy to see what we can get our hands on. I might need you, Zoe, to use your sexy voice to sweet talk him like you did Toni."

I laughed "It helps that I can sometimes hear what they're thinking. Makes it easier to give them what they want." For a moment I thought about trying to apply that in my own marriage. If I just knew what he wanted.. Or really it was the other way around. If he could hear my thoughts. If he just knew what I wanted.

Chapter 12: Time Machine

I snapped out of it when Tricia yelled "Booyah!" and threw her iPhone onto the couch. "We have to go meet him at the warehouse and they even said we could use the empty space there to work on our science project."

"Science project?" asked Holly curiously. "I told 'em you're a hotshot scientist who'd pay 'em off big time when you made your time machine available."

"Time machine?" I said laughing.

"Yeah these guys are dumber than Holly's boyfriend and I told 'em not only would we share the profits but we'd take 'em forward to learn scores of football games so they could make millions gambling."

Holly crossed her arms and looked fiercely at Tricia. "Says the girl who failed remedial math!" she said angrily, continuing. "And what happens when they come in to see what we're doing and see weapons?"

Allie answered that one. "I won't let them in," she said simply. We looked at her.

"No, I guess you won't," I said to Allie with a smile.

"And if they get in we'll shoot 'em!" Tricia said clapping her hands.

Allie turned to her "No one dies at our hands, okay?"

"Not if we can help it," I added. I reached out to my friends and grabbed Holly and Allie's hands. Allie reached out to grab Tricia's hand. Holly begrudgingly took Tricia's hand. Our eyes began to brighten and then glow.

"Listen up Falcons," I said. "The good guys never kill anyone but the bad guys. I know killing anyone is not ideal but we have to be realistic that it might happen. As good superheroes let's pledge right here and now that we will not harm innocents, but we will destroy the evils."

"Is evils the right word?" asked Tricia.

"I don't know," I replied "But I know we should all agree to this." Each girl nodded slowly.

"Put your hands in the middle now, like we used to do in high school." We each put our right hand in the middle of the circle one on top of the other.

"On three."

At the mention of three we all shouted "Go Falcon Five!" The word five hung in the air as we knew we were missing one valuable member of our club. But with or without Skylar the Falcon Five were engaged and ready.

I awoke later than usual. I was getting used to this staying up late and sleeping in routine that I'd slipped into over the last couple of days. I picked up my cell phone to see what time it was. It read, 9:00 a.m., October 31. Oh no, I thought, here comes the guilt. Today was Halloween, my favorite day of the year. Every year I treated Halloween as an extravaganza, decorating my house with pumpkins and goblins and bats and ghosts beginning on October 1st. The boys absolutely loved when I turned the house into Halloween town and we spent many hours cruising costume shops deciding what their costumes would be. This year I would be here in Washington D.C. without them and I felt terrible guilt and anguish over it. Jimmy had been very supportive of the trip and practically pushed me out the door to take it but it didn't mitigate my own "mother's guilt." It isn't like I missed one of their birthdays, I told myself firmly as I dialed my home number. It rang a few times and voicemail picked up.

"Hi boys and Daddy!" I said enthusiastically. "Happy Halloween! I miss you so much and know you're going to have a wonderful day and night dressing up and trick or treating! Be sure to have Daddy take lots of pictures. I miss you all terribly and I will be home tomorrow." I stopped for a second, then said very seriously, "Love you." I hung up and the tears spilled from my eyes onto my pirate shirt. There was ache in my chest. I wrapped my arms around myself and hugged, and but it did not subside. This trip had been such a whirlwind of all things unbelievable. A rollercoaster of highs and even highers, danger and suspense, mystery and excitement. All things I thought I needed in my life. But now that I had them I realized that taking my boys trick or treating sounded like the most important thing in the world. And talking to my husband was equally important. I vowed that I would be safe tonight, protect my friends and carry out our mission; but at the same time I would never spend another second not loving everything that I had. I knew that the only thing that would fill the empty black hole in my chest was my family and I would be home with them soon.

Right then my cell phone beeped. Jimmy had sent me a picture. It was the boys, Pierce already dressed as Darth Vader and Max as a Clone Trooper, sitting in a restaurant having breakfast. The caption read "Star wars and bacon. Happy Halloween." It hurt to see their cute faces but it was also comforting to know that they were safe, happy and well fed. It also reminded me that I hadn't eaten yet. I looked at the picture once more and decided to start the day. I slowly got off the bed and stretched, trying to remember what time we were supposed to meet downstairs for breakfast. We'd decided that we'd eat a big breakfast and then head over to Tricia's warehouse and get to work. I shuffled into the bathroom and turned on the shower. I splashed some of the water onto my face. I couldn't believe what we were planning on doing today. It all seemed like a long, crazy dream. I stepped into the shower and told myself that today I would live in our new reality and not question it anymore. I was more nervous than I had ever been but I knew we absolutely could not fail. Somewhere in my head I thought I heard a voice saying the exact same thing.

Last night we'd decided to dress down for the weapon making, to be sure we didn't stand out, just in case the guys at the warehouse were suspicious of anything. I pulled on my black yoga pants and grabbed another favorite t-shirt of mine, a Brad Paisley shirt. I never was a country music fan until I moved to Nashville and once I heard Brad Paisley's hit song "Ticks" I was hooked. He was a talented guitarist who didn't take himself too seriously. Jimmy had surprised me with tickets to his concert and that's where I got the shirt. It was short sleeved and black with Brad on the front sporting a big white cowboy hat. It would be a good shirt to work in and I smiled when I thought about what the girls would think when they saw it. I grabbed my Juicy Couture tennis shoes, pulled my hair back into a pony tail, threw on some make-up and I was out the door. As usual I was early, so I sat down in the lounge in the lobby and flipped through a magazine as I waited. I heard the elevator make its dinging sound and I looked up to see Allie and Holly striding toward me smiling. Holly was dressed in a light blue Nike track suit and had part of her hair pulled back in a silver rectangle barrette. Allie was looking like she was heading to work in her black yoga pants and green tea colored wrap top. Allie's hair was down and tucked behind her ears.

"You guys look great," I said. "Perfectly incognito." Both girls stared at my shirt.

"Who is that cowboy on your shirt?" asked Holly haughtily.

Allie gave Holly a sideways look "Now, now," she said. "Who is that guy Z?"

I stood proudly and said "Brad Paisley of course!"

With raised eyebrows Holly replied "You're into country music now?"

I smirked in Holly's direction and then spoke directly to Allie "I used to be a country music snob like some people in the room," I said motioning obviously to Holly. "But now I am not. Brad Paisley rocks my world."

Allie smiled "Whatever makes you happy, hon," she said.

"For the love of Pete don't make us listen to it, I'll lose my mind," Holly said snidely.

"Funny you should mention that Holly, I brought my iPod and speaker so we could have some music to drown out the weapon making!" Holly put her hands on her hips and waited for me to finish. "And you're in luck! It's Brad Paisley!!" with that statement I kicked my feet out left and right and pushed my fists down in rhythm. "yee haw yee haw yee haw" I brayed.

Holly couldn't help but laugh. "God help me," she said with a grin.

"Correction," I told her "*Brad* help you!"

Allie looked at her watch "Did we tell Tricia the right time?" she asked.

"Damn it," I said "I meant to give her the early time so she'd be on time but I think I forgot."

"Well it's been about 15 minutes," Holly said "She'll be here any minute." As if on cue the elevator dinged and out walked Tricia and our mouths fell open.

Tricia's hair caught my attention first. It was twisted up on either side of her head like Princess Leia from Star Wars. She was dressed in a fluorescent pink track suit with bright white stripes down the sides. Her shoes were also white and pink and very clean and bright. She smiled upon seeing us and did a twirl. When she turned around we could see the word "Trixie" had been embroidered on her derriere, in bright white letters of course.

"So much for trying to blend in with the crowd," said Holly sarcastically.

Tricia approached and all I could say was "You look like Fergie from the Black Eyed Peas." "I was thinking more of a pink Paris Hilton" added Holly.

"I think you look very, um, bright, Tricia" said Allie ever the peacemaker.

Tricia flashed a dazzling smile at Allie, "Yes Al, that's the point."

To Holly and me she shot a dark look, pursing her lips and spitting out the words "Ladies, jealousy does not become you!"

"Jealousy?" Holly spat back. "You look like a hot pink mess!" I nodded in agreement Tricia this is what you wear to disappear into the crowd? To go unnoticed?"

Tricia sighed loudly and with great affect. "I am a superhero, girls," she said sweetly. "I will be damned if I don't try to look like one."

"You look like Hannah Montana," muttered Holly. I grinned at Holly and she grinned back. We both knew Tricia would never change and half the fun of being friends with her were the opportunities she was always giving us to make fun of her outrageous outfits.

"Come on, Fergie," I said "Let's go eat."

Breakfast was long and delicious as we determined there might not be anyplace suitable for us to dine in near the warehouse. As true women, we skipped such delights such as bagels, bacon and regular eggs, opting instead for wheat toast, egg whites, fruit and yogurt. We all might have happily dined on bacon or bagels on our own, but women never eat junk food in front of other women. It is an unwritten code that when in a group of other women, one must dine on light, healthful fare only. After we'd had our fill, we headed out to the quiet room off the lobby that the hotel provided for traveling business people to work. We figured it would be a good place to listen to Tricia chat with her shady warehouse friend on the phone. We planned for me to be close by, to try and pick up his thoughts.

"You know what that means, choir girls," I said.

"Tell me we don't have to think sing again?" asked Holly.

"Look it's worse for me than it is for you, Holly, believe me. You guys won't be winning AmToddan Idol anytime soon and it's not because you're way too old to compete either."

"Not way too old," Holly protested.

"What shall we sing, Zoe?" asked Allie.

"Oh, I don't know. How about Mickey from the 80s?"

"Ooh I love that song!" said Allie excitedly "I know all the words!"

Holly sighed deeply and loudly "Must we always do ridiculous things?"

"Hey is that what the Spiderman said when he put on that hideous red and black, skin tight spandex costume-thingy and shot those little webs all over New York City? You're a superhero now, Holls. Might as well get used to things out of the ordinary!" I slapped her hard on the back when I said that, and she gave me a dirty look and turned away from me, shrugging. Tricia had her phone out and began to dial.

I heard Allie whisper 1, 2, 3 "OH MICKEY YOU'RE SO FINE," blasted in my head. "YOU'RE SO FINE YOU BLOW MY MIND, HEY MICKEY!" Holly and Allie were shaking their heads back and forth and clapping softly. I was glad they were enjoying themselves but decided on the spot that this would be the last time they would sing that song. There had to be something better for them to use. Their words began to blend and soon there was just a buzz from them and my mind was clear to hear Tricia's thoughts and the guy she was talking to. *How many times does his phone have to ring, 50,000??* Even Tricia's thoughts were impatient, I thought.

Suddenly he picked up and I heard her say "Sheesh, Sam that took forever. It's Tricia, I've got to get over to the warehouse, is it open?" *Come on Sam, let us come alone. Just leave us a key,* thought Tricia. I strained over the buzz of the song to hear what Sam was thinking. Gradually I picked up his tone and then his thoughts.

"I don't know, Tricia," he began. *I don't know. What are you up to?*

"Sam, you owe me from that time I pretended to not get that extra shipment of laptops for my office, do you remember? You got to keep them?" *It was Christmas. He said he was hungry and had hungry kids. I was too weak to argue.* She looked at me as she thought this. I nodded so she knew I could hear her. Allie and Holly had stopped dancing and sat down on some nearby stools still nodding their heads to the song.

"Look, I'll let you come down here but I'm sticking around. A time machine sounds huge and I want to be a part of it." *A real time machine! Wow!*

"Oh fine," replied Tricia giving in too easily "We're going to catch a cab over there and should be there in about 45 minutes. Meet us there?" *Jerk.*

"Can't wait to see your pretty face again, lady," he answered. *She is so pretty. I hope her friends are as hot as she is. Gonna be a great day!*

"Yeah whatever, bye" answered Tricia and hung up. Upon seeing Tricia hang up the phone Holly and Allie stood up and the background noise in my head stopped.

"While I actually enjoyed that song," said Holly "I think you need to work on picking up voices in a different way."

"Hey, I'm new at this," I answered "And we haven't exactly had time to practice."

"I don't mind the singing if it helps, Zoe," said Allie "So what's up? What was he thinking? Is he on the level?"

They all turned to me and I said "Well he doesn't think much at all. Also," I said, "He thinks the time machine is going to be something big. I bet he'll want to be in the room with us when Holly is working."

"Crap!" said Tricia "He obviously cannot see her working"

"His simple mind would not be able to comprehend what his beady little eyes will be seeing," I said.

"Well, we will just have to make sure that doesn't happen," said Allie "I will personally see to it!" she said making a muscle.

"I'm not sure we'll need to manhandle him right off the bat, Allie," I said. "It seems Sam has a bit of a crush on Tricia and he's hoping the rest of us are—in his words—as hot as she is!"

Tricia huffed "As if," she said "You guys are no slouches but you don't hold a candle to me," she said twirling.

"If we held a candle to you that outfit and your hair would go up in flames in 3 seconds," added Holly darkly. We all laughed at that, including Tricia.

"Ready to go?" I asked. Everyone nodded and we walked out of the room and back into the lobby. Outside we caught a taxi and gave him the address 939 Industrial Park SW. The dark-skinned cab driver regarded us suspiciously "You sure you want to go there?" he asked in a heavy Jamaican accent.

"Yeah," said Tricia speaking for all of us, "What's up?" The cab driver shrugged his shoulders and turned back to the wheel.

"Bad area," he said "I don't take my cab there at night. Get robbed." We exchanged uneasy glances. To ease their nerves and mind, I gave everyone a warm smile and even caught the driver's eye in the rearview mirror.

"We're pretty brave, sir" I said "You could even call us superheroes!"

The cabbie chuckled at that and the girls laughed as well. "Well you better be," he said solemn again "Dangerous town. I will give you my card and if you are not too late I will come get you. But if you are too late, never mind," he said. "There are few heroes and many villains," he added. This last statement from the taxi driver silenced all of us and we stared out the windows watching as the city changed from clean, crisp white buildings to run-down tenements and graffiti. The driver was right, I thought. This is a terrible area and we must be careful. Then Tricia, Holly and Allie whirled their heads around and looked at me strangely.

"I heard what you were thinking!" said Tricia. The others echoed her that they also heard what I was thinking.

"I couldn't do it again if I tried," I said with frustration.

"What were you feeling, Zoe, when you thought that?" asked Holly in her clinical voice.

"Um," I answered "I was thinking that he's right," I said motioning to the driver. "And I was feeling very deeply about taking this mission seriously."

"Well that may be the key to your communication through the mind," she replied. "I would like you to monitor your feelings when you're feeling fearful or on the defensive. I believe those may be the times when you can communicate with us clearly with your mind."

I nodded "Easy there Dr. Brainiac, I'm not one of those rhesus monkeys you do experiments you know," I responded to lighten the mood.

The cab driver cleared his throat and spoke incredulously "What you mean talking in your mind? That woman intuition? Ah, I will never understand women!" The girls and I chuckled at this, glad that we had something else to make us smile as we approached our destination. "Here you go, pretty ladies!" the cabbie said happily. "Take my card and call me before it gets too dark," he said gravely "I come get you girls, okay? Okay?" he said looking at each one of us.

"Yes of course," replied Allie warmly. "Thank you, sir." We exited the cab and approached the enormous warehouse. It looked as if it had been in a war. It was gray and grimy with many broken windows and what looked like bullet holes along the front wall. There was trash blowing around in the breeze around us and the concrete driveway leading up to the warehouse was full of cracks. A rotund, balding man dressed in suit pants and a button down shirt with the first five buttons open, showing a thick gold chain, appeared from the side of the building and walked toward us. Our bodies tensed at the sight of him and we approached cautiously.

"Sam!" yelled Tricia "How the hell are ya? How's your family?" Sam smiled widely showing off a gold tooth in the center of his top row of teeth.

"Family?" he asked puzzled "Oh yes! The family!" he replied with extra emphasis on the last word. "They are all doing great."

Tricia cocked her head to the side and said "Yeah, Sam. How is grandmother Fiona from Italy?" Sam cleared his throat and shifted to one foot and then back to the other,

"She's just great, Tricia, thanks so much for asking."

"Fabulous," she said "I'll do the intros once we get inside," she said, motioning to us.

"Lead the way, Sam!" Sam turned and walked ahead of us a few paces.

Tricia turned around to us and whispered, "There was no Grandmother Fiona! I made that up!"

"That's the laptop guy?" whispered Holly back. "You could have gone to jail for him? Obviously he's a liar!"

"Yes, thanks Dr. Obvious," Tricia whispered back fiercely. "I will have to consult with you the next time I want to help the poor!" Holly opened her mouth to respond but Allie put her hands on each woman and gave them a stern look to knock it off. They shook her hands off of their arms and huffed but remained silent as we continued around the back of the warehouse.

Sam had taken us to a large, red metal door covered in dents. "Always break-ins," he said motioning to the damage on the door. We stood silently while he unlocked the door and walked in when he stood aside like a gentleman.

The warehouse was a mess. Boxes and cartons were strewn all over the floor. There were huge pallets carrying giant wooden crates. Forklifts were parked next to wooden dollies that were next to file cabinets that were next to giant trash cans stuffed with packing material. Sam walked past all of the chaos and took us to a gray door that was padlocked shut.

"That's our regular cargo," Sam said glancing briefly back at the boxes and crates in the other room. "This is our piece de resistance," he said as he unlocked the door. Inside was a smaller room that was filled wall to wall with plasma televisions of all sizes. There were stacks of the 57 inchers, the kitchen plasmas, pink plasmas for your daughter and even plasmas that were being touted for the bathroom. I thought briefly of Jimmy who would have given his right arm to check out all of this merchandise. In the middle of the room was a large metal table that had several box cutters and measuring tape on top.

"Is this…contraband?" Holly asked Sam. Sam shrugged his shoulders and said "Did you have money for actual televisions? I was told you needed something free and fast." Holly snapped her mouth shut and looked pleadingly at Allie.

Allie responded by putting her finger up to her lips and mouthing "shh." I walked over to Sam and gave him one of my dazzling smiles.

"Sam," I said "This is all amazing. I have always wondered how people get a hold of these types of televisions when they simply cannot afford them!" I went on adding "You are a regular Robin Hood aren't you?" Sam's eyes lit up at this and he puffed up his chest and grinned.

"I suppose I am," he said grinning. Tricia jumped at this opportunity and touched his arm "Hey Robin Hood," she purred. "Think you could leave us alone so we can get to work on that time machine? Time's a wastin.'"

Sam looked back and forth at us skeptically "Yeah well, I'm not goin' anywhere, ladies." Allie boldly stepped forward "Sam?" she said sweetly "I would love a tour of the operations out in the main warehouse. Think you could spend a little time with me?" Sam looked dubious but relented the minute Allie put her arm through his. "We'll be right back Sam, you won't miss a thing," Allie said winking at us. I knew that once Allie got Sam out into the main warehouse that if he chose not to cooperate she could certainly use her new-found skills to hold him off from spying on us. I think even Allie was hoping he would be hard to keep away from us so that she could practice on him. I turned to Holly, who was staring at the towers of boxes.

"What do you need from us?" Holly crossed her arms and leaned back on her heels while contemplating.

"See those pink ones?" We nodded yes. "Get me those. I might as well make them pretty." Tricia and I obliged grabbing the pink boxes and dragged them to the table in the middle of the room. "Allie ... should ... be ... doing ... the... heavy ... lifting!" said Tricia breathing heavily. We used the box cutters to tear them open and we put the televisions on the floor in front of the table. Holly was pacing back and forth, deep in thought as she looked at each television we brought out.

"How many are you gonna need Dr. Nerdface?" teased Tricia. Holly's voice was barely a whisper "Give me five more for a total of ten." Tricia and I went back over to the tower of plasmas and grabbed more boxes.

"Why are we the only ones carrying these?" she grunted. When all ten televisions were on the floor lined up, Holly spoke.

"I would like you to leave while I work," was all she said. Tricia opened her mouth to protest but I stopped her.

"We'll go look for something that we can put the weapons in when we leave."

Tricia rolled her eyes and whispered loudly "Gawd she's a diva!" We walked to the door turning once to let Holly know we'd be back to check on her but she had already gone into her trance. Her eyes were bright white and her head was cocked to the side just like she did that first night we were all together.

"Here comes the tongue!" murmured Tricia. We walked out and shut the metal door tightly with a loud boom.

"I say we go find Allie and Sam, and get us a big box for our time machine," I said. "We can check on her periodically." Tricia nodded and together we wandered out into the huge main area of the warehouse. I could hear the voices of Allie and Sam echoing a short distance away. Her echo was high and chatty, his was low and gruff. I surmised that she was feigning intense interest in the warehouse business and Sam was eating it up. As Tricia and I wandered through the disorderly space I noticed the voices were harder to hear and I was getting worried. Tricia had noticed too and was looking around the room straining to hear them.

"Trix," I said with a knowing look. "Oh Christ Almighty can't you hear their thoughts without a terrible song from the 70s or 80s?"

I grinned "Not yet!" 1, 2, 3, *purple rain, purple rain purple rain purple rain.*

"Good choice!" I teased. Tricia rolled her eyes and pointed in the air in the direction we'd last heard the voices. *I never wanted to be your weekend lover.*

"It's not working!" I said frustratedly "Do it louder!" *I just wanted to be some KIND OF FRIEND EH. BABY I WOULD NEVER LEAVE YOU FOR ANOTHER.*

"Maybe because it's just one voice?" I asked. Tricia had thrown her arms in the air and was swaying back and forth in time to the silent song. *ONLY WANT TO SEE YOU BABY IN THE PURPLE RAIN.*

I reached out and grabbed her hand "Stop singing," I said.

"Why? Can you hear them?" she asked.

"No. They're right behind you." Embarrassed Tricia whirled around to see Allie and Sam looking at her. Allie was smiling but Sam was clearly confused.

"Sam was just finishing up the tour." We nodded. "Would either of you like to go?"
"Take me! Take me!" said Tricia jumping up and down. Sam looked thrilled to have her accompany him and off they went. I sat down on a wooden crate, dejected.
"What's up Zoe?" asked Allie, concerned. "You know I can't just have you guys sing every time I need to hear what people are thinking," I replied. Allie sat down next to me "Can you ever just hear voices if we aren't there? If we aren't singing?" I thought about it, remembering several times over the past two days that I could hear voices: our room service waiter that first night, Toni at the costume shop was one I heard all too clearly, and then I also heard Jimmy thinking about another woman.
When I said this to Allie she nodded slowly and said "Are you worried that he's cheating?"
I hugged myself tightly and said "Not yet..." Allie nodded "Look, I've been married just as long as you have. I know that you sort of...lose focus." Allie continued "And especially when you have been feeling disconnected like we all have, well, there just has to be a way out right?" I looked at her and shrugged my shoulders. "Z," she said "If this experience these past few days has taught you anything it's that life isn't always simple. We have to work at our powers just like we have to work at our lives."
I closed my eyes tightly. "Thank you, Oprah." Allie punched me lightly in the arm, knocking me clear to the floor, which cracked both of us up. Then we sat in silence for a few minutes "Practice makes perfect!" I knew she was right and I knew I needed to try. I distracted myself from thinking too hard and just opened up the ears in my mind. That image of ears in my mind made me laugh and relax. It occurred to me that I could hear those voices when I deliberately tuned out the noise and brought in the specific frequency of the other person's mind. With Christian, I was in distress. With Toni I was relaxed. And with Jimmy I was suspicious. Each time I tuned into those frequencies I was able to push the noise out. I just needed to focus as if I had a pressing reason to listen. My breathing was calm and my mind was clear. Suddenly I heard her loud and clear *What's so funny?*
"I can hear you..." I said warily thinking it would suddenly go away. *Don't give up* she thought.

I looked her square in the eyes "I won't." She smiled but did not speak *I think you have been able to do this all along. But you got used to tuning it all out and now you have to get used to tuning it back in.*

"You are absolutely right!" I said. *You're lucky that you can control it already. You didn't even know you were! By the way, your eyes are just a teensy bit shiny when you're listening..* I clapped my hands together like a child. I said, "Yay me!"

Sam asks, "Yay what?" He and Tricia returned from their tour.

"It's her birthday," Tricia said with a grin. Sam looked at me carefully. I stared back careful to blink so the glow wouldn't be too obvious. I opened up my mind to tune down the noise and bring only him in. *I bet she's 33.*

"I'm 35!"I answered happily. I was so excited that I was able to hear him I jumped up from my crate and sang "Happy Birthday to me! Come on Sam, it's my turn. Can I have a special birthday tour?" Sam looked confused at my enthusiasm but I could hear he was trustful in his thoughts. *Sure.*

"Sure," he said. *Let's go* "Let's go." Off Sam and I went for the very boring warehouse tour. I was hoping that practicing my listening skills on him would provide some entertainment but Sam was not the brightest bulb in the room and he thought precisely what he said out loud. We wandered in an out of stacks of crates and around to the loading docks and back around to the files and various other boxes and dollies. Returning to our starting point, we found Tricia and Allie sitting in the same place we left them.

"Think it's about time we check on Dr. Spencer?" I asked. I figured using Holly's professional name would impress and hopefully intimidate Sam.

"Yeah!" said Sam enthusiastically. "I'm ready to see what a time machine looks like." We turned to him and I said "Sam you can't see what she's done yet."

"Yeah Sam," said Tricia "It would ruin the surprise."

"Why don't you sit here with me, Sam," said Allie "Tricia and Zoe can go see if Dr. Spencer needs anything." Sam was about to protest when Allie grabbed his hand and pulled him forcefully down to the box where she was sitting. He looked surprised but shook it off. *I must have been off balance.*

"We'll be back in two shakes of a lambs tail!" said Tricia. As we walked away I glanced sideways at her.

"Two shakes of a lamb's tail?"

"I was trying to be nonchalant."

"Oh well done with that one, I'm sure if he was suspicious before, your lamb's tail comment eased his mind."

"Shut up."

We got to the big metal door and stood there.

"Should we knock?" I asked. "Hell to the no!" answered Tricia slamming herself into the door to shove it open. Our eyes scanned the room from left to right taking in all that was in front of us. To our left was a very tall, metal telephone booth type box. It had plugs hanging all over it and a glass door in front. Next to that, in the middle of the room, was the same table as before. Only now there were five tiny pink guns sitting on it. Holly was off to the right of the table, eyes aglow, working on something that looked like a cross between an Uzi, a Super Soaker water gun and a bayonet.

"Let's leave her alone," I said quickly and we backed out of the room and slammed the big door shut.

"What was that huge box?" whispered Tricia.

"I have no idea, Trix," I replied. "We'll just have to wait and see." We walked back over to Sam and Allie. Allie was still holding on to Sam's hand and she was talking in a relaxed conversational tone. Sam, however, was looking uncomfortable and confused as he tried to follow the conversation. I tuned him in to figure out what was going on. *Why can't I get up?* I realized that Allie was holding Sam in place by holding his hand and that he must be getting suspicious by now.

"I'm starved!" I said really loudly in their direction. Sam jumped but Allie just looked up and smiled.

"Sam and I were having a lovely talk about his Italian family," she said. "Now I feel like having a pizza."

Tricia balked "A pizza? Holy carbs..."

I gave Tricia a look to shut her up and said "Great idea! Hey Sam, if we buy, do you think you could pick us up some food?" Sam nodded slowly and tried to stand up but Allie held him firm.

"Let me walk you out, Sam," she said pleasantly.

"Okay," Sam mumbled awkwardly. Allie and Sam stood up and we all followed them to the outside door.

"I like pineapples on my pizza," I said "Is that cool with you guys?" Tricia and Allie nodded and Sam said nothing. I handed Sam a 50 dollar bill and said, "You can keep the change okay, buddy?" Sam brightened a little at the 30 dollar tip he would receive and walked out the door. Well, Allie kind of pushed him out the door.

"Come back soon, I'm starved!" said Tricia. Sam nodded slowly and shook his head clearly baffled at what was going on in front of him. We all waved big fake waves and smiled big fake smiles. The last thing our befuddled Sam did was blush before turning away and walking back out to the parking lot to the only car sitting there. The girls and I turned to go back inside and shut the heavy red door.

"Is he onto us?" asked Allie concerned.

"Honestly, he's about as smart as my shoe," I answered "His thoughts echo exactly what he says. And his facial expressions speak for him when he doesn't use his mouth. Even you guys can figure out what he's thinking." We walked slowly back to the main room and sat on the crates.

Allie asked, "What was Holly up to?

"She built a telephone booth," remarked Tricia. "I guess we can call people if we get in a bind."

"Wrong," said a voice behind us that made us all jump. We turned to see Dr. Holly Spencer with her blue eyes back to normal standing behind us. I immediately tuned her in. *It's a fake time machine.*

"A fake time machine!" I said "Brilliant!"

Tricia and Allie nodded "Of course!"

Holly look puzzled and then it dawned on her "You heard me? Were they singing some god-awful 80s tune? Let me guess, Hot Blooded by Foreigner?"

"Nope!" I replied proudly.

"Oh Zoe!" she said "You figured out how to hear us on your own!"

I nodded and said "I have to tune the noise out and tune the person I want to hear in. I still haven't figured out how to transmit my thoughts but I'm happy to have a least mastered this part."

Holly nodded "One thing at a time. I certainly had to make and remake our weapons in there as I learned what I am capable of. Shall I give you Falcons a tour?" Allie, Tricia and I jumped up and followed Holly to the back room. She pushed open the door and waved us in. Holly walked over to the large metal telephone booth box. "This," she said "Is our decoy time machine." We walked over to it studying it closely as she went on. "I spent very little time putting this together, but it's convincing enough to throw Sam off our trail."

Tricia looked skeptical "Does it do anything?" she said. "Well that's where you come in, Tricia. When we show it to Sam, I will ask him to get inside and press the black button." Tricia nodded. "Then you need to give this box a large electrical boost of energy, so much so that it sends sparks around and shakes the whole contraption."

We all smiled "And Sam will think he's going somewhere in time?" I asked.

"Well, I need Tricia to make this box charge strong enough to knock him out so we can get out of here without him knowing what we're up to. He'll come to and we'll be gone."

"And Sam's so dumb he'll probably think he went somewhere in time but that he doesn't remember," I added.

"Precisely," replied Holly. She walked over to the table where the five tiny pink guns sat in a line. "These are our weapons," she said, "I built them small so they won't be noticed at the festival. And in this case, ladies, size does not matter, because these tiny guns transmit a plasma ray that can blow holes through concrete." She picked up one of the small pink firearms and demonstrated its force by holding it with her right hand and pressing the bright white button on top with her left hand. Instantly a white line shot out of the petite gun into the door, leaving a gaping hole.

"Wow," breathed Tricia "And I can't help but notice it totally matches my outfit."

Holly ignored her and went on. "Now, this is a fantastic charge that can do a lot of damage, but we have no idea what we're up against with Charles or Christian. I needed it to do more." She turned the gun over and showed us a red square on the bottom of the handle. "Check this out," she said proudly. Holly pressed the button and the gun instantly expanded from its petite size to a large-barreled shotgun with a scope. "This allows for more precise, long range sniper shooting. Additionally, the charge is 100 times stronger and can do more damage. The only problem with this is that the gun charges slower for each shot." The gun vibrated in her hand as she once again pressed the white button on top. She turned to the door and aimed. A silvery line shot out of the gun and obliterated the doorknob on the door. Not only did she nail the doorknob precisely but it blew off half of the door.

"We're gonna have to get a new door," I said.

"We'll tell Sam to travel to the last Super Bowl where the Bears won and bet money so he can afford one," replied Tricia as she stared in awe at the weapons. Holly walked over to a small triangle shape sitting on the floor. "This weapon is mine," she said quietly. "It's a Swiss army knife of everything here." She began pressing the corners of the triangle. With one press a giant blade popped out and back in, another press revealed a small flame "Our lighter for Skylar's cigarette," she said. Another press revealed a small time-piece "This is a time bomb, if we need it." Tricia stuck out her lower lip. "Why don't we all get one of those?"

Holly turned to her and said "Because this has 10 times the plasma power in it and I'm not sure what it will do. I think I can control it but until I have a better weapons testing facility I will not put you in harm's way."

"Maybe you shouldn't use it then," said Allie.

"I can handle it," Holly said firmly. She flipped over the triangle showing us a red circle on the flat side. She pressed it and the miniature triangle flipped open and flaps unlocked revealing the Uzi Super Soaker bayonet weapon we saw her working on.

"That is huge!" I said.

"Yes," she replied "This is the charge of power that I cannot test here. It could be nuclear and I do not want to use it unless I absolutely have to."

Tricia's eyebrows knitted together "Why not? Let's blow Charles to smithereens!"

"Because," said Holly solemnly "This might not only destroy him, but like the bomb, it could also destroy us." The girls and I gave a collective "ahhh," as we nodded in understanding.

"Can we have our guns?" Tricia asked, bouncing up and down.

"Yes," was the answer. I, too, was very excited about getting my weapon and holding it close. I had never shot a gun in my life and this was going to be exciting.

"We should have target practice," said Holly.

"What the fuck happened to my door?" a man's angry voice bellowed. We whipped around to see Sam holding a large pizza box and a 2 liter bottle of diet coke staring wildly through the holes in the door. Thinking quickly, I approached him to block the sight of the weapons on the table. "Pizza's here!" I said "I'm starving! Clear the table girls!" Allie, Tricia and Holly moved quickly to clear the guns off of the table and Holly stuffed the deadly triangle into her purse. I heaved open the damaged door and let Sam in saying "We had a little trouble with the time machine." Sam dropped the pizza and the diet coke on the floor sending the bottle spraying. He stared madly at our fake time machine. *They actually built one!*

I smiled, "Yes, Sam," I said "This is our time machine. Would you like to try it out? Tricia was thinking we could send you back to last year's Super Bowl where the Ravens won. You could bet on it and make a lot of money." He turned to me with fear and greed in his eyes. *I could be so rich!* I could hear that the greed was far outweighing his fear, and he walked right up to the machine, opened the door and got in, pressing the button immediately. When nothing happened Sam was cautiously suspicious. "What the...?" he asked.

"Wait, wait," said Tricia jogging up to the big metal box. "Let me type in the information to get you back in time." Tricia pretended to type in the Super Bowl date, time and place on the frame of the machine. "Now you press the button," she said, emphasizing the word now as she placed her hand on the side edge of the box. Sam pressed the button and this time the time machine lit up like a firecracker. It shook and vibrated and Sam was grinning like an idiot, ready to go back in time to be a millionaire. Tricia's eyes lit up and she closed them tightly and gripped hard on the edge of the box. Blue sparks flew out from the corners of the box and the metal began to get white hot. Her shocks were working on the box but the charge was taking its sweet time reaching Sam. After a few minutes he started to look skeptical and the girls and I looked at each other not sure how to proceed. Suddenly, Tricia took her hand off the edge of the box and reached in to touch Sam. He turned to her when the box stopped shaking to say "What are you…" but she shot him with a bright shock and knocked him out cold. "We don't have all day!" she said grinning. "Enjoy the Super Bowl, Sam."

We had to get out of the warehouse before Sam came to. We carefully collected our weapons and I called our cabbie for a pickup. Even though dusk was approaching, he agreed to come get us. Relieved, we went out onto the street as the sun dimmed and the world around the warehouse suddenly became busy. There was a small bodega on the corner and I told the cabbie we would meet him there. Homeless men were sitting on the stoop outside the store, sipping from bottles in paper bags and talking in gravely voices about nothing in particular. Cars were driving slowly down the street blasting loud bass salsa dance music. A woman wearing very high heels and a very short skirt walked unsteadily past us. I could see the tears in her fishnet hose and the hand that held her cigarette was dotted with needle marks.

"Look Tricia, it's one of your coworkers," remarked Holly.

Tricia gave Holly a haughty look and held up her hand "Oh shit, look at this!" Holly moved closer to get a better look at Tricia's hand and Tricia gave her the finger.

"Dumb doctor always falls for that one."

Holly pursed her lips "Your mother must be so proud of you." Tricia was about to respond when Allie put her hand up to quiet them.

"Look," she whispered. A group of tough looking, young Hispanic men was approaching us as we waited near the front window of the store, looking very obviously like outsiders. The men had white baseball hats turned sideways over their red bandanas and each had a tank top of sorts on and low riding wide legged jeans. Their big tennis shoes dragged along the cracked sidewalk as they sauntered slowly over to us, looking us up and down.

"You not from around here," smirked the tallest one as he stared without blinking at Holly. The other three snickered and murmured their agreement in Spanish. "What you say, baby, you and me let's go for a ride in my car okay?" Holly looked down at him from the very tip of her nose.

"I don't want any trouble," she said finally "And believe me, you don't either. So go find someone else to harass, okay Pepe?"

Allie, Tricia and I exchanged confused glances. Holly's imperious tone and use of the word Pepe was out of character for her. I decided to tune her into my thoughts to figure out her plan. *I will be damned if I let a punk hoodlum like this mess with me or my friends.*

I stepped up to Holly and put my hand on her arm "Holly, we're fine." *Zoe we need to stand up for all woman targets out there in the world.*

"This is not the time to take a stand for all womankind!" I whispered. The men looked back and forth at each other and spoke quickly in Spanish and I stared at them to pick up their thoughts. *Vamos a amenazar con nuestros cuchillos y llevarlos de vuelta a nuestra casa.* The girls watched me waiting for my response.

"Well that was a bust," I said to the group, "I don't speak Spanish." *Zoe we can practice.* That last thought came through from Tricia who was holding her palms close together with a blue spark bouncing back and forth between them. Allie touched Tricia's arm, "I've got this one," she said softly. Allie pushed through our group and faced the one that seemed to be their leader.

The men shifted around, muttered back and forth to each other in Spanish "Diminuta mujer."

Allie began to speak but was drowned out by the sound of Holly shrieking "Get your hands off of me!" The leader and the other two had completely disregarded Allie and had grabbed each of Holly's arms. The fourth man had pulled out a very large knife with an enormous shiny black handle.

"You come now, women!" he said in a thick Spanish accent as his friends began to drag Holly away. Allie's eyes lit up bright white and in less than a second she'd ripped out an entire parking sign that was on the side of the street and began swirling it around over her head.

"LET HER GO!" she bellowed. She swung the metal piece at the man holding the knife knocking him clear into the street and onto the hood of a parked car. The other two men immediately let go of Holly and backed away slowly.

"We don't want no trouble, lady," they said. The leader of the group looked furiously at his cowardly friends.

"Volver aquí cobardes!" he said fiercely.

"No way man, she's the tiny hulk or something man." Allie smiled and began twisting the huge metal parking sign into a circle. That was enough for the gang leader. He grabbed his injured friend and took off. We stood in stunned silence for a minute.

"Everyone okay?" I asked looking around.

"Well that was certainly unexpected," said Holly. "Well done!" Holly patted Allie on the back.

Allie, who was still gripping the metal sign, looked up at her and grinned. "I love that no one suspects me!" "I love that we beat a bunch of jerks who would normally have done terrible things to us," said Tricia solemnly.

We nodded in agreement.

Curious about why Allie twisted the sign into a circle, "Were you going to lasso him or something?"

Allie smiled mischievously "Nah," she said "I wanted to see if I could actually do it. I figured if I did it would scare the pants off of him. And I could and it did!"

"Show off!" taunted Tricia.

"By the way Z," said Holly "You're going to need to learn some languages.

We heard the beep of a car horn and turned to see our faithful cabbie waving wildly. He rolled down his window down a teensy bit and yelled through the crack in his heavy Jamaican melody "Come on now! I am not rolling this window down any more and I'm not getting out to help you get in!" The girls and I walked over to the car and got in. Allie, who was still holding her parking sign, was the last to get in.

"Just a sec." She walked over to the prostitute who was sitting on the curb with her head hanging down eyes half closed and tried to rouse her. "Take this and protect yourself," she said breaking off a big chunk of the metal bar. The woman looked shakily at Allie and mumbled thanks before nodding off again. Allie, who suddenly looked as if she was ten feet tall, strode proudly back to the car and slid into the front seat.

"Back to the Oriental!" she said cheerfully. "What was you doing, girl?" asked the cabbie "That was a big stick you was holdin'!"

Allie tilted her head and winked as she looked at the taxi driver. "I work out a lot." We all grinned as the driver responded, "Remind me to never arm wrestle you, girl!"

Chapter 13: Parade of Terribles

We arrived at the hotel at 5:30 and immediately reserved our cabbie for our Georgetown visit, as we realized that we had very little time to get our costumes on and get down to the Halloween festival. The decision was made for everyone to meet in my suite and for us to get ready there. I rushed to my room to call my family before everyone arrived. Jimmy picked up sounding tired. "Hey," he said.

"Hi!!" I said trying desperately to sound enthusiastic. "How's Halloween?"

Jimmy brightened up a bit and replied "Kids already trick or treated. Instead of walking they ran from house to house and subsequently wore themselves out after about 5 blocks." My heart hurt.

"I miss them so much," I said. I wanted to say that I missed him too. I wanted to tell him I needed him. I wanted him to know that I was sorry for all of my sadness and I wanted to share with him about who I was becoming. And, I realized, I wanted him to be a part of this new person.

As usual though, I choked out a "What did you have for dinner?" instead.

"Pizza," Jimmy answered dryly. I heard a loud knock at the my suite door and I knew the girls were arriving.

"I don't have a lot of time to talk, Jimmy," I said. "The girls are coming over we're heading down to Georgetown for that big Halloween festival they have every year. We thought it would make a perfect last night of our trip."

Jimmy paused silently before answering "Well, you have fun." My heart hurt again.

"I want you to know something," I said, the words rushing out. "No matter what, you guys are the most important thing in the world, okay? Please tell them for me. Love you." I wanted to hang up the phone quickly because if I was to get hurt or worse tonight I wanted that to be the last thing Jimmy heard from me.

I heard Jimmy reply as I closed my phone "Are you okay?" As the phone snapped shut I wondered briefly if Jimmy would call back to ask me what was going on. I thought maybe he'd want to know what I was talking about. But he didn't call back. Poor Jimmy was so used to me pushing him away that this was protocol for us. I pushed him away and he stopped trying to reach out to me. I also realized that the hiding was catching up to me. Pushing it deep down made it stronger and harder to control.

I walked to the door and let Allie in.

Immediately she saw my sadness "What's the matter, hon?" she asked. "The usual," I replied.

"Jimmy?"

"Yes."

Allie put her arms around me and hugged. I laid my head on her shoulder and began to cry.

"I am destroying us, Allie."

Allie pulled back and looked me straight in the eye "Zoe, enough of the blame game. You're a new person now. It's time to act like it." With that she gave me one more squeeze and pushed me out of the way as she walked into the main room with her duffel bag. She surprised me with that comment and I came to the realization that she was right. It was time to start taking control. I promised myself that as soon as I saw Jimmy again (if I saw him again) that I would.

There was another knock at the door and I pulled it open to reveal Holly and Tricia. Tricia was visibly irritated and was sticking her tongue out at Holly.

"You're on time?" I said flabbergasted.

"Holly forced me," Tricia replied.

"You're a giant child," retorted Holly. "It's time you grew up."

"If growing up means I have to dress like a geek then count me out."

"I dress like a grown woman not a character from high school musical."

"A grown OLD woman."

They continued to bicker as they passed me in the hallway and I followed them into the main room where Allie had already put on her costume.

"Ladybug!" said Tricia enthusiastically.

"Did you know that if you squeeze a ladybug it will bite you but the bite won't hurt?" asked Holly.

"Mine will," muttered Allie as she walked into my room heading toward the master bathroom mirror. I walked into the bedroom after her, reaching for my beloved Elvis costume. As I slid into the shiny white jumpsuit I giggled at the sight of myself in the mirror next to Allie who was busy applying big red circles on her chubby cheeks.

Tricia walked into the bathroom, already dressed in her skimpy hooker costume "I would be one expensive hooker," she announced to the two of us. I grabbed my lopsided wig and secured it to my head. I didn't look quite like Elvis without the wig but I still didn't look quite like him with the wig either. Still, I needed some sort of hair to complete the look so I decided to keep it even if it did look shaggy and kept sliding to the right. Tricia turned to me and surveyed my costume closely.

"What?" I asked sharply. Suddenly she reached out and grabbed the top of the costume at the chest and ripped it open.

"Tricia! What are you doing?" I asked grabbing at her hands. It was too late. Tricia had successfully torn a slit in my Elvis costume that made a 'V' all the way to my stomach.

"Much better!" she said cheerfully as she turned and teetered on her hooker heels out of the room. I gaped at my new look in the mirror. While I was irritated that Tricia had torn my costume, I couldn't help but smile at how much sexier the costume had become. Certainly Toni and Jimmy would agree. Now I had cleavage showing and the "V" stopped in a place that made my stomach look flat. I guess there was something to be said for having a little sexy in your Halloween costume. I still wasn't going to hop on the hooker bandwagon but this was actually kind of fun. I wasn't about to admit it though.

"I didn't want to be a sexy Elvis!" I called after her, even though I secretly loved the new look.

Allie turned to me. "You are a terrible liar," she said with a smirk. She finished her cheeks, shiny red lips and put on her ladybug antenna.

"Holly told me that a male lady bug is smaller than a female ladybug," I said grinning "That would be one small dude."

"Shut it, sexy Elvis," Allie replied as she squeezed her ladybug shell costume out the door and headed into the living room. In came Holly, dragging her duffel bag slowly behind her.

"I need some privacy, if you please" she said darkly. I nodded and walked out closing the door behind me. I found my blue moon boots and pulled them on and my outfit was complete. I clomped loudly out to the living room and saw a hooker and a ladybug chatting quietly on the couch.

They looked up and me and grinned "I'm all shook up!" said Tricia in a horrible Elvis imitation.

"I hope I can fight the bad guys without my boobs falling out," I retorted, annoyed but secretly happy to be looking so hot.

"Oh lawdy," said Tricia looking past me "Wonder Woman is turning over in her grave." I turned around to see Holly standing behind me in her poor man's Wonder Woman costume. She stood utterly fuming in her faded leotard complete with pink beehive wig, one gold wrist band on her right arm and the green fake leather cowboy boots. She stood stiffly as if she was accepting an honorary degree at Harvard but her expression was contemptuous and humiliated.

"Wonder Woman is still alive, you idiot," Wonder Woman said darkly. "At least the actress who played her is."

"Oh for chrissakes, relax!" yelled Tricia "You look awesome!" Holly seethed.

"Why on earth do I have to wear this atrocious wig?"

"Because your actual hair makes the costume look lame," responded Tricia.

"Oh?" replied Holly "Because the dirt on the fabric, the single wrist band and these ghastly boots make it look that much better?"

Allie stood up "Holly, look at me. Look at us. Do any of us look great? No, we don't." Tricia snorted "Speak for yourself," but Allie ignored her and went on chastising Holly. "We have to fit in at this festival. So you're either going to have to fake it or actually let go and enjoy it."

Holly rolled her eyes and her nostrils flared "Very well," she said between clenched teeth "Do we have any more of that tequila left from the other night?" I grinned, readjusted my wig for the tenth time, and stomped over to the table where our bottle of tequila from that first night was still sitting. I poured four shots but paused as something interesting occurred to me.

"What is it?" asked Allie. "I'm not a huge fan of superhero movies," I began "But I don't remember the heroes shooting tequila before going on a mission."

Holly abruptly pushed past me and grabbed the shot closest to her "Hey Green Lantern's weakness is yellow, mine is tequila. Cheers!" We all hurriedly picked up the other three shots and drank them down. In my heightened state of excitement, I barely noticed the burn of the tequila as it trickled down my throat. I was grateful when Holly poured another shot for us. We drank the shots, gathered our weapons and headed down to the elevator.

The festival started at 7:00 and it was already 6:30. The girls and I made our way down to the lobby. "This is mortifying," Holly mumbled under her breath when the elevator doors opened and we strolled into the lobby. I was thrilled and said so.

"Own it Holly!" I encouraged "Just act like they are the ones who are wrong for not dressing up."

Holly's eyes narrowed as she nodded at this lesson "Fine."

"That's the spirit!" Tricia said sarcastically. The onlookers, who were mostly male, business men stopped in their tracks as Elvis, Wonder Woman, a hooker and a ladybug sauntered through the lobby. We acted as if we wore these outfits every day and we milked each stare, gaze and gawk with grace and celebrity. My moon boots, Tricia's hooker heels and Holly's cowboy boots made a terrific racket, so even if we wanted to be inconspicuous we didn't have a snowball's chance in hell.

We headed out to the circle where our beloved cab driver was waiting. Marques was amused by our costumes and said so.

"You girls are goin' down to Georgetown" he said. We nodded and didn't say much. "I will get you there in no time and if you don' stay too late I will get ya again and take ya back here." Marques's thoughts were honest and clear and it gave me an idea. I leaned in close to him from the back seat.

"Marques," I began "We might need you to help us out but we'll need you to keep what you see to yourself. Can we trust you?" Marques looked suspiciously at me in the rear view mirror.

"I don't know girl," he answered. The girls looked at me confused.

"We may need a getaway vehicle," was all I said.

"Getaway?" said Marques, his voice lowering "You gonna rob someone?"

I smiled. "No, Marques. We are going to save someone from someone terrible. Can you help us?"

Marques looked away from me in the rearview mirror and looked straight ahead. "I will help ya, girl. But I don' wan' no trouble."

Allie patted him on the shoulder gently "We'll do our best." He smiled at that and we rode in silence the rest of the way.

"I can't go no further, street is closed," Marques said. The girls and I looked up at the festive orange and black sign hanging from tall, dark green lampposts at the end of a shut-down M Street; "15th Annual Georgetown Halloween Festival and Drag Queen Race," it read in big, shiny rainbow-colored letters.

"I never thought I'd be afraid of men in high heels," said Tricia to no one in particular. Neither did I, I thought as I we got out of the taxi. I realized we were all trembling and afraid, but it wasn't enough to slow us down.

"We can only go forward—we are superheroes," I said to my friends. "We are the Falcon Five." In my overly dramatic show of bravery I strode boldly forward and walked right into Tricia who was bent over, re-strapping her shoe. I knocked her clear to the ground and she cussed a blue streak at me when she realized she scraped her knee and it was bleeding.

Suddenly a deep effeminate voice rose from behind us "Oh stop, child," the voice said. "Let Nurse Nancy fix it up!" We turned around to see a black man in a red wig - who without heels was well over six feet tall but was now even taller in black patent leather high heels - wearing a very short white nursing costume complete with name tag (Nancy), stethoscope, blood pressure cuff and medical black bag.

Nurse Nancy gently picked up the whimpering Tricia and set her on a nearby bench. The drag queen opened her bag and pulled out some antiseptic and a Band-Aid.

"Can't have a boo boo at the Festival, girl!" she said in her deep voice. Tricia was thrilled to be getting so much attention and used this opportunity to garner sympathy from Nurse Nancy while the rest of us shifted back and forth on our feet and rolled our eyes at each other.

"Oh Nurse Nancy I love you!" she fawned. Nurse Nancy helped Tricia to her feet "All better now," Nancy boomed proudly.

"You're officially my first patient of the night!"

Tricia smiled an overly grateful smile "Well thank you! Are you running in the race tonight?"

Nurse Nancy looked quickly at her giant wrist "Girl, the race is in five minutes! I have got to go!"

"I hope you win!" Tricia called after Nancy as she strode away.

"Do we have time to race?" Tricia asked the rest of us.

Holly protested immediately "I will not..." she began but I interrupted her.

"Hey Wonder Woman, we have to head down that way anyhow. Might as well race our way there."

Allie had started walking in the direction of Nurse Nancy "Come on girls," she called back to us "The starting line is over here." I took a few minutes to take in our surroundings. Georgetown is one of the most beautiful parts of Washington D.C. It's streets are lined with colorful historic townhouses, each with its own unique style. Some are brightly colored with black shutters, others are more conservative looking with vivid colored shutters. Some townhomes are broken up into apartments while others are single family homes. M Street isn't residential however. It was designed for shopping, eating and nightlife. Irish pubs are popular on this street as well as hipster shops, piano bars, and dance clubs. On a normal night M Street is usually crammed with the many university students in the area, as D.C. boasts American University, Howard University, Catholic University, Georgetown University and George Washington University to name a few. In addition to college students there are always tourists from all over the world strolling on the streets, window shopping and exploring bars and restaurants. Georgetown is notorious for major traffic jams as well, but not tonight. Tonight, instead of traffic, the street was alive with dazzling bright costumes, voices and music. I had never seen so many tall, beautiful men in my life. And the dresses they wore! These were not your run-of-the-mill queens. These were the professionals who spent hours tucking, primping and applying make-up. The dresses, skirts, tops and shoes were expensive and stunning and the drag queens played their roles like Oscar-winning actresses. Marilyn

Monroe was walking next to me speaking to a non-queen gay man in a breathless voice about diamonds being a girl's best friend. In front of Marilyn was another famous blonde—Madonna. This was Madonna from her late 80s golden cone bra days, and this queen was a dead ringer for her. I gazed at her as she strolled confidently through the crowd. That was a person who knew who she was. How beautiful she looked! She radiated confidence. I looked at my hero sisters shuffling through the crowd in our pathetic costumes and told them to walk proud.

"We may not compare to these spectacular costumes but we have astonishing gifts," I said "So act like it, damn it." We straightened our spines, I adjusted my wig now for the now fiftieth time and we took our places at the starting line. On either side of our group was Cher and a newer drag queen, Rhianna.

"I have been running in heels way longer than you, Cher," Tricia said, taunting the queen closest to her.

"Bring it on honey," answered Cher. The starting gun sounded and we were off in a flurry of muscled arms and clacking heels. Rhianna easily muscled past me and took on Barbara Bush, who had pulled out in front. This was no longer a silly little race, this was an all-out Olympic sprint. Not to be outdone, the girls and I steadied our gaze and pushed ourselves faster. The ladybug overtook Rhianna and I saw Wonder Woman blow by Barbara Bush trying to catch up to Tina Turner, whose strong calves were swiftly carrying her to win the race. As we neared the finish line we were suddenly overtaken by a hooker who was screaming her bloody head off.

"Out of my way princesses, a real woman is coming through!" Elvis bowed out of the race at this point because I was laughing too hard to run, and of course I had to fix my wig. Again. The prostitute's long legs carried her closer to the finish line but a huge hulking nurse blew past her and everyone else to take the lead. The hooker slowed down grinning, as did the ladybug and finally Wonder Woman. The three winners were Nurse Nancy, Barbara Bush and a sneaky runner who was clearly a former track star, Angelina Jolie. Breathless and smiling, the girls and I congratulated the winners and grabbed some water from a volunteers' table at the finish line.

I looked down the street and noticed we were only two blocks away from our target. I could see the bank on the corner, which was right next to Toni's Costume Shop. When I pointed this out, our smiles faded and we were instantly serious.

"Anyone see Mother Theresa?" asked Allie. "Zoe can you hear anyone?" My head was buzzing with noise from the busy festival.

"I can't just find a random voice," I replied "I have to at least see where he is or know where he's hiding."

"Maybe you should hide," suggested Holly. "He might see us and appear, but he'll grab you first so you don't know what he's up to." I looked around quickly for someplace to hide, finding nothing.

"Where?" I asked them.

"Here!" said Tricia grabbing me and pulling me into the Costume Shop.

"Since it's right next to the bank!" said Allie "You should hang here to listen and we'll go down there and try to remain inconspicuous. Listen to our thoughts while we're there and we'll tell you when he see him and you can figure out his plan!" I thought this was a horrible idea and I said so.

"But I want to fight! I want to help you!" I started to say but was interrupted by a familiar gruff female voice.

"Hey gorgeous," it said. We all turned to see Toni standing there in her regular t-shirt, tight black jeans and converse shoes. "Whatcha fighting for?" Tricia, Allie and Holly looked at me each one thinking the same thing *This is the only way to hear his plan without him catching us.*

"We'll see you in a few minutes, Z!" said Allie as she held the door open for Tricia and Holly.

"But…" I protested weakly. As much as I wanted to stand with them and fight I knew that this was a smart way to catch Christian and figure out his plan. Once I was able to zero in on his frequency I could keep listening even after he disappeared. I turned to Toni who was busy checking out the new look of the Elvis costume.

"You ripped it?" she said "That's gonna cost you." She stepped closer "Although I do like the changes."

I put my hand up gently pushing her back "Listen, Toni," I said. "What I'm about to say will sound ridiculous, but I am short on time so I'm hoping I can trust you." Toni waited to hear what I was going to say. "To put it simply, we're superheroes. Well, sort of accidental superheroes." Toni raised an eyebrow but said nothing. "And we're battling a bad guy who kidnapped our friend. He's got someone helping him and we're going to meet that guy tonight and try to figure out where the other bad guy is keeping her and how we can get her back." Toni smiled.

"Why are you telling me?"

"Because I need to hide out here and listen to the thoughts of my friends so that when he appears I can listen to him and figure out his plan."

"What do you mean, listen?"

"I can hear thoughts."

Toni considered this for a moment "What am I thinking?"

I stared at her picking up her frequency "You're hoping my boobs will fall out of this costume." Toni swallowed, surprised but then laughed.

"True."

"Can I hang here?"

"Sure, baby, sure. Can I help you find this guy too?" I thought about this. In other superhero movies there always seemed to be a non-hero who would help the real hero. In Spiderman and Superman it was a love interest. That wasn't exactly the case here but I figured it was close enough. "Actually, yes you can," "This guy can make himself invisible. He said he'd be dressed as Mother Theresa. So we're looking for a Mother Theresa costume that suddenly appears."

Toni's eyes grew wide "I just saw that costume go by the store a few minutes before you guys got here," she said her low voice shaking.

"That's our guy," I said forcefully. "I need to listen."

Toni backed away and pulled up a chair next to me as I stood with my eyes closed trying to find the voices of my friends. I picked up Holly's thoughts *We're just waiting. No sign of anyone yet.* I stood with my hands on the window of the store, desperately straining to hear her next thoughts and I picked up Tricia's. *I'm sending out small shocks to open spaces in case he's invisible so we can see him if he's here.* Toni cleared her throat and distracted me for a moment.

"Shh!" I said vehemently. *He's here!!!* I heard Allie's thoughts say. Frantically I searched my mind to hear him but he was silent. *He's spotted us and he has a gun. He wants us to follow him. He says he has Skylar close by. We are going with him. Please God I hope you can hear us.*

"No!" I screamed. Where were his thoughts? I ran out the door and snuck down the block trying to get a look at them. I could see Holly Allie and Tricia's backs but not what was in front of them. They were slowly walking around the corner and when they made the right turn I saw his costume. It was all I needed to zero in. *That was easy. Dumb whores. Wait, where is the other one?* Christian whirled around and grabbed Holly who instantly put her hand on her pocket.

"Where is the fourth girl?" he asked panicked. The girls froze and no one answered. I went to step forward but a hand stopped me. I turned around to see Toni holding me back.

"Let me help you, baby" she whispered.

I shook my head "No! He's dangerous."

Toni pushed past me "You'll protect me," she said smirking. I watched in horror as Toni walked self-assuredly up to the group.

"Jugs!" she said loudly "Girl is that you from the bar the other night?" Holly's eyes were wide and confused for just a second but then it became clear to her what was going on. Toni continued "Listen I am sorry I left so early this morning but I had to get to work. I didn't even get your number, baby!" Holly stiffened as Christian pulled her closer to him. "Leave, dyke or you're going to get hurt," he threatened.

"Oh Hooters, you're kidding me—you've got a man on the side too? That's okay! I'm all about the threesome!" Toni strode boldly forward to grab Christian's hand in an effort to shake it.

"Allow me to introduce myself..." she began. As soon as she touched Christian's hand he disappeared and dropped his clothes in a single motion and dragged Holly off in an invisible embrace. The crowd swelled behind them and the music and noise blocked any screaming from Holly. They were about to vanish when Tricia moved quickly.

"Toni! Duck!" Tricia commanded. Toni hit the concrete just as Tricia's electric shock flew across her and into the blank space pulling Holly away. In a brief instant we could see a flash of Christian taking the blow and then disappearing again. I heard Christian think, *Son of a bitch! I am not supposed to kill them yet!*

"We've got to keep at him!" I yelled running forward "He's panicking!" I turned to Toni "You've done enough, this is too dangerous now. Go back!" Toni sat up on the sidewalk and looked up at me.

"Go get 'em, baby." Allie, Tricia and I rushed past Toni and chased the figure of Holly as she was pulled farther into the darkness behind the bank building. *I will kill this one now. I have no choice. Charles will understand. They must comply.*

"No!" I cried "He's going to kill her! Holly! He's going to kill you. FIGHT HIM!" Holly did not need to hear any more. She grabbed at her pocket for her tiny pink gun and struggled to pull it out. Suddenly she dropped violently to the ground as her invisible captor released her. *Kill her.* "He's going to shoot!" I shrieked. I heard a pop and felt a buzz past my ear. "Shit, he's shooting at me!" I ducked to the ground and Tricia sent a new round of blue sparks into the air. Christian swore as one hit him and he lit up briefly. A ripping sound was heard as Allie pulled out a nearby parking sign and swung it where he was standing and hit him with a satisfying thunk, lighting up his naked figure once again. A bright white line flashed through the air and I turned to see Holly brandishing her gun and shooting the plasma ray directly at him. *Kill me. You'll never find her.* The ray lit him again and hit him square in the shoulder and blew a hole right through it. Christian howled in pain but dropped his gun instantly. Allie and Tricia moved in quickly.

"Stop!!!" I screamed "If we kill him we won't find Skylar!" Allie continued forward and grabbed Christian's naked figure off of the ground and shook him hard. His head whipped back and forth and he started to go in and out of consciousness.

"Where..is...she... you...stupid...mother..." she was grunting in between shakes.

"Allie!" I said forcefully "Calm down! You're going to kill him." Allie's bright white eyes dulled and she slowed down her violent shaking.

"What...am I...?" she stammered "Doing?"

Holly approached still pointing her gun at Christian. "Allie, I got it," she said. "Just hold him tight so he can't get away." Allie twisted Christian around and held him to her with his back to her stomach. She wrapped her strong arms around him and held him tight. I was struck by the pose she took as it looked remarkably like a mother hugging her child closely. But Christian was no child and Allie certainly was not his loving mother. The look in her lightly glowing eyes was fierce and dark. Tricia, Holly and I stood side by side facing Allie and Christian.

"Tell us where she is," I said simply.

Christian lifted his lolling head "She's at the White House," he said sarcastically. Tricia sent a spark flying that hit him right in the chin. He convulsed violently but Allie held strong.

"It's no use fighting," I said calmly "Tell us where she is, or we will torture you until you do." *Oh god no more. I am in pain. It hurts so bad.* Christian said nothing. I shook my head in disappointment and nodded at Tricia. Delighted, Tricia sent another spark, but this one was directed at his badly injured shoulder. Christian howled and convulsed and this shock left him shaking and in tears.

"Okay, okay," he said weakly. "She's at the Cathedral. Up the road about 10 minutes by car." *She's in the basement.*

"In the basement, eh?" I remarked "Well that was easy, I guess Charles picked himself a real wuss as a sidekick." At the mention of Charles' name Christian lifted his head and stared me deeply.

"You have no idea who you're dealing with." *He will destroy them.*

"How will he destroy us, Christian?" I asked. But Christian was no longer looking at me. His head fell to the side and he slipped into unconsciousness. A police officer happened by "Every thing okay, guys?" he asked nonchalantly, looking at Christian's naked, bleeding figure. "Oh, he's just a teensy bit drunk, officer," smiled Tricia, standing in front of the damaged shoulder. Allie quietly ripped part of the back of Tricia's scarf skirt and fashioned it as a loin cloth for Christian. The cop moved closer to study Christian's body.

"What is he, Jesus?" the cop asked.

"Yes, Jesus. See the fake blood?" answered Tricia brightly as she felt the new opening in the back of her makeshift skirt. "And he was in the midst of turning all the water into wine tonight when he managed to lose his loin cloth and passed out cold. We're taking him home now, right girls?" We exchanged glances and nodded and I took out my cell phone.

"I'm calling the cab right now," I said as I dialed Marques, our faithful cab driver. The officer smiled "Good thinking, and get some clothes on him," he said with a nod. The policeman moved to walk down the sidewalk but turned around once more.

"You sure he's okay?" Holly pointed past him down to the corner of Wisconsin and M where it looked like gigantic versions of Sharon Stone and Glenn Close were about to throw down.

"You might want to break that up, officer," she said convincingly. The cop took one more doubtful look at Christian but then fortunately for us went against his instincts and headed down the sidewalk to the brewing battle.

In order for Marques to pick us up we had to walk down a few more blocks on Wisconsin Avenue to where traffic was flowing freely. The ladybug held tight to her hostage and the hooker walked alongside her, just in case he came to. Wonder Woman and I walked closely behind them, scanning the many taxis looking for Marques's. Holly had the idea to head back to where Christian left his costume and was able to fashion a tourniquet for Christian's shoulder and a sarong for the rest of him with the Mother Theresa costume he'd left behind. We didn't want him healthy but we certainly didn't want him naked or dead either. We heard Marques yelling in his musical accent before we saw him.

"Hey you girls!" we heard him say "I'm over here!" He turned the corner, stopped the cab and got out as we approached. "This is your bad guy?" he asked me softly.

"He's one of them," I replied. "Marques, our friend is in grave danger. Can you take us to the National Cathedral?" Marques nodded.

"I proposed to my wife in the gazebo up there! What you need at the Cathedral?" We slid into the cab and Allie held tightly to Christian, who was still out cold.

"Marques," I said "We need your help." Marques nodded and listened. "We have to get into the National Cathedral basement to save our friend. I don't know how long we'll be but we will need a fast ride when we get our friend out of the basement. Can you wait for us?" Marques pulled the cab away from the curb and turned left back onto Wisconsin heading toward the Cathedral.

"I will help you, girl," he replied.

Tricia leaned forward "We'll pay you," she said plainly.

Our driver smiled "Good girl, I am not doin' this for free ya know." I listened to Marques's thoughts briefly. He felt affection for us and honest concern. I knew his money comment wasn't serious but of course we fully intended to pay him for his time. Aside from Christian's ragged breathing and the steel drum music playing softly on the radio the car was silent. We had no idea what we were going to find when we got to the Cathedral.

"What if she's not there?" Tricia finally asked.

"Christian's thoughts say she is," I replied firmly.

"What is the plan?" Holly asked me "We have no idea what we're up against or if we are even going to make it out alive."

I considered this for a moment before I replied. "It's impossible to make a solid plan because we don't know what we're facing," I agreed. "However, I think there is power in our numbers. We must stick together at all times. Stay close to each other."

Allie nodded "Definitely. Stick together and we must listen to each other."

Tricia asked dubiously,"Stick together and listen? That's all you got?" "We're gonna die." Tricia's words hung in the air ominously.

"That's absurd," Holly announced. "We've got stronger weapons than the U.S. Military, we've got actual real powers that are stronger than the U.S. Military, and we've got three brilliant minds at work here."

Tricia furrowed her brow. "Three?"

Holly grinned, "Yes three. Have you met you?"

Marques spoke. "We're getting close to the Cathedral, girls," he said softly.

"Marques," I said to him "Do you know about the Cathedral? Like how to get to the basement? Do you have to go inside to get there?"

Marques responded immediately. "Well, no," he replied "It's more like a cellar over there. They got those big hatchway doors you open up from the outside to get in."

"We'll have to sneak around back and try to get in through those doors," I said to the girls. "I will go in first and I promise to use every ounce of concentration I have to listen to what is going on inside. Allie, can you stay close to me?"

Allie nodded "Of course."

"Good. Tricia, you stay close to Holly." Tricia nodded, winked and squeezed Holly's knee. Holly gave her a testy look and brushed her hand off.

"Wait," said Allie "What about him?" she motioned to Christian's mangled unconscious body.

"Hmm …" I mulled over what to do with him.

Tricia said, "I say we bring him in. Maybe we can use him as a hostage!" "If we show how we've hurt him and threaten to do more, maybe Charles will hand over Skylar?"

"It's worth a shot," I answered looking out the window. My eyes searched the darkness as we came upon the magnificent National Cathedral. The first things I could make out were the tall trees surrounding the building. Behind them rose magnificent giant square towers adorned with decorations carved in stone and stained glass windows that were now dark. The Cathedral was lit by outdoor lighting that gave the sand-colored stone an appropriately celestial glow.

"I never realized how enormous the Cathedral is," said Allie.

"It had better be, considering it took 83 years to build," replied Holly her head bent over her iPhone. "I just Googled it."

"Good thinking!" I said. "Anything in there that we can use?"

"110 gargoyles, 288 angels…" Holly mumbled as she searched the screen. "Huh. This is interesting. Evidently there's a sculpture of Darth Vader on top of the Cathedral's west tower."

"How does that help us?" asked Tricia impatiently.

"Oh it doesn't," Holly absently replied "I just thought it was interesting."

"Ugh!" said Tricia "Anything about the cellar Dr. Vader?"

Holly clicked a button and stared closely at the screen once again mumbling random facts she was reading "1,500 separate pieces of needlepoint … center tower 30 stories tall … Cathedral is home to one of the few old-growth forests still standing in the nation's capital, Olmsted Woods ..." My skin prickled at the mention of Olmsted Woods.

"Read that last part again?" I asked. Holly repeated herself and slowed down as she realized the connection.

"Does it say anything about the Gazebo?"

Holly clicked a few more times and shook her head "It calls it the Shadow House and all I can see from this picture is some stone and a wooden roof. It does mention the renovation that we saw on that flier in Skylar's place."

Allie observed, "He's surrounded himself with plenty of wood, hasn't he? Why?"

Tricia responded enthusiastically. "Pencils, wooden deck, more friggin' pencils, wooden gazebo – talk about a fetish."

Holly looked up from her iPhone irritated. "Tricia, calm down. You're making this fade in and out." Tricia who was pushing a little blue spark around on her palm, looked up sheepishly and extinguished the spark immediately.

"Sorry."

"Does it mention the cellar?" I asked Holly again.

"Not that I can see," she replied. "There's a map of the garden though, and I can see a place that looks like two cellar doors at the top of it." I took her iPhone and examined the picture.

"That's it," I told them. "This is where we have to go."

Marques dropped us off in the circular drive in the darkness of the trees and promised to stay close by for our getaway. Before we got out of the car we each gave him our home numbers and the names of our loved ones.

"In the event we don't make it out of here tonight, please call these people and tell them we love them dearly," I instructed him. He wasn't happy about the task but agreed to it. Into the darkness we went—Elvis, Wonder Woman, ladybug with hostage and a hooker.

"We don't look very intimidating," Tricia whispered.

"At least you're not a ladybug," Allie replied. Finding the back garden was simple. We just stayed in the shadows of the trees and followed their line until we reached the back of the Cathedral. Autumn had just come to the Northeast and leaves had begun to change colors and fall to the ground. Fortunately for us, the Cathedral garden was cared for meticulously and the ground was soft and quiet. We found ourselves at the edge of the garden near a bronze sign that read "Bishop's Garden." Under the name was a brief history etched in the metal. The lighting in the back of the garden was minimal but it was enough for us to see where the back of the Cathedral was. Silently, we padded along the top of the garden trying to see through the giant bushes and trees that decorated the part of the building where the map said the cellar doors would be.

"According to this map," Holly whispered looking from her iPhone to the back of the Cathedral, "The cellar doors are right there." She pointed across the garden to the back right side of the building. From our vantage point all we could see were lush bushes and flowers.

"Look!" Allie whispered sharply. She was pointing out away from the Cathedral into the middle of the garden. There sat the Gazebo, or Shadow House. It was completely devoid of its wooden roof and many of the stones had been removed during the renovation. The grass was flattened around it. It looked as if debris had been scattered there but had recently been removed. Behind it, I noticed several large holes where trees must have been. I walked over to the pressed ground and ragged holes and told the girls my suspicions.

"I bet he has all that wood down there with him." No one responded. There was nothing to say at this point. We knew where he was and that he'd probably amassed quite a bit of wood. A scurrying sound in the bushes startled us and an enormous rat came running out from under the bushes near the cellar. I thought I was going to be sick.

"Oh I HATE rats," I said swaying to the side.

"Pull it together!" hissed Tricia. More rats came running out and scurried away.

"I think they must be running from something," said Holly.

"Fantastic," I said darkly. Christian started moaning and writhing, startling all of us. Tricia jumped so hard that blue sparks flew from her hands and zapped holes into the ground.

"Shh!!" We all urgently hushed each other.

"We have to go through those bushes," Holly said, pointing to the map on her iPhone.

"How?" Frightened of the rats and other nasty rodent creatures and bugs hiding within, I asked.

"We just have to crawl through there," she said, her tone letting us know she was stating the obvious. I stood staring at the thick, green bushes. There are spiders in there, I thought to myself. Horrible, crawling spiders and their webs. Ever since I was a child I was terrified of spiders. My fear of them was so intense that even if my sons found a spider in the house they had to be responsible for its removal or death because I couldn't go near it. A spider scurrying across the floor would send me into hysterics to the point I'd be standing on a chair screaming like a banshee.

"But…" I stammered. "Spiders." Holly, Tricia and Allie stopped and looked at me as if I had four heads. "Have you lost your fucking mind?" Tricia snapped at me.

"Guys," I pleaded to no avail, "I really have a terrible paralyzing fear of spiders … " My so-called friends were not interested in my fear and they stared at me with unflappable expressions. "Can we throw Christian in there first?" I offered "To scare off the big ones?" Each girl shook her head slowly and Tricia pointed sharply at the bushes.

"You need to go first, remember? You have to listen!" "But…" I replied. My unfeeling, unsympathetic friends ignored my feeble plea and all three of them pointed to the lush bush in front of me. Allie took it a step further acting as a puppeteer, taking Christian's hand and pointing it in the same direction as theirs. I took a deep breath and let it out slowly. I had no choice but to go in and face the spiders. At this point Charles was a distant thought as I made my way into the spider's lair. I stopped one more time and gave them one more beseeching glance but they remained unmoved.

"This is not fair! I have no way to protect myself from spiders!"

"Try smushing them with your hand," scoffed Holly.

"Fine!" I spat out at her. I held my head high and grabbed the outside branches on the thick bush pulling them open slightly. Was that a spider web I saw? It wasn't, I realized, it was just my imagination. I ducked down and laid on my stomach to slide underneath the bush to get to the cellar doors. Leaves and branches scratched my face and arms as I wriggled through, trying to get to the other side. Up ahead I saw a small clearing and a path. I strained my eyes in the dark to see the end of the path and thought I could make out the cellar doors. Right then the worst possible event on the face of the earth happened. A spider dropped down on a strand of its web and swung right in front of my face. It was so close to the bridge of my nose that my eyes crossed as I tried to get a look at it. Was that a Black Widow? Was it a Brown Recluse? Rationally, I knew it wasn't a tarantula but irrationally I wondered if Charles might have planted one there just to scare me. Could a tarantula swing like this spider was doing? The spider swung gently in the breeze of my breathing and mocked me. My heart was pounding and I could barely breathe as I tried to efficiently scoot back away from it and back to the relative safety of my uncaring friends. Then the next worst possible thing that could happen happened. Another bigger spider dropped down near my left eye. Oh god, oh god, oh god I began to pray as this new spider swayed gently in the disturbed air of my panicked breathing. Behind me I could hear the girls calling to me quietly.

"Zoe? What's going on?" "Can you see the doors?" If they only knew I was utterly frozen in fear at the two enormous spiders that were planning an attack on me. "Ssspiders … " I stuttered. The "s" sound gave the murderous spiders an extra boost out away from me and I relaxed for a split second. But that consonant boost swung them back even faster than when they swung out and they abtuptly landed right on my face. Panicked, I shook my head, slamming into branches on either side of me. I could feel them crawling around, looking for a place to leave their poisonous bite. This was it! Never mind Charles, I was going to die right then and there from spider bites. Who hasn't seen the internet horror stories with pictures of infected spider bites. Everyone knows that you suffer a horrible infection prior to death after one of them gets to you. I smacked myself in the face and head as my throat closed and my breath quickened. I knew that meant I was having an allergic reaction and most of what I'd read on the internet taught me a victim had merely seconds after a reaction before dying. Mercifully, I felt someone grab my ankles and I had the sensation of being dragged backwards. Valiantly I fought the spiders, smacking myself and twisting my head around wildly. The hands on my ankles flipped me over and I looked up to see Holly, Tricia, Allie peering curiously at me.

"I've been bitten," I hissed at them "I'm pretty sure it was two Black Widows. My throat is closing, it's an allergic reaction! Holly, can you help me??" Holly squatted down next to me and brushed my cheeks gently. She stood up and showed her open hand to the others, sighing loudly.

"Parasteatoda tepidariorum," she said.

"I knew it!" I wailed "Am I going to die? Oh god we didn't even get a chance to save Skylar!"

Holly looked down at me "Parasteatoda tepidariorum is a common house spider. It's about as menacing as a kitten. I trust you're not afraid of kittens?" The girls chuckled quietly. Indignant, I sat up, brushing leaves from my hair.

"They bit me!" I said unconvincingly.

"Hardly," said Holly "Once taken from their webs their poor eyesight and body type renders them completely helpless."

I stuck out my lip and pouted, humiliated. "But my throat closing!" I protested "My quickened breathing! That's certainly an allergic reaction!"

"It's called a panic attack, you enormous chicken." Allie patted me on the head "I know it must have been scary," she was patronizing me, but gently. "But we have bigger tasks at hand and you're going to have to go back in there. Time is running short for Skylar." The mere mention of her name brought me back to reality. I had to face my fear of disgusting, creepy biting spiders and get back in there.

"I saw the doors," I told them. "Once you get through the bush there's a small path that leads to the cellar doors."

They nodded and Holly said "Could you hear anything?" Ashamed I shook my head no. I had been so preoccupied with the spiders that I hadn't even bothered to listen.

"I'll get back in there pronto," I replied sheepishly, determined not to disappoint them. I understood that being a superhero was serious business and facing fears like spiders was just the beginning. I shimmied under the bush again, this time covering my head with my hands so that if the spiders were to come down again they would at least just bite my fingers. I shut my eyes and breathed deeply and listened. At first I could only hear the girls thoughts of fear and worry but then I began to pick up something new. *I have to get out of here before he kills me.* It was my first attempt and already I had heard her. Skylar was inside and from the sound of it, she was trapped and in grave danger.

Attack spiders were now a distant memory as I wriggled back out of the bushes to report what I had heard.

"We need to get to the path," I told them. "Can someone shut him up?" Since my spider debacle Christian had been making all sorts of moaning noises so we had Allie conk him once more on the head to quiet him.

"Am I killing him?" she asked Holly.

"Of course not. He's out cold and he's going to have one bad headache when he comes back to us." I scooted under the bushes and reached back for Christian's dormant body so I could drag him into the pathway while the others followed. He was heavier than I'd anticipated and it took quite a bit of pulling, pushing and untangling to get him over to my side, but we managed. The girls and I were completely silent now as we padded softly to the cellar doors. My heart was pounding so loudly I was sure that everyone could hear it, but from the frightened looks on their faces their hearts were pounding just as loud. When we arrived at the big, copper, cellar doors I motioned for the girls to stop. I pointed to my ears mouthing silently "I'm going to listen." I closed my eyes to concentrate. *I am a little pencil in the hand of a writing God who is sending a love letter to the world* I shook my head hard trying to remember where I had heard that quote before. *I am a little pencil in the hand of a writing God who is sending a love letter to the world. Oh god please help me get out of here.*

"I hear them," I whispered "But it's not helping me figure anything out that would help us. He's spouting off some quote about a pencil and God.."

"That was the Facebook quote," hissed Holly.

"She's scared and wants to get out! I think we just have to go in and face him, " I said as I went to grab the handles of the cellar doors. Allie stopped me.

"If we find ourselves losing this battle," she said to all of us, "then we should stay close and go out together, agreed?" We nodded and swallowed.

"This is it," I said. "Ready Falcons? Let's show this fucker what he made when he tried to kill us." With that I grabbed the handle of one door and Allie grabbed the other and we heaved the doors open. They creaked softly and fell loudly to the side causing us all to jump and sending a few more blue panic shocks into the air from Tricia. We peered in and saw an old wooden stairway and hand rail leading down into darkness. *I am a little pencil in the hand of a writing God who is sending a love letter to the world. Am I going to die here?*

"Me first," said Allie hoisting, Christian onto her shoulder and stepping carefully onto the first step. I followed, and close behind me came Tricia and Holly. I fingered the weapon in the pocket of my jumpsuit trying desperately to remember how to work it. Did I press the white button to shoot? Or was it the blue? I could hear Tricia and Allie thinking the same thoughts. Too late now, I thought.

At the bottom of the stairs was a long, dark tunnel-like hallway with tan concrete walls and a floor covered in dirt. A warm, yellow light shone through from the end of the tunnel and it was the only direction for us to go. *I am a little pencil in the hand of a writing God who is sending a love letter to the world. I wonder if I can break this lock?* I noticed that this time the thoughts were coming through louder and I knew that meant we were heading in the right direction. I wondered what Skylar meant when she said 'break this lock?' We shuffled quietly down the hallway, coming to a doorway that was so small we had to duck to go through it. No sooner had we stepped in but a loud, sliding swoosh came from behind us the air pushing us forward. A thick wooden panel with a flat metal cross adorning it had dropped behind us covering the doorway and leaving only a small cave-like entry way.

"We're trapped," said Tricia softly.

I stared in awe at the room in front of me. The only light came from a medieval-style wooden chandelier hanging from the high ceiling. I noticed it was not lit with real candles, however, but instead was powered with fake-looking electric flames. They flickered rhythmically, creating a backdrop of dancing shadows and dark corners. Along the back wall was a high stage. It resembled Shakespeare's Globe theatre apron stage as it thrust out into the middle of the room. Also similar to the Globe theatre were two large columns on either side and where the Globe had a roof, this stage had purple velvet curtains that were pulled open to reveal stacks upon stacks of wooden arrows with metal tips, axes, and smaller pieces that I couldn't make out from my vantage point. And the similarities to Shakespeare's Globe theater ended there, because in lieu of balconies were long, thick wooden walls with what looked like thousands of metal spikes jutting out of them. The walls reached almost all the way to the ceiling and stretched from the stage to mere inches from where we were standing. I shuddered as the spikes glinted in their sharpness.

I glanced at my friends. They seemed entranced as they stared straight forward in utter horror. At the foot of the stage was a giant wooden cage. Its bars were thick, round and rough looking. At the front of the cage was a strange looking lock. It looked like an Irish Celtic symbol with metal pieces intertwined with wooden pieces. Inside the cage it was dirty and bare. And standing at the back of the cage, looking out at us, was Skylar. *You came.* In a split second Skylar appeared at the front of the cage. She didn't walk, jog or run that I could see. One second her body was at the back of the cage and the very next she was standing at the front bars looking just as surprised at her speedy movement as we were.

"Her power…" Holly whispered. "It's manifesting itself because we are all together!" Skylar took one small step back and then in a blur she was at the back of the cage, then the right, then the left then the front again and then the back. Each time she moved there was a hazy iridescent shadow that followed her but faded by the time she made it to her destination. *What the hell?* I heard her confusion and longed to explain it to her.

"Well if there was ever an ironic moment," Tricia muttered "It was the time that the girl who was so slow we named her Turtle became the fastest woman in the world." I looked around, straining my eyes in the dim light to find Charles, to no avail.

"Where is he?" asked Holly from next to me.

"I can hear him thinking. He's here. But we can't wait. We have to rescue her." The girls nodded and we inched slowly forward dragging Christian with us along the way. *The earth also was corrupt before God, and the earth was filled with violence.* The change in his thoughts startled me and their new aggressive content gave me an overwhelming feeling of dread.

"He's getting angry," I said softly. We exchanged glances as we inched forward our boots, heels and shoes making gentle scuffing noises on the dirt floor underneath our feet. We stared ahead watching Skylar who was darting furiously around her wooden cage unable to contain her new power of speed. "What is happening?" she screamed to us. We didn't answer as we slowly and carefully walked forward. *Oh god are they deaf? How is Allie carrying him?* At this point we were in the wall enclosure and the only escape from the razor-sharp pointed spikes was to retreat. There was room for the four of us to walk side by side and our closeness gave our eyes the now comforting bright glow we'd become accustomed to. *Their eyes...* Skylar looked at us in terror, shrieking, "What is wrong with you?" She was unable to see that her own eyes had taken on the gleam. "We're okay!" I called out to her. "We've come to get you out!"

THE END OF ALL FLESH HAS COME BEFORE ME; FOR THE EARTH IS FILLED WITH VIOLENCE THROUGH THEM; AND BEHOLD I WILL DESTROY THEM WITH THE EARTH. I stopped in my tracks and shivered violently, causing the group to stop and look at me.

"He's thinking something bad?" asked Tricia.

"He's thinking he's God and that he is going to destroy us with the earth."

"What the hell does that ...?" Something whizzed past my ear and landed behind me. Sticking out of the ground behind me was a long wooden spear with a blade tied to the end.

"Get your weapons," said Holly roughly.

"If he's going to throw sticks at us I think we're going to be just fine, Doc," remarked Tricia eying the spear. It was true that the spear looked crudely constructed. The blade was loosely tied with twine to the very tip of the crooked stick and even the blade looked shoddy as if it had been carved from a dull stone.

Holly asked, "Was Charles smart in high school?" We had begun to move forward again, picking up the pace, taking faster steps, and we could now see and hear Skylar clearly. Our friend was racing around and around in her cage so rapidly that it looked like a tornado of colors.

"Hamster in a wheel," I remarked causing Tricia to cough out a laugh.

"Hamster on crack," she replied. A few more spears came whizzing by us, but we barely noticed them. They appeared to come directly from the piles of debris on the stage. Each one lifting shakily from the pile as if a nervous invisible hand was holding it. When they were launched they came at us with no target at all and they were easy to duck or just swat out of the air. I even caught one for posterity when it came close enough.

I twirled it around like a baton "This superhero stuff is a breeze!" We weren't even next to each other anymore as we jogged the rest of the way to the cage. When we got to the bars, Skylar stopped flitting around long enough for us to get a good look at her. She was barefoot and filthy from head to toe and had clearly been wearing the same clothes for days. Her dark blonde hair was a mess of frizz, tangles and grime.

"Your hair looks ridiculous," said Tricia dryly.

"Nice outfit, whore," deadpanned Skylar in her deep Eeyore voice looking over Tricia's hooker costume. "In fact, you all look like Halloween ate you, got food poisoning and then diarehaed you back out" she added grinning. "In other words, you look like shit. Let's get down to brass tacks, shall we? she said now very seriously. "Why am I here? Why am I running around like I've lost my mind and why are your eyes doing ... doing that?!" I looked at the group.

"We haven't got a lot of time to explain," I said as another spear lifted up and whizzed clumsily by my ear. "Shortest version is Charles made us accidental superheroes. We have powers that we discovered at dinner the other night. For some reason, when we're close together our eyes glow. They also glow when we use our powers."

Tricia interrupted. "Zoe can hear your thoughts, Holly can fix things and design killer weapons, Allie is stronger than the Hulk and I am the coolest. I can do this!" Her eyes brightened as she flipped her palms up shooting blue boomerangs of light into the air and causing the chandelier above our heads to lose some of its fake lights.

"Coolest indeed," replied Holly snidely as she motioned to the lights going out "Never mind the hassle of taking down your Christmas lights this year. Just invite Tricia over to boomerang them off." Skylar looked skeptically at each one of us. We stared back at her through the wooden bars, unmoving. In a flash she darted to the back of the cage, to the right of the cage, to the left and then back to the front.

"I'm fast."

"And master of the obvious," I told her. *Thou stretchedst out thy right hand, the earth swallowed them.*

 "He's thinking some serious violent bible shit," I told everyone

"Let's get her out of here now before he brings down his path," added Tricia.

I looked at her strangely "What are you talking about?"

Holly scoffed swatting another two shaky wooden spears as they came at her "I think she means wrath. It's wrath, not path Einstein."

"Look the last time I went to Mass the priest put his hand on my knee," Tricia said. "I'm not exactly up on the correct terminology."

"You don't have to know the bible to know what wrath…"

"Enough! Wrath, path whatever it is I don't want us to be here when it gets handed down. Allie, do you think you can break these bars?" I said.

Allie nodded vigorously as she dumped Christian onto the ground with a thud.

"Honestly, wood? It might as well be marshmallow." She ducked another rogue spear while walking over to the bars "Stand back," she commanded to Skylar. In a flash Skylar was at the back right corner of the cage. Allie reached up to the two wooden bars that were part of the front door of the cage, effortlessly plucked them out and tossed them on the ground. She turned to us, triumphant. "This is easy!" None of us responded except to motion to Allie to turn around. Just as she'd tossed the bars to the ground the wooden bars lifted and hurled themselves violently back into place with a loud crunch.

"Whoa," I whispered. "How did that happen? Unwavering and determined Allie turned back to the cage and grabbed the bars again, only this time she didn't stop at two. She grabbed more and more and yanked them off the cage frantically but each time the bars came hurtling crazily back and landed precisely where they'd just been. We ran forward to help by trying to grab the wooden bars as she pulled them off, but they were simply too strong. They would twist forcefully as we held them, leaving long crooked bloody splinters in our hands. And once they were free of our grip we had no control over them—they would send us ducking to the ground as they barreled past us.

"Damn!" wailed Tricia after wrestling a rod.

"What?" I said "Are your hands bleeding like mine?"

"No!" she snapped "That friggin log tore up my boa. There's like, one feather left!"

"Lemons into lemonade," chided Holly "What's the saying? A boa with no feather is a rope with which to hang yourself," sniped Holly.

"I'm pretty sure that's NOT a saying."

"I'm pretty sure it is."

"Girls please!" I chastised them as I bobbed under another crude spear. "Holly, can we use our guns?"

Holly nodded "You bet we can. I am not going to use the 'you know what' because I can't risk Skylar's life. But the gun is designed for this sort of thing." She stepped forward and slipped the small pink gun out of her pocket. Skylar darted defensively back to her corner for safety. Holly backed up a few feet motioning us to follow and then aimed the gun at the top of the door.

"If I hit it right here, it should disintegrate that piece holding the door up. The door should come down immediately, so be ready." We waited anxiously as she gently pressed the button sending out a white hot shot right to her target. It hit the wooden piece square in the middle sending the pieces flying out, but for just a millisecond. For as soon as it disintegrated it was repaired as if nothing had happened. We stared in horror as the pieces were sucked back to their original placement. The door never moved an inch. Skylar raced back up to the front of the cage.

"The lock!" she cried pointing to the Celtic looking metal wood combo. Swatting spears we advanced forward as a group, leaving Christian snoozing behind us on the floor. We huddled over the lock, discussing various ways we could open it.

"It is a puzzle?"

"Can Allie just tear it off?"

"It will just fly back!"

"What about the guns?"

"What if it just builds itself again?" The five of us were very close together and while the rest of them bandied about lock ideas I noticed that not only were our eyes brighter than they'd ever been but there seemed to be something in the middle of us. It looked a little like a fuzzy blur and I rubbed my eyes roughly and opened and closed them to see if that would help me see it clearly. There was still a slight blur in the air in front of us. Christian groaned, causing us to break our circle as we turned to look at him. Allie returned to him to give him another bonk. When I turned back to focus on the blur, it was gone. Maybe I hadn't seen anything, I thought. It had been one hell of a long few days and I was certainly due to have tired eyes and blurry vision. But still, as I listened to them debate the best way to break the lock, I wondered. After much deliberation we decided that we would try the guns on the lock but this time we'd all use them at the same time to increase our chances of breaking it. We stood side by side in a half circle and aimed our tiny, girly guns at the lock.

"Hey don't cross streams!" I joked.

"Oh no you did not just make a Ghostbusters reference," replied Tricia "Gawd, you're old."

"Hey ding dong, I picked that up from your own thoughts!" I replied. Tricia blushed and sent a small shock in my direction that inadvertently hit a spear on its way to bump into me.

"Hey, you saved my life," I said in a mock dramatic tone.

Holly shushed us, pointed her gun and aimed at the lock. The rest of us did the same. "On three…1, 2, 3!!!" Four white lights shot out simultaneously and nailed the lock right in the core center of it. The metal on the lock grew white hot and the lock itself shivered and shook. I noticed a new type of arrow coming out from the stage. This new sleek shiny arrow flew past my cheek and my skin burned as it went by.

"It cut you!" shouted Allie. "It wasn't like the others!" I put my hand to my cheek and felt the blood trickling down. More sleek arrows shot at me, barely missing my hands and face.

"These are new arrows! We need to take cover!"

Skylar wailed "Nooo please don't leave me!"

"Skylar," I yelled to her, "I'm bleeding! We will take cover but we will return. We will not leave you!" We dragged Christian back to the doorway with us where we retreated into the small cave entrance. *THOU HAS ALSO GIVEN ME THE NECKS OF MINE ENEMIES, THAT I MIGHT DESTROY THEM THAT HATE ME.*

"He thinks we hate him," I told them breathlessly "And that we're his enemy and he wants to kill us."

"Now who's Einstein," snapped Tricia "I think we can figure that one out by the new spears that cut your face, my left ear, tore up wonder woman, and caused Swartzenegger over there to get a bloody nose ducking them."

"Well, I'm just telling you what he's thinking! Don't shoot the messenger!"

"Please!!!" we heard Skylar cry. "Please don't go!" I peered around the doorway to see her collapse on the ground sobbing.

"We have to get her!"

"How?"

"Guys," said Holly excitedly "I totally forgot to tell you this! Our guns have shields!" We turned to her, eyes wide "Go on!"

"Well, remember when I was demonstrating the guns and their functionality and then Sam came in?" We nodded.

"Remember that we had to hide the guns? Well, I never got a chance to tell you about the gun's defensive capabilities!" We waited as she went on "If you squeeze the gun, putting more pressure on the left side, a plasma shield will form in front of you." She demonstrated using her own gun. As she squeezed the gun it trembled slightly and then produced a large umbrella shaped dome. It was butter colored and shimmered slightly in the darkness. I used the spear I had collected from the other room to test it. First I poked it with the metal tip and watched as the shield accepted it briefly but then forced it back out. Then I put the shield down on the ground and backed away to throw the spear. It glanced off the front of the shield and hit Tricia right in the butt.

"Dude!" she said angrily.

"Sorry!" I sang, "Just testing it out! Evidently your ass is as dense as the shield." Tricia gave me a sideways look but said nothing.

I turned to Holly "This is great news," I said "So we use our shields, head back in there and try to break the lock again! If we'd had just a few more seconds I think it would have blown!"

Holly bit her lower lip "Well…" she said "It's not exactly going to work that smoothly."

"Why? What do you mean?" asked Allie.

"You see, you can't have a shield and a gun at the same time."

Our faces fell. "So we're screwed. Either we shoot or we hide and we can't do both," mumbled Tricia.

"Well we just have to be creative," Holly replied "Some will have shields and some will use guns." Tricia and Allie exchanged knowing glances. *We will carry guns, we don't need shields. We have powers that they do not.*

"Wait a minute you two," I said. "Holly is a way better shot than you, Allie. If you hold the shields she can get in there and destroy the lock in no time." Holly nodded in agreement. They looked at each other again and Allie spoke.

"When we get closer we can switch. But for walking to the cage, there is no discussion. You will carry shields, we will carry guns. I can hit spears out of the air with ease and Tricia can deflect them with her sparks."

"But who will carry Christian?" I asked finding a loophole in their plan.

"He will stay here," said Allie firmly "He's not our concern right now. Skylar is." *Zoe. Just do it.* "Fine," I harrumphed. "Let's just do this." I pulled out my gun and activated the plasma shield. I held it close enough to me to protect my body and motioned for Tricia to walk with me. Holly activated her shield and Allie stood next to her as we walked back to the doorway. The room was silent. No spears, crude or sleek, were anywhere to be found. The room was silent aside from Skylar sobbing into her folded arms. *Skylar doesn't notice us. Maybe it will keep him off guard.* I thought this thought as hard as I could and tried desperately to send it to her. She didn't move an inch and kept on sobbing so I had no real way to know if it did.

"We have to run, deflect and shoot the lock," I said. The girls nodded. Christian gasped for air. It was time to go.

"GO!" I shouted and we ran quickly into the room. Instantly spears came flying at us, hard. They had continued to evolve as well. I vaguely noticed that they were almost totally metal now, with the only wood visible being at the very end. That must be how he's controlling it, I thought. He's still got the wooden component but he's made it more dangerous with the metal on the outside. *I heard that I heard that I heard that.* My friends thoughts were telling me they'd heard my thoughts! I didn't know how but I was able to tell them something important. I only hoped I could do it again when the time was right. The next batch of spears we couldn't even call spears anymore. They were more like large missiles. They came out low, heavy and smooth. Every time one of them hit the shield I had to stop mid run and brace myself with both feet. I could see Holly doing the same. Tricia and Allie were solidly playing defense. Tricia fought back by sending her blue boomerang out, systematically deflecting several missiles at a time.

Then she would dart back behind the shield with me to wait for the boomerang to return. Allie fought by making a fist and pounding missiles to the left and the right. I heard Tricia curse loudly.

"What is it?" I shouted.

"There's something new coming! It's small and sharp and damn it hurts!"

I could hear the new attack weapons pummeling the shield so loud and fast at first I thought it was a machine gun. I put my shoulder up against the shield and pulled Tricia behind it with me. Next to us, Allie and Holly did the same. I watched as what seemed like millions of little pieces flew by us at breakneck speed making soft high-pitched whirring noises. Allie reached out with a missile she'd caught and deflected one over to me. It made an arc in the air and landed in my lap, burning a hole in my Elvis jumpsuit. I swore softly as I lifted the object lightly with my finger tips and blew furiously on it. As it cooled I picked it up and studied it closely. It was three curved blades joined at the center by a 'y' shaped wooden piece with an ornate, jeweled cross carved into it. Tricia reached over to grab it and accidently touched the tip of one blade, instantly slicing her finger. Swearing once again she put her finger in her mouth and sucked gingerly.

"I am not sure but I think this is some kind of throwing star," I yelled over the din of whizzing missiles and whirring blades.

"We'll need to use all shields!" Tricia activated her shield and Allie followed suit. With four shields in a row we slowly inched our way up through the pounding and pummeling attack. We reached the cage and Allie and Tricia deactivated their shields. With two behind each shield we huddled close as the attack worsened.

"I have a clear shot!" yelled Allie. She grabbed the shield and handed Holly her gun. Tricia and I did the same. *Z. Activate the rifle feature. Red square bottom of handle.* Holly nodded to me and I nodded back. Together we turned our guns over and pressed the red square. Making hardly a sound the guns unfolded in front of us into the sniper rifle Holly had demonstrated at the warehouse. I poked my head ever so slightly out from behind the shield and pressed the plasma shot, just as Holly did. The lock began to shake harder than ever before.

The blades were coming at us now without mercy. They whirred a breath way from my ears and face. So close that the blood on my cheek moved in their direction when they passed. The shield was taking a beating but the blades either bounced off or stuck directly in it, only causing its light to falter and then brighten again. Tricia did her best to hold the shield and use her other hand to throw sparks to deflect the attack. Allie punched forcefully at the flying blades whenever they were too close to Holly. As they fought to defend us the lock shook violently and rays of light were appearing from its corners.

"It's breaking apart!" I shouted. Through the excessive amount of weaponry raining down I could barely make out Skylar's figure but it looked as if she was sitting up close to the door. We could only hope that the instant the lock broke she could use her super speed to break out before the lock repaired itself again. Suddenly I was thrust forward, losing my aim. I looked quickly over my right shoulder to chastise Tricia who looked bewildered.

"What are you doing?" I shouted.

"The spikes on the wall pushed into me! I fell!" I looked behind her and to my great horror saw that the walls were trembling and sliding, inching their way toward us. We would have to get in a single file line, I thought. Allie and Holly were already motioning us to the middle of the room.

"The walls!" bellowed Holly "They're closing in!" I had hoped naively that it was only our wall that was moving. That perhaps theirs was stable and that we would have more time to rescue Skylar. I was sadly mistaken. Not only were they moving, but they weren't moving slowly at all. They'd picked up speed and were grinding the dirt around us as they crawled forward.

"We're running out of time! Shoot it again!" I screamed as I positioned myself behind the shield in my sniper position. Since we were single file we only had my plasma rifle to use. I aimed and sent the ray directly into the lock. Once again it shivered and shook and this time, out of the very middle of the lock a ray of light shone through. I knew we were getting close to destroying it.

"I need more time!" *I will stop the walls Zoe.* Behind me, Allie and Holly had begun to piece together missiles. Holly would slide them over to Allie with her feet and Allie would use her super strength to yank the wooden piece out of them and then she would smash the wood-free missiles together, creating a line. Brilliant! I thought to myself. I thought I saw Allie smile a little and once again I wondered if they could hear me. Soon Allie had built a long enough barrier and she laid it between the walls as they came upon us aggressively. A loud metallic sound was heard and the walls ground and moaned to a stop. The metal pieces shuddered under the pressure but they held fast. For now, I thought to myself. Holly gave me an alarmed look. Did she hear that? I made a mental note to try and keep negative thoughts to myself. I turned my attention back to the lock that had more and more light coming out of it.

"It's about to blow," I screamed as loud as I could. "Skylar you're going to have to move fast!" *That I can do.* The missile barrier whined and the metal pieces on the lock began to fly away. We were still being attacked with flying blades and the combined sound was deafening.

"Once the lock goes and she gets out we go get her!" I shouted to Tricia. Charles Mitchell has tried to beat us tonight, I thought to myself. He thought he could get us but we're going to set her free, and we're going to get out of here. In the midst of my mental cheering I failed to notice the male figure that had slowly risen on the stage as if on a platform. *Thou stretchedst out thy right hand, the earth swallowed them.*

"He sounds louder! He's close!" I screamed to them. The lock suddenly broke on the door, loudly exploding, but the man on the stage moved a finger and what looked like fifty or so wooden spears jumped up and made an even stronger, thicker wall in front of the cage. Defeated, I depressed the button on my gun, changing it back to its original form and sank back next to Tricia behind the shield. Allie and Holly were also behind their shield. Together we sat listening to the blades cut the air as they flew by, as well as the groaning of the walls straining against the metal barrier. Suddenly, the throwing stars stopped, the walls gave up grinding and the figure on the stage called to us.

"Let us pray..." said a raspy voice. We pulled back our shields tentatively and peered at the stage behind Skylar's wooden jail. I could make out the figure of a man standing behind what looked like a pulpit. "Let us pray..." he repeated more forcefully. Carefully we stood up one at a time and together we stood side by side, squeezed between the walls. Skylar had her back to us, up against the front bars of the cage. *Zoe. The walls stopped because they got to the cage.* I nodded ever so slightly to Tricia. I, too, noticed that the walls were pushing up against the bars on the cage. If the metal barrier gave way Skylar would be crushed in her wooden jail just as we'd be crushed along with her. We had little time to waste. Once standing I could see him clearly. He was tall and fit looking with wavy medium brown hair that was tossed loosely to the side. He was dressed as a priest, complete with the black shirt and white collar peeking out from underneath. His shirt was sleeveless, revealing taut curved biceps that flexed as he shifted from foot to foot and flipped through some pages of a book sitting on the pulpit stand. I stared long and hard at his face, studying it to see if I could remember Charles Mitchell from way back when. The man who stood before us had bright green eyes, flushed cheeks and pouty, pink lips. He was stunning. I heard a low whistle from my left.

"Girls," Tricia remarked. "My Mother always said be nice to the dorky guys because they all turn out hot. The football stars get fat, the nerds get rich and handsome." The rest of us nodded slowly with our mouths open wide. He wasn't just good looking, he was drop-dead gorgeous. "He could be a movie star!" she added.

"Trix, calm down" I said "He's crazy as a loon."

"I SAID LET US PRAY!" his voice boomed around us in echoes causing us to jump. Instantly, a long thick rod came up from the pile on the stage and hurled towards us. We flinched as it stopped abruptly above our heads, lowered itself to just behind our heads and then conked us hard on the back of our necks forcing us to our knees.

"All he had to do was ask," said Tricia.

"Dear Lord God our Savior I have waited my entire life to carry out your plan and rid the world of SINNERS..." he screeched the word sinners and a chill darted up my spine. "There are devils in your sanctuary tonight, Lord. I will rain righteousness upon them in YOUR NAME." I tried to move to look up to him but the rod held our necks in place stiffly and we couldn't put our heads up even if we tried.

"Allie! Move the bar!" I said.

Allie reached back and screamed "Duck!" as she yanked the bar from the back of our necks and threw it at him, hard. But when it reached him he moved one of his fingers ever so slightly and the rod stopped in front of his face and then fell loudly on the floor beside him. I looked sideways at Tricia.

"Those are some fingers," I whispered. He walked out from behind the podium and over the top of the cage to get closer to us.

"Who among us has heard the cry of hell?" He stared coldly down at us "You know nothing of hell. For if you knew the cry of hell you would know GOD!"

"CAN YOU HEAR IT?" A shower of pencils poured down on us from a place I couldn't see. But they weren't just run-of-the-mill pencils. Instead of lead they had small, sharp metal points that pricked us, leaving stinging, bloody dots all over my Elvis jumpsuit. "SHIELDS!" I commanded and the girls complied.

"Son of a…" I exclaimed to them as I ducked underneath, "Blood all over my Elvis." The pencils were also falling on the stage only they curved gently around the priest, not touching him at all. Then they stopped as quickly as they started and we cautiously deactivated the shields.

I took a look at the girls to gauge how well we were doing. As a group of first-time superheroes we were not doing very well. Tricia was twisting her bare boa around and around her fingers and also biting her nails, I was rocking back and forth on my heels covered in bloody dots. Holly was unconsciously twisting her Wonder Woman wrist band around and around nervously. And Allie? Well, her costume was still perfectly intact but because of it the stern look on her face was probably not being taken very seriously. It was no time for humor, I told myself, but if I'm going to die tonight I might as well go out having a little fun.

"Charles!" I called to him causing the girls to startle. "Do you remember me?" Charles' head snapped up and he stared a long, steely gaze that felt as if it was piercing my soul. His next words came out rushed as if he'd been thinking of us for years. "Of course. Zoe Lewis. Dance team captain, class president. Leader of this mess," he motioned to the girls. Then Charles looked at the rest of us and began calling out our names one by one. "Tricia Salmons," he growled "Class clown. And whore, I might add." Holly stifled a laugh causing him to look at her.

"Holly Spencer…stick-up-her-ass-smart and also whore." Tricia gave Holly a triumphant look. "And Allie Coen. Mommy Dearest." Pleased with himself Charles looked back at his bible.

"I am surprised you even know my name," he said between clenched teeth not looking up. *Popular girls. I was never liked. No one liked me. The Lord loves me. I have HIM.* "Charles," I said cavalierly "It's true, we didn't like you. And if you're trying to win us over now you're really going about it the wrong way." I saw the muscle in his left bicep flinch slightly. A long flat 2 x 4 board appeared with the words, "Board of Education" written on the side in cursive letters. In less than a second it was behind me and I felt a hard stinging smack on my bottom. I yelped in pain, trying not to let him see me suffer, but it was difficult. The board had hit me hard enough that I could feel a long welt swelling up and pumping with blood.

My face turned red with rage and I screamed at him "DON'T YOU EVER DO THAT AGAIN!!" I moved to turn around and stop the board, but Charles had anticipated this and sent the praying rod back for us. It shoved us to the ground and held us still. I heard the board of education whoosh back and then whip loudly forward as it smacked me hard once again. I buckled forward onto my hands trying to catch my breath. The stinging was intensely painful. At that point I was pretty sure I would never sit again. He walked over the top of Skylar's cage.

"Charles!" she yelled "Take me! Let them go!"

"Quiet, Sinner!" he snarled. A bar on the side of the cage snapped open and moved quickly in an effort to hit Skylar, but her new speed allowed her to dance easily out of its way.

"Too fast for you," she said. Charles looked mildly irritated. With one tiny flinch he sent an entire wall of bars on top of her head knocking her out cold.

"Charles," I moaned "What is your problem? Why are you doing this?" Charles looked pleased.

"I'm glad you asked, Elvis," he replied. "You are the soul torturers. You ignored me. You ridiculed me. You allowed others to abuse me." *Todd the hammer.* It dawned on me that the paddling that Charles gave me was all too familiar. Charles was punishing me the way he was punished so many years ago.

175

"Charles, we told you to leave that night." *Ha ha ha Charles you're a loser. We hope you die on the street Charles.* Charles turned his chin slightly up and the paddle came whooshing back, cracking me on my lower back. I buckled over in agony.

"Hey man," I said in pained voice "We told Todd to leave you alone! We told you to leave the party. We were the ones who called the police that night." The handsome priest's eyes bore into me darkly.

"You left me to rot in the street like some animal," he replied. "However, I should thank you for that. It was because of that I was inspired to make my powerful compound and discover my heavenly power of the forest. And kill Todd…the…Hammer," he sighed a contented sigh.

"But Charles," I sputtered "You gave us powers that night too. We are just like you, don't you see?" The board of education made another whooshing sound and walloped me once again. I fell flat to the ground and rolled over moaning.

"Don't you EVER COMPARE YOURSELF TO ME, EVER AGAIN DO YOU HEAR ME? YOU KNOW NOTHING OF MY LIFE, MY SUFFERING." His voice was a gravelly screech and was very disconcerting. I could only compare it to the sound and effect that chewing on tin foil creates.

"You are supposed to be DEAD," he pouted. "I knew when I'd heard about the accidental antidote and the…" he paused and then said sarcastically "..miraculous recoveries that you'd likely picked up something that resembled simple powers." He balled his hands into tight fists and stomped on the floor like a child. "WHY DIDN'T I TAKE TIME TO TEST THE COMPOUND?" he howled indignantly. "Although truly it doesn't matter now. I just saw your measly powers. Strength, electricity, speed.." He looked at Holly and cocked his head to the side "I can only assume that since you're a natural shot that you built these weapons, yes?" Holly didn't reply but started boldly back at him. "And you," he said to me "What can you do?" *The leader doesn't seem to demonstrate anything. Perhaps she is powerless…*

"I can hear you, Charles. I am far from powerless and every fear you have, every secret you're hiding, every thought that crosses your mind also crosses my mind. You can hide nothing."

"That is it?" he scoffed. "I was hoping to have a real battle tonight before I delivered you to our Savior."

I made a big show of squinting my eyes and holding my fingers to my temples acting like a two-bit mind reader as I faced him. "Aw, Charles, you big baby." I patronized. I turned my head to the side to look at the girls. "You guys, he's terrified. He knows he's about to get beat up by a bunch of girls," I said. Turning back to him still motioning like I was listening to his brainwaves I continued with my teasing. "I just love being in your head, Charles you little scaredy-waredy punkin pie. You're whining and crying so loud on the inside I can't believe the whole room can't hear it." The girls snickered loudly taking my cue. With Skylar out cold it was going to be difficult to rescue her. If I could keep him talking a little bit more I was hoping she would come to. My joke was short lived when the board of education delivered four brutal smacks on each of us, knocking the breath out of us.

"Stop it!" yelled Tricia. "Charles please … " she said softly and breathlessly. "Don't hurt us any more okay baby?" Charles looked up at this Marilyn Monroe voice and his lips curled on one side in a grotesque smirk. *Look at that body on the whore. She cannot seduce me. God says a priest shall not take a widow, or a divorced woman, a profane or a harlot these he shall not take but he shall take a virgin of his own people to wife*

"He says he can't marry a harlot. Only a virgin." I whispered to her. Tricia nodded slightly to my words.

"I mean let me tell you I remember you Charles and boy have you blossomed into one delicious man. And I know I had a reputation in high school but the truth is I have never been with a man." *She is lying. She is lying to you.*

I groaned softly to Tricia "He thinks you are lying." Tricia put her hand up to her neck next to the bar "Baby, can you please move the bar up a little bit? I can't get a good look at your biceps like this." Charles blinked and the bar lifted only on her side allowing her to stand up. She walked forward seductively thrusting out her chest and swinging her hips. *She is beautiful. I would have killed for her in high school. Charles remember Mother always said giving into lust leads to sexual perversion.*

"His Mother thinks he's a pervert. But he's interested!" I hissed at her.

"I'm not lying, baby. I really l never met a man powerful enough to give myself to."
Never known a woman. THOU SHALT NOT....
 "He's a virgin!" I whispered.
Tricia went on talking "We could learn together" she demurred tracing her finger along
the valley of her cleavage. "You could teach me." *Blood pumping. My dick is hard..*
THOU shalt NOT .... I listened to the arguments in his brain and rolled my eyes.
"I mean really. Here he's set up this whole thing, he's planning on murdering us and one
mention of sex has thrown him off course," I said to Holly and Allie who shushed me.
She is lovely.
"It's working Tricia!" She flipped her hair and showed him the side of her neck as she
looked at him from the side.
 "Would you like that Charlie?" she asked. Charles' eyes narrowed and he bellowed
"MY NAME IS CHARLES!" A long flat board with a c shape at the bottom rushed down
from the ceiling and pinned Tricia by the neck to the dirt at our feet. "Shit," she
mumbled. *Hammer called me Charlie. Mother was right! The slut was deceiving me.*
"Calling him Charlie killed the boner," I told them. "And I think he's a real momma's
boy." I smiled at my own snarky comment but cut off the grin at the dirty looks from my
friends.
"Hey Charles," I yelled "Your momma's so fat she had to get baptized at sea world!" The
board of education punished me severely for that one.
"Stop screwing around and tell us what to do next!" Holly spat at me. I moaned softly
"When he talks the weapons stop. So let's keep him talking so I can think," I replied.
"How?" hissed Allie.
"Talk to him so I can listen to his mind!"
Allie looked terrified but began to speak. "I knew your Mother, Charles" she said
carefully. "Where is she these days?" Charles squatted down at the end of the stage to get
a closer look at Allie.
He asked, "What are you? A bug? Do not speak of my mother ever again you dirty
vermin!" he growled. *Thus sayeth the Lord, behold I frame evil against you. Time for*
punishment. Charles was about to do something horrible so I screamed for Allie to throw
the rod. Once again Allie pulled the rod out from behind our heads and whisked it at

Charles. This time a wooden door with a metal panel flipped up from the floor, blocking Charles. The rod smashed loudly into it, shattering it into pieces. Charles was not amused. *Stronger than I thought.* We ran to Tricia and Allie lifted the board off of her and threw it like a Frisbee at Charles who flipped up another thick door to block it.

"SINNERS!" he howled. "YOU WILL NOT DEFEAT ME. I AM THE LORD!"

"I'm pretty sure saying that is a sin!" I replied, "Shoot him!" We took out our guns and sent our white plasma lines at him from different directions. The doors flew up around him at different times blocking each shot. First left, then right, then center.

"Keep shooting! Tricia! Boomerang him, get behind the doors!" Tricia rubbed her hands together and the blue energy grew. She threw it immediately and precisely. It whirled around and around lightning fast as it moved behind his barrier doors. Charles barely moved and his own wooden boomerang rose up and knocked hers out of the way, sending it careening back at us. It hit Holly, knocking her out cold. We lost Skylar and now we'd lost Holly. I ran over to her and screamed for her to get up but she just laid there silently. I grabbed her gun and activated her shield while the others continued to shoot at Charles. When the shield appeared it knocked her leg over to the side and out of her pocket fell the other weapon that she'd built that day in the warehouse. I grabbed it and stuffed it in my pocket and ran back to the girls.

"Stop shooting!" I said when I got to them. "He's only playing defense right now. We should save the plasma for when he attacks. I'm going to get him talking. When I tell you to, Allie, hoist Tricia up high in one of those cheerleader flips."

Tricia looked confused "I wasn't a cheerleader, remember? I slept with the co-captain's boyfriend and got cut from the squad."

"Does everything always have to be about your sexual history?" I replied. "Look, figure it out. Allie, you flip her up high and Tricia you look for a clear shot where you can get him behind those doors and hit him with all that you've got."

"What are you going to do Zoe?"

"I'm going to get into his head and see if I can manipulate him."

"Be careful!"

"I will."

I walked over to where Charles was standing and I put up my palms so that he could see I wasn't going to shoot.

"Charles," I began "We have your little invisible friend, Christian. He is in terrible shape due to our torturing him. We are going to kill him if you don't hand Skylar over." *He is nothing to me.* Plain as day Charles' thoughts came through to me. That son-of-a-bitch couldn't have cared less about his lackey.

"Tell me you haven't hurt him too badly?" he replied feigning fear. "I could never live without him. You see, he was my biggest fan at that dreadful asylum I was sent to for all of those years. He was weak and often the staff bullied him. Poor Christian always had to do the grunt work of cleaning up vomit, feces and blood. Particularly when it all happened at once. Perhaps you heard of my male nurse victim?" he paused dramatically. *Kill him. I do not care. I do not need weakness.* "He saw me murder with my power that very day. He was devoted to me completely. When I ran out of the compound shots, it was Christian who delivered them to me. I rewarded him with a special compound of his own. Thanks to Christian I have been able to perfect it so that we only need a shot once a year!" he paused, visibly proud of himself. "When I needed to practice my skills, it was Christian who allowed me to bring him to the brink of death over and over again. And when it was time to plan my escape and hunt you down, it was Christian who assisted me. I simply cannot live without him, you must tell me where he is!" *He was used. I don't need him any more. Turn your backs on me to go get him, whore. See what happens when you turn your backs to me.*

My eyes darted to the left where I saw several shapes rising. I could only see for a split second, but it looked like wooden sharks' jaws opening and closing slowly. I pretended not to notice as they flew noiselessly above our heads and hovered there. In the cage in front of us, Skylar stirred slightly. While I could hear quite clearly how Charles had no use for Chrisitan, this dialogue between us was distracting him and I knew I had to act in order to save Skylar. I had to turn my back and act as if I was going to get Christian. Distracting Charles was the only way that Allie would have a chance. I took a deep breath and called out to him.

"I can hear what you're thinking, Charles. I know you value Christian as a brother, that's why I'm going to KILL HIM!" I turned my back to run, forgetting to tell Allie and Tricia to try the cheerleader trick. *Do it!* I thought desperately hoping they'd hear. The shark jaws came down fast and snapping as I ran back toward the open hallway. One of them dropped directly behind me, lurching and nipping. The other was at the top of my head floating along and making periodic darts down to bite dangerously close to my head. Charles was playing with me, I realized. He could make these these jaws kill me whenever he wanted. The only way to survive was to keep moving and hope that Tricia could get a clear shot. As I ducked and weaved I saw that I was a mere 10 feet from the entryway. If I could just get into the that little entrance I could outrun the jaws. Somewhere deep down inside, I knew this was not going to happen. I tripped and stumbled, giving the shark jaws behind me an opportunity to land squarely on my back, biting in deeply. I fell to the ground in utter agony as I felt the splinters of the teeth push deeply into my skin and muscle. I flailed wildly and screamed, trying desperately to get it off of me. I knew that the other jaws were about to pounce, with my neck as their target. There would not be another chance for me if that happened, so I had to move fast. *Die!* I rolled over onto my back the best I could, sending searing pain up and down my spine. The other jaws were waiting for me, dashing in and out snapping and snarling trying to get a clear shot at my neck. I pulled out my gun and shot random shots, but it did nothing to slow the jaws down. They came at me, biting my arms and shoulders each time, cutting deeply and letting go. The teeth continued to pull back and attempt another dive to get to my throat. The jaws on my back were squeezing in tight.

If they connected, a chunk of flesh would be torn from my back and I would surely bleed to death. *And out of his mouth goeth a sharp sword, that with it he should smite the nations: and he shall rule them with a rod of iron: and he treadeth the winepress of the fierceness and wrath of Almighty God.* I twisted and turned and screamed and fought for my life. For my children. For my husband. For my friends. *Go go go go.* Allie's thoughts came to me loud and clear. From the corner of my eye I could see her motioning to Tricia as she bent low and entwined her hands. Tricia's long legs sprinted her forward and she placed her foot into Allie's hands. Allie's hands lifted and she propelled Tricia high into the air. Gracefully she soared and I saw her flick a blue light diagonally down where Charles was standing, consumed with ecstasy at my suffering. The blue boomerang accelerated quickly and dove sharply to hit Charles square in the back of the head, sending him crashing to the stage floor just above Skylar's cage. Tricia ducked into a flip and sailed downward into Allie's arms. I cheered silently, feeling the jaws tightening and knowing that I wasn't going to win the battle against them. I felt like giving up and letting go. We'd rescued Skylar and I was the sacrifice. *Do not give up Zoe!* I lifted my head and once more swatted weakly at the wooden mouth, when it unexpectedly and violently fell to the floor and the other jaws on my back released. I rolled off of the sharp teeth leaving a pool of blood as I turned. I struggled to sit up on one arm and was shocked to see that the cage bars had fallen down in a big splintery mess. The iron doors Charles had used to defend himself disengaged and fell to the stage in a thunderous boom. Skylar was sitting up looking dazed, while Allie picked up the cage rods and easily tossed them aside to get to her. I struggled to listen for Charles to be sure we had gotten him. I heard nothing from him, no thoughts were coming through. I groaned in pain as I dragged myself up and limped weakly over to them. Tricia had revived Holly with a simple smack to the face which visibly irritated Holly who was horrified at once when she saw me.

"Oh my God! What the hell happened to you?" I motioned feebly to the back of the room where the bloody shark jaws sat. She looked briefly at the jaws and then at me, sizing up the damage.

"You need a hospital," she said fiercely.

Allie lifted Skylar out of the cage debris and set her on the ground. In a flash she was next to me, crying.

"Oh no no no," she said deeply "I am so sorry, Zoe. He is so awful. I am so sorry."

I gave her a wobbly smile "How hilarious is it that you are fast? You have no excuse to be late ever again." I could see the fear and terror in their eyes. I didn't want to know what they were thinking, I didn't want to know how bad it really was. "Let's get out of here," I said to them. Allie gently put her arm around me to help me walk to the exit. Next to her stood Tricia, Holly and now Skylar. I noticed their eyes were bright and pulsing. "Am I hallucinating or are our eyes white like lightning now that Skylar is here?" I asked.

Holly looked at us. "Probably a reaction to having one more person with us who has the same blood composition."

"Nerd."

"Hey way to say you were a virgin back there. I'm surprised the whole cathedral didn't collapse with that lie."

"Too bad he's nutso, I could teach him a thing or two."

"Remind me to tell him to wear 10 condoms."

I shushed them. "I thought I heard the walls creak. Did you hear that?" We quieted down and listened.

"I don't hear anything," said Allie. *Hear the cry of hell!*

"He's awake!" I shrieked, "Turn around!" No sooner had the words come out of my mouth than the ceiling opened up and his entire weapons arsenal came swirling around us like a hurricane. The room thundered as the walls lurched forward and the metal barrier groaned and creaked under the weight. Charles was standing at his pulpit shrieking and pointing but the room was so loud I couldn't make out his words. I activated my shield as did the others, with Skylar sharing Holly's. Tricia was sending out huge blue explosions that pushed back against the hurricane, allowing us to push forward toward the stage. Allie was able to grab a large flying missile. She pulled the wood out and handed it to me and I used the metal to feebly defend myself from the storm as we pushed forward. The star blades were cutting our ankles and calves, the rods were beating against the shields and pounding us on the head and shoulders.

Skylar screamed "My light! Did you bring me a light?" Holly fumbled in her pocket looking for her special weapon.

"I have it!" I screamed.

"Light it!" Skylar cried.

I pressed the switch activating the small flame. The wind blew and I accidentally lit the rod in my right hand. We heard a loud wail of pain coming from Charles.

"HE HATES FIRE!" Skylar yelled to us. I realized this simple army knife weapon could be the key to take Charles down, only I didn't know what to light that would take him out completely. I hid behind my shield and hobbled lamely around, waving the flame at as many wooden pieces as I could without getting abused by them. I was able to light a few pieces of wood on fire and they promptly flew back into the hurricane lighting other pieces on fire. Charles once again howled in pain but the storm only grew worse. The wind picked up and pushed us back and forth and the walls seemed to be leaning in on top of us. Smoke was everywhere and we could hardly see each other. *Give it to Tricia let her add her electricity to the flame. It will give it maximum power.* Holly's thoughts came in loud and clear.

"Tricia! CATCH!" I flipped the tiny lighter through the air. It cut through the wind and Tricia reached up and stretched out her hand to catch it. I thought, once she has it, we can break him down! I watched helplessly as the lighter was snatched midair by a wildly snapping set of jaws. Charles laughed maniacally and raised his arms into the air. Instantly the walls heaved forward causing the metal barrier Allie had made to give way. "WE HAVE TO FIGHT!" I screamed, taking down my shield. I heard what I thought were Allie's thoughts. *Zoe no. you'll die!*

"I'll die if I don't fight. I would rather die because I do!" I shouted. "SHOOT HIM!" The rest of the girls deactivated their shields. Tricia gave Skylar her gun and as we sent plasma rays buzzing through the air, Tricia followed suit with her electric sparks and boomerangs to block us as much as she could from the wooden storm surrounding us. "HEAR NOW THE CRY OF HELL!" he shrieked pounding his fists on the podium. With each blow the stage shook violently and the walls groaned and slid closer. An enormous thick round rod with wooden thorns on it came spinning up behind us. It pounded us on the back of our heads and necks, tearing at our flesh. We were taking a severe beating and I couldn't see a way out of it. We'd rescued Skylar but we could not defeat Charles. I was bleeding profusely and my head was spinning. Allie and Tricia couldn't keep up with the weapons swirling around us and I saw Tricia fall to the ground, exhausted. Skylar and Holly were in no better shape. Wounded and weak, they stumbled blindly, shooting at anything and nothing at the same time. With my mind, I called to them. *Girls, we're about to get the biggest splinter of our lives. All for one or up, up and away or whatever those superheros say. Take my hand – we're going out together.* In the midst of the pummeling I reached out a shaking hand. Tricia took it and I managed to pull her up from the ground. Allie was on the other side of me. Holly and Skylar joined hands and then connected with Allie. Together we stood side by side, feeling the warmth and strength in our hands. Our eyes lit up the darkness of dense dust with their brightness. *It's the brightest I have ever seen* I heard someone thinking.

"What is that?" Holly shouted above the noise. In front of us was an orb-shaped sun, floating and bouncing along the waves of the wind. It was as large as a basketball and I could feel heat coming from it as it danced in front of each of us individually.

    What is that? I heard Charles think.

"It's not his!" I yelled "He doesn't know what that is." It danced over when I spoke and floated in front of my face beckoning me. It was light and dark green with flowing white streams swirling around it in constant motion. I thought I heard whispers coming from it, whispers and echoes, but I wasn't sure if they were in my mind. The noise around us was thunderous, so that I couldn't figure out how I could possibly hear a noise as soft as a whisper. Charles quickly lost interest in the orb, as it looked harmless and gentle in the storm around us. He put his arms up into the air making a V shape and as he did the podium he was standing in began to rise slowly. With a twitch of his muscles the podium rose above us and the storm pounded harder and with furious intensity. We were being hit from all sides and I could see the girls staggering, going in and out of consciousness, trying desperately to remain standing. The orb was not at all affected by the thunderous storm. It glowed brightly in front of me and moved in so close I could feel its intense heat and its green flames licked at my skin leaving little burns.

"Ow!" I cried, head butting it out of the way. It was bad enough I was cut, bruised and bleeding from all sides but now I was being burned. The orb jetted backwards bouncing off a circling 2 x 4, burning a hole through it. Charles' head turned sharply and he arched his back wailing, in agony. I watched the fiery orb next bounce off a metal door and dart directly into one of the advancing walls, ricocheting off a spike, blowing through several spinning rods, systematically setting each of them aflame. Charles went into a frenzied fury at this. He roared so loudly that the room itself began shaking, the walls closing in even faster. The thorned pole pushed hard on our bloody, bruised necks, trying to force us down to our knees as he brayed bible verses at us. I spoke to the Falcons. *This is it my sisters. Do not fall. Hold hands tightly. We'll meet again.* My eyes drooped and my head sagged under the pressure of the thorned weight behind me. A bright green heat forced my eyes back open and the orb was back in front of me at waist height, lightly whispering words that I could not hear. It got closer and closer and the searing heat began to burn at my cheap, polyester jumpsuit. I was at the end of my rope. I would not let us be taken down by this mysterious ball and I knew that if I fell to my knees that my friends would too. With one last burst of energy I kicked the ball as hard as I could to get it away from me, from us. It went bouncing madly around the room hitting rods, poles, arrows. It burned through the snapping jaws and lit the throwing stars it passed. The wind was filled with green sparks as the orb flashed from corner to corner.

Charles was spinning around in his podium in the middle of the raging cyclone slamming his hands on the podium and screaming "DO YOU FEEL THE ACHE OF DEMONS? FOR GOD'S SALVATION I SACRIFICE YOU TO THE DEVILS. I DAMN YOU TO ETERNAL HELL. THEN YOU WILL KNOW GOD." Curved blades with wooden handles appeared and positioned themselves on our throats. Suddenly the orb flashed by us all, lighting up our faces with green heat as it passed. The flames singed our clothes and faces but it never slowed down. My body was weak and my eyes drooped as the green ball collided with a flat metal door that was flipping around and around in the air. The orb ricocheted off the flipping door and blew right through the chest of Charles Mitchell.

Instantly the thorned bar let up from behind us but the storm only eased back a little bit. We watched in horror as the ball hit the back wall and sailed through him again, this time through his right thigh. Flames engulfed his body and the wooden pulpit. The sound he made as he burned was like nothing I had ever heard before. It started out as a long, deep, guttural moan. The pulpit began to spin faster and faster, and as it did, his low moan rose higher and evolved into a ear piercing wail that sounded like a small child crying. Faster he spun and higher his voice rose until it resembled a screaming, cursing demon shriek. It was a sound filled with pain, violence, evil and death. He fell on his back to the floor of his spinning pulpit with his head dangling off the side. Charles' mouth drooled blood and spit and his tongue stuck out unnaturally to the side. He was dying, that I could plainly see. I watched as he closed his eyes and his head fell back and the pulpit slowed to a stop. I wouldn't let myself turn away from his suffering; I wanted to be sure he was dead and gone. The girls also watched intently and as the flames covered his body we sighed, relieved. As the others looked away and at each other, I remained on guard, keeping my eyes trained on his face; entranced by the green and white flames that were melting his skin. To my absolute horror, Charles suddenly and hideously slurped his blackened tongue back into his mouth, jerked his head upright and stared down at me with his bloodshot eyes. Even though the sight of him looking into my eyes would be in my nightmares for years, I bravely met his insane, diabolical glare. He spoke his final disturbing words as blood poured from his lips.

"I will also send WILD BEASTS among you," he wailed. "WHICH SHALL ROB YOU OF YOUR CHILDREN."

Everything in the room began to smolder and burn, and quickly the room filled with rancid smoke.

"He's dying but still has powers!" I screamed. "We have got to get out of here!" We turned and stumbled forward amidst the approaching spiked walls and the darkness of thick smoke. Single file and still holding hands we made our way forward to the open hallway. I turned back as the walls closed tightly crushing everything in their path. With my own two eyes I saw the almost lifeless, burning body of Charles Mitchell free fall from its blackened pulpit stage directly between the walls just as they snapped shut. The crunching sound of his body was sickening to hear. In that moment, Charles Mitchell was no more.

I tried to tell the girls what I had just witnessed, but the thick smoke entered my lungs and I began to cough fiercely. I freed my hand to cover my mouth and instantly the orb - which had followed us into the tunnel - was gone. We shuffled and dragged each other over the collapsed door, through the dark tunnel and out into the dark, cool night

.

"Who's hurt?" I asked, coughing. A chorus of "me" answered. "I'm calling Marques," I rasped digging my cell phone from under the bush where I'd left it for safekeeping. "He can take us to the hospital." We walked feebly forward as I made the call to Marques. When we rounded the corner he was there. We basked in the warm glow of the yellow lights from the taxi.

"Never thought I'd be so happy to see a cab in my life," coughed Tricia. Marques jumped out of the cab and looked at us with fear in his eyes but he didn't say a word. He gently helped each one of us into the cab. He slid behind the wheel and we drove away. "If you can't tell, Marques," I croaked, "We need a hospital."

"I'm not blind, girl, I'm takin' ya there now." I sank back into the cool leather seats and breathed in the air freshener scent trying to empty my lungs of smoke.

"We're going to tell the hospital that we were taking a walk after attending the festival because we wanted to walk off some of the booze before heading home. We saw an injured dog run to the back of the cathedral and down to the open cellar doors," I rasped. "We went down there together to see if we could help it and also because we were too scared…" I coughed heavily before finishing the sentence "…to go alone and someone had started a terrible fire. We tried to put it out but it overwhelmed us, blah blah blah we got hurt blah blah blah. Got it? I'll make the call to 911 now. Marques will you back our story?"

He nodded. "I am just a cabbie picking ya up is all."

"Why are we lying?" asked Allie.

Holly answered throatily, "Because if they find out what we are they will dissect us into pieces. We'll be freaks. They'll call your kids the spawn of freaks. Do you want that?"

"No," she replied.

"So we lie then," chimed in Tricia wheezing. "They'll find Charles' body and they'll think that's where he escaped to and he'll be blamed for it."

"It's actually pretty accurate," I added, beginning to relax. *We forgot Christian.* My body stiffened when I heard this. In the midst of the chaos, smoke and severe injuries we had forgotten to get Christian out of the building. "Yes," I said "We forgot Christian." We sat for a moment coughing intermittently.

"I'm sure he perished in the fire," said Holly unconvincingly. "Did anyone see him on the way out of the cathedral?" No one answered. *I didn't I didn't I didn't I didn't.* "Well I'm sure that's what happened," she said again.

The police met us at the hospital and interviewed us there. We had no trouble selling our story as they were more interested in the arsonist they would have to catch. I listened to several of them thinking about how this story would be huge news and they would be on the hook to solve it immediately. They took our accounts of the night's events and then went on their way in a hurry. It took the medical staff several hours to treat us all. Out of the five of us, Skylar was the least injured, only needing treatment for smoke inhalation and bumps and bruises. Tricia and Holly also got off relatively easy. Holly had a concussion and some big cuts and bruises. Tricia needed stitches on the back of her neck but was otherwise doing well. Allie had extensive damage to her arms and hands and had both arms wrapped tightly in bandages. I was by far the one who suffered the most extensive injuries, needing 153 stitches to the bite marks on my back. The nurse who stitched me up was very suspicious.

"Looks like a shark bit you," he'd said.

"Big, sharp stones were falling everywhere," I said innocently. "I got knocked out for a little while and woke up with this horrible cut!" The nurse pursed his lips together but said nothing. Neither did I.

After we were stitched up and bandaged, we were forced to get back into our tattered and torn Halloween costumes. I wasn't sure what was more upsetting to us, battling Charles to the death or putting on mismatched, burned, bloody and holey Halloween costumes. Skylar once again got off easy as she just had to put on her ratty regular clothes. I supposed she was getting her due, seeing as she'd been living in a wooden dungeon as the captive of a psychopathic villain. Our wonderful cabbie, Marques was running late, so we sat in the emergency room lobby while we waited. We peppered Skylar with questions, begging her to explain what she'd been through the past few days.

"Start from the night you worked late," I told her. Skylar began to talk softly about that night. She was supposed to meet us and as usual she was running late and still wrapping things up at her school. She recalled needing to write some interim grades in her book and needed a pencil. When she looked in her drawer, it was empty. So she walked around checking students' desks looking for an extra pencil and found none. She was distracted when her phone buzzed with a text from one of us and when she went to answer it that's when she felt a sharp point at the back of her neck. Christian was there poking a blade tipped pencil into her skin. He was the one who forced her to put her hair up in pencils, he was the one who forced her to text us and give up her passwords on Facebook. Christian was the one who covered her head and dragged her screaming and kicking into his car and to the wooden cage in the basement. It was there Skylar met Charles and he delighted in torturing her with thoughts of our impending deaths. How he would kill us, how we would suffer. At first Skylar said she was sassy and fearless. But the day came when Christian wandered into the wooden dungeon with a lit cigarette. Skylar used to smoke and she begged him for a cigarette of her own. Christian obliged, giving her one out of his pack and striking a match to light it. She told us when the match was lit how Charles appeared in a violent rage and then how he relentlessly punished and abused Christian with his many wooden weapons in ways she had never imagined, for hours upon hours. He showed no mercy. He didn't say why he was punishing him but it was clear to her that for whatever reason, fire intimidated him. "Christian almost died that day," she'd said "All because he lit a match. I figured if I could get you guys to bring a match, maybe we could figure out what Charles was afraid of." Skylar went on to describe what happened when she was allowed to write her note to us. "Christian told me exactly what to write," she said "But I added that last line in the hope Christian and Charles wouldn't see it." She recounted that Christian stared at the words she'd written, confused, and demanded that she read it back to him or he'd punish her severely. "Now I know when a kid in my class can't read," she'd said. "I know that blank look in their eyes, the complete unfamiliarity with the words on the page. I knew immediately that he couldn't read. So I read him the note and told him the last line was me telling you to water my plants. He bought it and that little tidbit about the cigarette light slipped past Charles and out the door into your waiting hands.

"Brilliant!" Tricia had replied.

"My turn," Skylar had replied. "Tell me what in the world has happened." Excitedly we recapped our last few days for Skylar, constantly interrupting each other to explain each experience we'd had. The dinner, our eyes, the encounter with Christian and our first battle, how we realized she'd been kidnapped and how we fought among ourselves about whether we could even save her. She chuckled when she heard about Tricia's silly outfits and how we met the lecherous Toni at the costume shop. That chuckling turned to all-out laughter when she heard why we were dressed the way we were and how miserable Holly had been during the costume gathering process. We relayed the events at the warehouse, Halloween night and how we ended up at the Cathedral to rescue her. I even made a special point to share with her the other experiences we'd been having with regard to our personal feelings of boredom and depression; realizing that we felt stuck and how we each thought the other one had it better. I wasn't surprised when she, too, echoed the feelings we'd been having. When we finally brought her up to speed, Marques called to tell us he was waiting outside.

We limped and hobbled outside to Marques's waiting cab and slid into the soft taxi seats, grunting and groaning.

"Those cops believed the whole story!" said Allie "I hate that we lied but I'm glad it was so easy."

"Look," said Tricia "Those guys are going to discover the fried Charles Mitchell and get a freakin' purple heart or something. He's a wanted man!"

"Purple heart is for saving someone's life, genius," teased Holly.

Allie interrupted her "What am I going to tell my husband? Do I lie?" she asked. "What are all of us going to tell our loved ones about how terrible we look?" I shared with them that laying on the table for two hours getting stitched up had given me a lot of time to think.

"These past few days I have felt more like myself than I have in years," I told them.

"Gone are the days of darkness and excuses," I said. "I'm confident, strong and ready to take on the world." I grinned broadly "What that means is I am going to come clean and tell Jimmy everything. About the marriage, about my sadness and about my powers. I'm back and better than ever and he's not going to know what hit him!"

"I can't wait to hear what Tate thinks," said Tricia.

"My man is going to love the fact I carry both kids and groceries and the car if I want to!"

"Dave is a writer, are you kidding? He'll probably develop a comic book about it."

"And Myles will write a song and smoke pot," added Skylar sarcastically. We pulled into the circular drive at the hotel. I could hear Marques feeling sad.

"Marques, thank you. For everything. For your protection, your concern, your silence…" I handed him a check for $400. "This is not nearly enough for what you have done for us. You've gone above and beyond being our driver, you're a protector and a dear friend." The girls echoed my sentiment and gave Marques kisses on his cheeks, embarrassing him.

"My wife won't like this much!" he accepted the check and said "I only have one request: That the next time you need a ride you come call Marques, okay girls?" I had a feeling that we'd be calling him very soon.

"Of course," I said hugging him tightly.

We limped into the hotel turning to wave to Marques as he drove off. *I'm going to miss him.*

"Me too, Allie," I said putting my arm around her. "What time does everyone have to be at the airport tomorrow?" I asked.

"How can we ever be apart after this?"

"I am going to cry, this is awful"

"Everyone needs to just move here!" I grinned at my friends with my own tears welling up.

"I listened to your thoughts and it sounds like with the exception of those who live here, we need to be there early, about 7AM."

"Gawd that's annoying."

"Group hug!" We threw our arms around each other and hugged tight as tears came streaming down our faces. The Falcon Five stood hugging in the middle of the Mandarin Oriental Hotel lobby covered in bandages, dressed in tattered, burned, very unwholesome Halloween costumes and we didn't care. As bystanders stared curiously, we held each other tight.

"I love you, girls," I said to a chorus of "I love you too!" We put our heads forehead to forehead smiling and crying through our glowing eyes.

"Let's all sleep in my suite tonight, okay? You too Skylar. Let's stop the hugging because we're going make that big green ball again and set this place on fire."

"I know! What was that thing?" asked Tricia as we walked to the elevator.

"It materialized as a reaction to our collective power, we created it. When we broke our physical chain, it disappeared," replied Holly.

"So it's our baby!" Tricia replied.

"I don't want to see what kind of poop comes out of that thing," Skylar laughed. The elevator doors closed and we chatted aimlessly until we arrived at the door of my suite. That night we all slept in the bedroom, some on the floor, some on the couch and me in the bed alone because I was terrified someone might touch my painful stitches. The morning came quickly and it was time to go. I made a quick call home to remind Jimmy when to pick me up. He mentioned that the kids were going swimming with my parents and that we'd meet them at the pool after he picked me up. I hesitated thinking about my sensitive stitches but figured I'd be better off explaining them to him in person. And this time, I was definitely going to do it..

Skylar stayed with me to help me shower and pack while the rest of the girls went to their own rooms to gather their things. We met in the lobby and Skylar decided to ride with us to the airport on the shuttle, saying she'd call Marques for a ride back to her place just so she could see him once more as comfort when we were gone. Washington D.C. traffic was horrendous as usual, making us late for our flights, so there was no time for long, tearful goodbyes.

We hugged one another tightly and said, "See you on Facebook, call me when you can, come visit soon." My flight was the first to leave, so I grabbed the Washington Post and waved my final goodbye as I went through security. Being in the airport doing non-hero things jarred me back into reality. I'd been so busy using my powers and spending time with others who had similar magic that I was having a little trouble adjusting to regular people. I did find it rather comforting to hear thoughts that weren't murderous or frightened. Just your run-of-the-mill nerves about flying or wondering about bringing McDonalds on the plane. Once on the plane I settled in uncomfortably and my pain medicine lulled me to sleep. I dreamed of green fire and wicked eyes; of Georgetown and Halloween; of my friends and their warm hands. I awoke with a start and stretched forgetting I had major injuries on my back. I cursed softly and put my hands back in my lap where they rested on my newspaper. I rubbed my sleepy eyes and read the front headline. It read "NATIONAL CATHEDRAL BURNS: Charred remains found inside thought to be Charles Mitchell, recently escaped murderer and mental patient. Police are investigating to determine whether Mitchell started the fire." The front-page photo showed the Cathedral gardens enclosed with yellow police tape. Several uniformed officers were pictured looking at notepads or walking cadaver dogs. I stared closely at the photo, remembering all that had happened just the night before. I could even see the bushes that we slid under to get into the Cathedral cellar and later to escape its firestorm. The gazebo was also in the shot, toward the back right side of the picture. Something peculiar caught my eye in that corner of the shot. Behind the gazebo, peering at the police, was a fading figure of a man who the photographer probably didn't even realize was there. And the reason the photographer didn't know that anyone was there was that this figure was fading to the point of being almost invisible. There in the corner picture I could see Christian; alive and well and evidently still quite able to disappear.

My plane landed thirty minutes later and I immediately sent a text message to the girls that I would be in touch very soon with some news. I recommended that they pick up the Post themselves and look at the picture on the front page.

For now, however, I wanted to focus on other things. I got off the plane and limped stiffly out of the gate. Far away I could see him—his head bent over his BlackBerry, reading casually. His hair was tousled, just the way I liked it, and he looked muscular in his gray t-shirt and jeans. I deliberately didn't alert him to my presence until I was practically on top of him.

"Kiss me," I said putting my arms around his neck. He was surprised but then pleased and obliged, taking me into a sweeping embrace. And crushing my poor, cut up back.

"Oh ow ow ow ow," I cried pulling back gently. Jimmy put his hands on my shoulders and stared at me intently. *What the hell happened to her?*

"What the hell happened to you?" he asked looking at my bruised face and lacerated cheek.

"We have a lot to talk about," I replied.

"Did you have an accident?" he pressed.

"First things first, Jimmy," I said sternly. "Tell Jenny from work to quit calling our house." Jimmy's mouth dropped open.

"How did you know?" *Nothing happened. Nothing. She must believe me.*

"I can hear your thoughts, that's how I know. "I said matter of factly. "Tell her to scram. I'm back, Jimmy, and I'm better than I have been in a long, long time." *She seems different. Something has changed inside her. Something good.*

"I..I will," he said. "Nothing.."

"Happened," I interrupted. "I told you I can hear your thoughts."

"How?" he asked frowning.

"I'll explain on the way home. I want to see my baby boys, have some lunch and maybe a margarita. And you and I have a lot to talk about." *I love her boobs.* I looked at him sideways "Really?" I said "I look as if I've been through a nuclear war and all you can think about are my boobs?"

Jimmy laughed "Just wanted to see if you could hear that. And I do love them."

I rolled my eyes "Come get my bags and help me to the truck." Like a good husband Jimmy did what I asked and took great care to help me get into the truck, lifting me up to get inside. *She smells like antiseptic.*

"Yeah well you'd smell like antiseptic too if you had 152 stitches on your back."

"Jesus," he replied. "Stop doing that. And tell me what happened!" *Wonder if the stitches will put a damper on the blow job Monday?*

"I think we'll have to figure something else out for blow job Monday you pervert," I teased.

Jimmy raised his eyebrows "You know your eyes get all bright when you're doing your little mind trick."

"They do not!"

"Yeah they do." *Operating systems must employ optimal connectivity.*

"Stop thinking boring stuff because you know I'm listening!"

"I have to get some control!"

"Thinking boring things does not give you control, try again." *I love you.* Tears welled up in my eyes and I reached out to touch his hair. "I love you, too."